THE WORLD BANK
A Third World View

THE WORLD BANK

A THIRD WORLD VIEW

H.N. RAY I.C.S. (Retd.)
Former Executive Director,
The World Bank
&
Former Finance Secretary
Govt. of India

INDUS

INDUS PUBLISHING COMPANY
NEW DELHI

ISBN 81-7387-058-6

Published by M.L. Gidwani, Indus Publishing Company
FS-5, Tagore Garden, New Delhi 110027, and printed at
Elegant Printers, Mayapuri Indl. Area, New Delhi

CONTENTS

FOREWORD

It gives me great pleasure to write the Foreword for the book 'The World Bank—a Third World View' written by Mr. H.N. Ray. He served as the Executive Director, representing our Constituency comprising India, Bangladesh, Bhutan and Sri Lanka, on the Board of the World Bank during 1980-85, and I had the opportunity of assessing his work during my tenure as Minister of Finance, Government of India.

The World Bank is a unique organisation, owned by the member-Governments, with the primary objective of promoting development, and not wedded to the generation of profits. Unlike many other publicly-owned organisations, the World Bank has been by and large successful, though its activities have also aroused the ire of environmentalists, and of politicians of various persuasions, and engendered controversy, often arising from misconceptions.

With his insight into the internal working of the World Bank, Mr. Ray has given a readable account of the many influences that operate on this multilateral body, and the pulls and pressures it has to contend with. While outlining the many achievements of the Bank, the book also draws attention to some of the shortcomings. The author calls for simplification, easing of the policy dialogue, and concentration on basics, without distraction by trivia. He draws extensively upon studies carried out by the World Bank itself, and it is to the credit of this organisation that it has set up its own independent Operations Evaluation Department, and subjected its activities to impartial and objective analysis by various Task Forces etc. Commitment to transparency and openness recently announced by the World Bank is to be welcomed.

There has been a tendency in recent years for World Bank lending to stagnate, and influential bodies have discouraged more lending, questioning its role in the context of globalisation, and the general consensus on liberalisation and privatisation. The author makes out a strong case for continued and enhanced lending by the World Bank group, especially in the light of the requirements of the countries of Eastern Europe and the former Soviet Union, for making the transition to market driven economies. He stresses that resources for these transitional economies should be additional to the levels of current lending to traditional Third World borrowers, so that there is no diversion from the latter. He points out that though the flows of private investment to the developing countries may have increased, these flows are skewed, and are concentrated mostly in some middle-income countries, while low income countries, whose needs are greater, are being ignored by private investors. Continued multilateral assistance to the second category is, therefore, required, according to the author. It is also argued that in order to create an enabling environment in which the private sector can thrive, the State has to play an active role, and the infrastructure has to be developed to acceptable standards. The activities call for massive fresh investments, and could benefit enormously not only from World Bank financing, but also from its expert advice and guidance provided by a team of experienced and dedicated professionals, built up over many years.

My hope is that the data and facts collected and the analysis by the author, will help to generate a more informed and objective debate on the proper role of the World Bank group in the vastly altered conditions of the present day world. His objective approach should help to remove misconceptions about the World Bank and to further streamline and simplify its operations, so that it can be instrumental in improving the quality of life of many more people in the Third World. In particular, it should help to create the climate for enhanced concessional lending, and the more equitable allocation of these much sought-after funds.

Finally, I must clarify that the views expressed in the book are those of the author alone, and do not necessarily indicate the views of the Government of India.

April 1996

PRANAB MUKHERJEE
Minister of External Affairs
Government of India

PREFACE

I had the privilege of serving for some five years in the early 1980s as an Executive Director of the World Bank representing our Constituency, comprising Bangladesh, Bhutan, India and Sri Lanka. The World Bank is a co-operative institution owned by the member-Governments of both the developed and developing countries, having as its objective, furthering the development of the less developed countries, and improving the quality of life there. By and large, it can legitimately claim to have operated successfully during the last five decades, though some critics would differ sharply. After having seen the institution's functioning at close quarters, I found it commendable that the World Bank should voluntarily impose upon itself a process of continuous review of completed projects, and also study the final impact of some selected projects, after achieving their full potential, upon the economies of the host countries, through an independent entity, viz., the Operations Evaluation Department. After I demitted office, I thought I should write about this institution as we had many lessons to learn from the way the World Bank conducted its affairs, especially since so many of the public sector enterprises in the developing countries, also owned and managed by the Governments, were performing far below expectations. I also thought that the World Bank was unique in systematically collecting an immense amount of data about a multitude of projects executed in different countries at various stages of development, and about the economies, as well as the public finances of its many borrowers. Such data were retrievable, and would permit cross-country comparisons, which in turn, should enable resources to be used more efficiently. Besides the financial resources provided by the Bank, its impact in the form of expert advice was also significant. It appeared to me that more information presented in a readable form about the functioning of the World Bank would enable the developing countries to take full advantage of their membership of this world organisation, and also to avoid possible pitfalls. The book refers to the project cycle followed in dealing with various proposals, to the influences that operate within the organisation, and to what transpires at Board meetings. It is hoped that these references will help prospective borrowers to better prepare their projects and forewarn them about the issues likely to be raised in the subsequent negotiations with the Bank representatives and the inevitable policy dialogue. Hence my attempt to write this book.

I had not then realised the size of the task I had undertaken. While I was trying to proceed with it, momentous developments occurred, including the dissolution of the erstwhile U.S.S.R., the building up of a remarkable consensus on liberalisation, and widening the scope of the private sector. There were also unforeseen developments such as the unification of Germany, the initial deepening of the debt crisis, and its subsequent easing, the growing economic prowess of Japan and the Gulf War. These developments commanded attention while writing the book, and necessitated substantial rethinking. Having retired from service, and with many family ties and obligations, as also varied other interests, the writing of this book proceeded with many interruptions, but was eventually completed.

Now that the book is ready, my hope is that it will help to clear misconceptions about the World Bank, and lead to a more informed and reasoned debate about its future role. There has been stagnancy in World Bank lending in recent years, and there are indications that an influential body of opinion in the industrialised countries would prefer to see its future role greatly circumscribed in the light of the consensus on liberalisation, privatisation and globalisation, and the primary role assigned to the private sector. Also negotiations for the next IDA replenishment are encountering heavy weather. The book argues the case for continued World Bank lending, preferably at a higher level, even under the altered conditions. The finding with regard to adjustment lending, that it was the middle income countries which benefitted more than the low income countries is mentioned, as also the reason attributed viz., the initial low level of development in the latter group. Despite the surge in private capital flows, data are presented to show the highly skewed pattern of distribution of these flows, the countries of East Asia and Latin America being the main beneficiaries. The poorer countries just do not attract private capital in adequate measure. Development is a long term process, and calls for massive investment in infrastructure and the social sectors. To redress the balance, achieve a minimum threshold level of development in the social and financial sectors, and to create an enabling environment for the private sector, the State has to play a major role, particularly in the low income countries, and would require assistance from multilateral financial institutions, including the World Bank for several years to come. Part of this assistance has to continue to be in the form of concessional aid, as many low income countries are no longer capable of servicing loans at market-related rates. The book also calls for a more equitable allocation of such assistance in replacement of the present inequitable system.

The needs of the transitional economies of Eastern Europe and the former Soviet Union are commented upon, and it is suggested that additional resources should be raised for these countries, as there is a grave risk of diversion of the already inadequate resources from traditional Third World borrowers to the former group because of cultural affinity and propinquity to the European Union in particular. Additional World Bank lending to all developing countries is possible without any direct impact on the budgets of member-Governments as adequate resources can be raised from the financial markets according to responsible expert opinion.

The book examines the findings of the Wapenhans task-force and suggests that there is scope for improvement in the approval and supervision of Bank-assisted projects. Examples are cited where two comparable countries have performed very differently despite the supervision exercised by the World Bank, and it is suggested that the development process cannot be fully captured by statistics alone, and much depends upon the perspicacity and competence of the decision-makers in the host countries, and their commitment to the development process, the implication being that the safety of the loan depends more on these other factors, rather than on analysis based on statistics, sometimes of doubtful reliability, and on routine visits by Bank missions. It is further suggested that the World Bank should concentrate on essentials rather than on trivia, as evidenced by the host of legal covenants which remain unfulfilled, with no sanctions enforced.

The World Bank has been continuously increasing the scope of policy dialogue with its borrowers, and probing sensitive issues such as military expenditure, and the quality of governance. The book advocates that the World Bank could, with advantage, ease off on policy dialogue, where it does not possess the required comparative advantage, and pay greater heed to the political implications of the advice that it may be tendering. The attempt should be to carry the political masters along with the strategy proposed.

The point is made that the body of expert and dedicated staff built up over the last 50 years by the Bank should be fully utilised to improve the efficiency of Third World projects in both the design and execution stages, so that the maximum benefit is derived by the borrowing countries. This objective will be achieved only if lending continues at the current or a higher level.

Public consciousness of environmental issues has now been aroused, and the World Bank seems to have developed cold feet about financing multi-purpose developmental projects. The book pleads for a balanced approach, as sound projects should not be discarded on emotive grounds. The objective should be greatest good for the greatest number, and of course, displaced persons should be resettled humanely and their original incomes safeguarded, while every feasible effort should be made to minimise damage to the environment.

I am deeply grateful to the Hon'ble P.K. Mukherjee, Minister for External Affairs, Government of India, and Deputy Chairman, Planning Commission for graciously agreeing to write the Foreword to the book, despite his many and urgent preoccupations. My gratitude is all the deeper, because for a good part of my tenure as Executive Director, World Bank, he was holding charge as the Minister of Finance, Govt. of India.

I am indeed fortunate that I was able to lay my hands on some relevant documents, which are not widely distributed, and without which it would have been impossible to write this book. I must express my grateful thanks to my friends and colleagues in the Ministry of Finance, Government of India, and to the staff of the World Bank's Resident Mission in Delhi for supplying me some publications. Though it might be invidious to name individuals, as so many have helped me, yet I must record my special thanks to Mr. N.K. Singh, Addl. Secy., Ministry of Finance, (now Secretary, Expenditure) and to Ms. Bimla Bissell, External Affairs Officer of the Resident Mission, Delhi. Former friends and colleagues in Washington, D.C. have also been most helpful, and I would like to take this opportunity of expressing my gratitude to successive Executive Directors, who succeeded me in our Constituency at the Bank, and to their staff, for keeping me informed. My particular thanks are due to Mr. Alexander Shakow, Director, External Affairs, (now Executive Secretary, Development Committee) of the World Bank. Meanwhile, the new policy of openness and greater transparency adopted by the World Bank made important documents more accessible, and therefore enabled me to make more meaningful and informed comments.

All my efforts would have been in vain but for the invaluable assistance rendered to me by the Indian Council for Research on International Economic Relations (ICRIER). I am deeply indebted to its Chairman, Mr. R.N. Malhotra, and to the Director & Chief Executive, Dr. S.P. Gupta, for permitting me to use the facilities of the Council, including their library and the word processors, etc. My special thanks are due to Mr. Manmeet Ahuja for undertaking the laborious work of processing the manuscript.

Last, but not least, I would like to express my thanks to my understanding family for bearing with me while I was trying to write this book, tolerating my many quirks, and helping me with the manuscript and the index.

Needless to say, I am solely responsible for the views expressed in this book, and these views do not necessarily reflect the views of the Government of India or of the World Bank, as these views are held by me in my personal capacity.

H.N. RAY

List of Acronyms

ARPP	—	Annual Report on Portfolio Performance
BWC	—	Bretton Woods Commission
CAS	—	Country Assistance Strategy Statement
CIS	—	Commonwealth of Independent States
CPPR	—	Country Portfolio Performance Review
DAC	—	Development Assistance Committee
DFC	—	Development Finance Company
ED	—	Executive Director (of World Bank)
EMDB	—	Emerging Market Data Base
ERR	—	Economic Rate of Return
ESMAP	—	Energy Strategy, Management and Assessment Programme
FIAS	—	Foreign Investment Advisory Service
FDI	—	Foreign Direct Investment
GCI	—	General Capital Increase
GEF	—	Global Environmental Facility
IBRD	—	International Bank for Reconstruction and Development
IDA	—	International Development Association
IFC	—	International Finance Corporation
NAFTA	—	North American Free Trade Agreement
NEAP	—	National Environmental Action Plan
ODA	—	Official Development Assistance
OED	—	Operation Evaluation Dept.

PPAR	—	Project Performance Audit Report
PSE	—	Public Sector Enterprise
SAL	—	Structural Adjustment Loan
SAR	—	Staff Appraisal Report
SCI	—	Selective Capital Increase
SDR	—	Special Drawing Right
SECAL	—	Sector Adjustment Loan
SLL	—	Sustainable Level of Lending
VLR	—	Variable Lending Rate

CHAPTER 1

ARTICLES OF AGREEMENT OF IBRD

The basic document, which created the International Bank for Reconstruction and Development (hereinafter also referred to as IBRD and by its popular name the World Bank, or even as 'Bank' for brevity, where no confusion is likely), and which regulates its functioning, is its Articles of Agreement. For a proper appreciation of certain developments, as they are considered subsequently, it is necessary to have some knowledge of these Articles, and how they were negotiated. As long ago as April 1942[1], Harry White of the U.S. Administration prepared certain proposals for the creation of an international organisation, which foreshadowed the Articles of Agreement as these eventually emerged. Much work followed these preliminary proposals, e.g. the constitution of a Technical Committee in Nov. 1943 to formulate the proposals of the U.S. Administration, the framing of a series of questions and answers in elaboration and clarification of those proposals, and the amalgamation of the suggestions of Lord Keynes and of Harry White in a joint statement. The next development leading to significant progress in giving concrete shape to these ideas was a conference held at Atlantic City, USA to prepare an agenda for the proposed conference at Bretton Woods, New Hampshire. The work of the agenda committee continued till 30th June 1944, when the delegates repaired to Bretton Woods. The U.K. and several other countries were represented at this preliminary conference, and in fact some of their representatives collaborated to prepare a draft set of proposals, which was worked upon during their trans-Atlantic voyage on the 'Queen Mary'. Interestingly enough, this set came to be known as the 'Boat Draft'. Invitations to attend the Bretton Woods conference in July 1944 were issued by the U.S. Secretary of State, though the U.S. Secretary of the Treasury, Henry Morgenthau, had earlier circulated a preliminary draft outline of a proposal for a United Nations Bank for Reconstruction and Development. Though greater emphasis was laid on setting up the International Monetary Fund (IMF), the conference did get around to considering the constitution of the proposed International Bank for Reconstruction and Development. The stress laid in the 'Boat Draft' on development generally, seems to have helped to maintain a balance between the needs of reconstruction after the devastation caused by the war on the one hand, and the needs of the developing countries on the other. The draft of the Articles of Agreement as these emerged from the Bretton Woods Conference were similar to the Articles as eventually adopted by the founder Members and appears to have been the collective work of Dean Acheson, Lord Keynes, Pierre Mendes France and several others, together with their aides.[2]

In retrospect, it is fitting that tribute should be paid to the remarkable foresight, and statesmanship of these leaders in the concerned Governments that they should have initiated measures during the dark days of the Second World War, culminating in the successful conclusion of the Bretton Woods Conference, so soon after D-day when even victory in the European theatre of operations was still in the balance. Though the Articles are said to be primarily the outcome of work in the U.S. Administration, especially the U.S. Treasury, other Governments also contributed, including those of the developing countries. It is noteworthy that the foundations laid down were basically sound, and the Articles have stood the test of time, with very few amendments since their adoption. They have enabled the IBRD to grow from strength to strength so that it is today an institution with an unrivalled financial standing, and its views carry weight in both the developed and the developing countries. Its impact on the entire process of development has been massive, and its reputation as the premier developmental institution is both well-earned and fully deserved.

The Articles of Agreement constitute a binding document signed by the various Governments who became or agreed to become 'Members' of the World Bank. The first article sets forth the purposes of the World Bank, with the express direction that it "shall be guided in *all* its decisions by the purposes set forth" (Emphasis added).

Pride of place amongst the various purposes goes to the reconstruction and development of territories of members by facilitating the investment of capital for productive purposes [Clause (i)]. These include:

(a) the restoration of economies destroyed or disrupted by war;
(b) the reconversion of productive facilities to peace time needs; and
(c) the encouragement of the development of productive facilities and resources in less developed countries.

Having regard to the time when these Articles were drafted, the reference to wartime destruction and disruption can be fully appreciated, but it is noteworthy that simultaneously, the needs of the less developed countries also find mention.

The second purpose is the promotion of *private* foreign investment by means of guarantees, or by participation by the IBRD in loans etc. by *private* investors. However, where private capital is not available on reasonable terms, the Bank is enabled to *supplement* private investment by providing finance for productive purposes out of its capital, or from funds raised by it. Both here and subsequently [Art. III, Sec. 4 (ii)], the Articles only contemplate direct lending by the IBRD, if private investment is not forthcoming on equitable terms, and the philosophy underlying the Articles is the promotion of private investment. A refrain which occurs repeatedly in this Article is the use of resources for productive purposes, and this is in keeping with the general thrust on securing the highest standards of efficiency, prudent lending, and the ability of the borrower to meet its obligations.

The third purpose is to promote balanced growth of international trade, and the maintenance of equilibrium in the balance of payments. The device suggested is the encouragement of international investment for the development of productive resources, from which was expected to follow, higher productivity, an improved standard of living and better conditions for labour. With the setting up of specialised agencies such as General Agreement on Tariffs and Trade (GATT) and now, the World Trade

Organisation (WTO), as well as the United Nations Conference on Trade and Development (UNCTAD), the international trade aspect is no longer of the same direct concern to the Bank as before. Also, the balance of payments situation, especially in the short term, more directly concerns the International Monetary Fund (IMF). Nevertheless, these aspects as well as the promotion of international investment remain at the core of the World Bank's economic philosophy, and permeate much of the thinking that goes into policy dialogue with the various borrowers, and the preparation of country reports giving advice and counsel to different countries regarding the management of their economies.

The fourth and fifth purposes need not detain us unduly. One lays down the priority that the more useful and urgent projects will be dealt with first. The framers of these Articles were aware that international loans would be available through other channels as well, and the suggestion to the Bank is to use its financial power in relation to these other loans so as to achieve the desired priority. There is also the express direction that the World Bank should conduct its operations with due regard to the effect of international investment on business conditions in the recipient country. In the short term, the objective was to bring about a smooth transition from a wartime to a peace-time economy.

ARTICLE II deals with Membership in the Bank and its capital. It will perhaps suffice if only the salient features are referred to here. An essential pre-requisite for membership in the Bank, is that the applicant should be a member of the IMF. The authorised capital was put at $ 10 billion[3], which was a relatively modest amount, and it was specified that the capital stock would be in terms of United States Dollars of the weight and fineness in effect on July Ist, 1944. As we shall see later, this provision led to complications because the USA delinked the U.S. Dollar from gold in 1978. The capital of the World Bank can be increased but this requires a three-fourth majority of the total voting power. The capital was divided into shares of $ 100,000 each. The Articles specified the original members in its Schedule A and also fixed the minimum amount each was to subscribe (with the exception of Denmark). The total amount allocated was $ 9.1 billion, the balance being available for new members, as and when other countries joined the Bank as members. The USA was by far the largest shareholder, subscribing $ 3.175 billion, followed by the United Kingdom and the USSR with $ 1.3 billion and $ 1.2 billion respectively. The fourth largest was China, i.e. Nationalist China, the People's Republic of China joining the Bank only in the late 70s or early 80s. The fifth largest was France, and the sixth largest was India. There were 45 countries included in this Schedule, but obviously none of the Axis powers could be included at the time, though Japan and Germany (FRG) in particular have played an increasingly important role in later years, with Italy also displaying growing interest. Poland and Yugoslavia were included, as was Norway, though Sweden was not one of the original members. The Articles also envisage members subscribing to shares of the capital stock in addition to their minimum subscriptions, subject, however, to the rules framed by the Bank.

Clause (c) of Section 3 of this Article incorporates an important safeguard, popularly known as the 'pre-emptive rights' clause. From time to time the practice has been to increase the authorised capital of the World Bank so as to reflect the economic strength of the member, and bring about a degree of correspondence with the revision of the IMF quotas. This provision allows a member an opportunity, whenever the Bank's capital is increased, to subscribe to a proportion of the increase of stock, equivalent to its own proportionate share in the total capital stock, *before* the increase was authorised, i.e. to maintain its original share of the total capital, and hence its relative voting power, despite the increase. This is a safeguard which operates in favour of countries which may not be growing economically as rapidly as others, or whose IMF quotas are getting depressed relative to others. India in particular has made repeated use of this provision.

Section 4 provided that the minimum shares of the original members shall be issued at par. Normally other shares will also be issued at par, though in special circumstances the Bank can decide otherwise. An important provision (Section 5) divides the subscription of each member into two parts, viz: (i) a 20 percent portion which is to be paid in, or in the alternative is subject to call, as needed for the operations of the Bank, and (ii) the remaining 80 percent portion, which though subject to call by the Bank, is only to be raised when it is required to meet the obligations the Bank incurred,

(a) by raising funds in the market of a member, or by other borrowings, or
(b) by guaranteeing loans made by private investors.

Liability on shares is limited to the unpaid portion of the issue price. During the earlier stages of the Bank's operations, the full 20 percent portion was paid in by the members, but as the finances of the Bank improved, and in order to induce members to agree to an increase in the capital stock, the paid-in portion was reduced initially to 10 percent, then to 7½ percent, and currently to 3 percent, for the 1988 General Capital Increase (GCI). The balance viz: 10 percent, 12½ percent or 17 percent can still be raised, should it be needed for the operations of the World Bank. This has not happened yet. The 80 percent portion represents a contingent liability, and would be raised only if the IBRD were to default in the repayment and servicing of the loans it raises, or if it were unable to honour its guarantees. Because of the healthy state of its reserves, and the circumstance that the loans sanctioned by the Bank are given only to member Governments or are guaranteed by these Governments, the risk that the recipients would default in their obligations to the Bank is small, and in turn, the risk of default by the World Bank is still more remote. Nevertheless, creditors are comforted by the assurance that the 80 percent portion is also available to them as backing, should it be required. As the share-holders comprise sovereign Governments, including the Governments of major industrial and economically powerful countries such as the USA, Germany, Japan, France and the U.K., the comfort derived is significant. These considerations serve to strengthen market perceptions of the IBRD's credit-worthiness, and enable it to borrow funds at favourable rates, which also helps the borrowing countries, as the rates charged by the Bank from its borrowers reflects the costs incurred by the former.

Out of the 20 percent share, 2 percent of the price of each share is payable in gold or in U.S. dollars, and, when calls are made the remaining 18 percent is to be paid in the currency of the member. However, when a call is made on account of the 80 percent portion, the member has the option of paying either in gold, in U.S. dollars, or in the currency required to discharge the obligations of the Bank for the purpose for which the call is made. As earlier mentioned, such a contingency is remote. The Articles have made transitory provisions for payment of the subscriptions, with relaxation for members whose metropolitan territories are still under enemy occupation, or who have not recovered possession of their gold reserves, etc. These clauses may have lost significance with the efflux of time but were highly relevant during the early years of the Bank's functioning. In fact, Czechoslovakia maintained that it came under Sec. 8(a) (ii) not having recovered possession of its gold reserves, and thus did not have to comply with a mandatory time limit for paying in its 2 percent contribution in gold or US Dollars. The Executive Directors, however, decided that Czechoslovakia was governed by Sec. 8(a) (i) which is applicable to cases where the country's metropolitan territories had suffered enemy occupation, and as such could postpone payment of its contribution by five years only. As a result, Czechoslovakia was suspended from membership in December 1953 and its membership formally terminated in 1954.[4] These clauses serve as a reminder of the problems facing the original members, and heighten the significance of the agreements hammered out even before the cessation of hostilities.

Section 9 of Article II provides an important safeguard for the World Bank. Since currencies of various members may be devalued, or may otherwise get depreciated, this provision is designed to insulate the Bank's finances from such currency fluctuations. An obligation is imposed on each member to maintain the value, as of the time of initial subscription, of its currency held by the Bank by paying in additional amounts of its own currency, whenever the par value of its currency is reduced, or the foreign exchange value of its currency within its own territories has, in the opinion of the Bank, depreciated to a significant extent. This obligation relates both to the subscription made by the member towards the Bank's capital in its own currency (usually 18% of the 20% portion), and held by the Bank, as well as to the amounts loaned out from its capital subscription to other borrowers, and repaid by them in the form of principal. Clearly the intention is to safeguard the full value of the capital subscription in a member's currency, whether it is being held by the Bank or has been lent out to some borrower. The safeguard is further reinforced by the stipulation that even those amounts paid in under these provisions to maintain the value of the member's currency originally held by the Bank, would be subject to the same obligation, and would require to be 'topped up' in the event of a future devaluation or depreciation. However, a member can avoid the maintenance of value obligation if it opted to repurchase its currency held by the Bank either against gold, or against the currency of any member acceptable to the Bank.

A converse provision applies when the member's currency appreciates and the Bank is required to return a corresponding amount to the member. However, a significant asymmetry exists between these two provisions. The member's obligation arises both when there is a change in the par value, and also when in the Bank's opinion, its currency has depreciated to a significant extent. The Bank's obligation to return the extra amount arises under the articles *only* when the par value of the member's currency is increased, and the possibility of an appreciation in value otherwise is ignored. Finally, these provisions could be waived if a uniform proportionate change in the par values of the currencies of all its members is made by the IMF.

A reference has been made earlier to the provisions requiring the capital stock of the Bank to be expressed in terms of the United States dollar of the weight and fineness in effect on July 1, 1944. This provision became obsolete with the amendment of the Articles of Agreement of the IMF, and the simultaneous changes in the Par Value Modification Act of the United States in 1978, which effectively repealed the legislation linking the current US dollar with gold.

The consequence was that while before 1978 the Bank had a workable standard of value in which all members' subscriptions to the Bank's capital stock could be denominated, after 1978, there was no such standard of value, and the basis for converting 1944 gold dollars into current US dollars ceased to exist. As a corollary, maintenance of value settlements for members' subscriptions were suspended from 1978. The situation was clearly anomalous, and had its effect on the market perceptions of the IBRD's financial position. In the absence of a strong and stable common standard of value, bond-holders could become concerned about the prospect of an erosion overtime in the relationship of callable capital to the debt of the Bank, and such a concern could affect the Bank's ability to borrow from the financial markets, and thus hamper its role of financial intermediation, and perhaps simultaneously, raise the cost of borrowing. It was estimated in 1981 that the Bank's subscribed capital would have been $ 8 billion lower at the end of FY 1980 if members' subscriptions had originally been denominated in their own currencies rather than in 1944 dollars or SDRs. There could be other operational difficulties also. As will be mentioned later, the total loans and guarantees outstanding is limited by the Articles, and the Bank's capital is an important determinant of this limit. In the absence of a common standard of value, this limit could not be computed precisely, and by way of abundant caution, a conservative view was adopted, which constrained the Bank's lending. As an interim measure, the Bank accepted subscriptions to its capital at the rate of 1.20635 current US dollars for one 1944 US dollar, this rate being the last official value of that dollar in terms of the current US dollar.

The confusion arising from these arrangements eventually led to the formation of an *ad hoc* Committee of Directors in 1983, to resolve the issue. It was able to report only in 1986. The preference of most countries was to adopt the SDR as the common standard of value, as it was recognised internationally, and was devised by the IMF itself. However, the USA was adamant in rejecting this suggestion, primarily because under the original dispensation, with the US dollar as the standard of value, the USA was unique in that it had no maintenance of value obligation, though all other members had this obligation. From 1974, the currency basket method of valuing the SDR was adopted. Hence, the adoption of the SDR as the common standard of value would treat all members equally. This position was unacceptable to the USA as it was said to impose an open-ended commitment in dollar terms on the USA.

The eventual solution proposed by the *ad hoc* Committee and adopted by the Board of Executive Directors was to interpret the words "United States dollars of the weight and fineness in effect on July 1, 1944" to mean the SDR introduced by the Fund, as the SDR was valued in terms of the US dollar immediately before the introduction of the basket method of valuing the SDR on July 1, 1974, such value being 1.20635 US dollars for one SDR.

In effect, therefore, the common standard of value thus remained the US dollar. However, the Committee and the Board did envisage the possibility of a substantial appreciation of the SDR against the US dollar, and provided for a review of the adequacy of the Bank's capital every three years, or at any time in the intervening periods when, in their judgement, such a review became warranted. The object was to ensure that negative effects on the Bank's capital owing to the fluctuations in the US dollar were avoided. With such an arrangement, the US objection was satisfied, and it remained unique in continuing to have no maintenance of value obligation, unlike all other members. The maintenance of value payments were also resumed on the basis of this decision, though certain transitional measures were adopted to spread out the payments needed for meeting these obligations.

Certain calculations were made at the time (May 31st, 1986) which estimated these obligations at $ 643 million for the Part II (developing) countries, and at only $ 71 million for the Part I (developed) countries. The asymmetry in the literal wording of the Article between the members' obligation to the Bank on the one hand, and that of the Bank on the other, to those members whose currency appreciated has been noted earlier. The Committee and the Board took a broad view, and as a policy, decided that the Bank would make maintenance value payment to members whose currency had significantly appreciated, on the ground that the reference to par values in the wording of the article was outmoded in the changed circumstances.[5]

These developments throw light on the functioning of the IBRD, and have, therefore, been mentioned at some length. A clearly anomalous situation arising out of the delinking of the USA dollar from gold in 1978 was resolved only in 1986, and even then in a somewhat transitory manner. Despite the long time that elapsed, there was no amendment of the Articles, which would prima facie appear to have been the correct and straightforward remedy. On the contrary, reliance was placed on the interpretative authority of the Executive Directors contained in Article IX, and a somewhat strained meaning was given to the outmoded words in question. Such a devious course had to be adopted to obtain a consensus. Clearly, even before the dissolution of the USSR as the second Super-Power, the USA had an overwhelming say in the functioning of the IBRD and was thus able to protect its unique position, by virtue of which it continued to avoid maintenance of value obligations binding all other members. Experience suggests that any significant amendments to the Articles will be difficult to make, as reaching the requisite consensus may face even more formidable obstacles in the present altered situation. Later in this chapter, the provisions in the Articles concerning their amendment have been discussed. These provisions were apparently inserted to ensure that amendments were not proposed lightly, and reinforce the statement made here.

The imbalance between the maintenance of value obligations estimated for the developing countries ($ 643 million) and those for the developed countries ($ 71 million), has already been noted. It is noteworthy that according to these estimates, the only significant amounts that would have to be returned by the Bank to the members are $ 178 million to Japan and $ 25 million to Germany. This pattern may continue to hold in future also, at least for some time. Developing countries can be generally expected to have weak currencies in the foreseeable future because of the demands made by the development process itself, and they will therefore face the full rigour of the resumption of maintenance of value payments, while economically strong countries such as Japan and Germany (especially after the strain of unification has eased) stand to benefit. Owing to their weak bargaining position, and need for additional funds, developing countries will probably find that even their genuine difficulties will receive short shrift at the hands of the international community.

ARTICLE III relates to loans and guarantees by the IBRD. The first Section provides that the resources and facilities of the Bank are to be used exclusively for the benefit of members. Thereafter, follows the remarkable statement that equitable consideration should be given to projects for development and projects for reconstruction alike. The framers of the Articles were content to add that for determining the terms and conditions of loans for those members whose metropolitan territories have suffered great devastation from hostilities, the Bank will pay due regard to lightening the financial burden and expediting the completion of projects for the restoration and reconstruction of their economies. It is noteworthy that the framers were not unduly influenced by the enormity of the war damage, and the immediacy of facilitating reconstruction work, to the extent that they were impelled to accord priority to such activities; on the contrary, they looked at the issues in a longer term perspective and called for consideration of all projects, whether for development or for reconstruction, on an equal footing. The next Section is procedural, laying down the channels of communication and calls for no further comment.

The third Section imposes an important limitation on the IBRD's authority to lend or to extend guarantees. Briefly, it enjoins that the total amount of the outstanding loans, and guarantees shall not be increased at any time, if by such increase the total were to exceed the aggregate of the unimpaired subscribed capital, the reserves and the surplus of the Bank. The phrase "at any time" has given rise to the concept of the sustainable level of lending, which predicates that the Bank should not increase the level of its annual lending to such an extent, that it subsequently has to cut back sharply in order to remain within the limit imposed by the Articles. The "sustainable level of lending" is supposed to constitute the maximum annual level which can be sustained indefinitely by the Bank without exceeding the mandatory limit, at a given level of capital stock. Clearly, this sustainable level depends upon many factors including the grace period for a loan, its maturity, the speed of disbursement, the rate of interest, and the reserves and surpluses that can be accumulated. The concept furnishes an argument for inhibiting additional Bank lending even though there is still considerable cushion between the mandatory limit determined by the Bank's capital stock, reserves, etc. and the amount of loans and guarantees outstanding. Ostensibly, on the grounds of continuity and stability, the concept serves to curb Bank lending some years before the time when the mandatory limit may be reached, and does not take cognizance of factors such as a possible capital increase in the interim, or a change in any of the other determinants of this level.

The criticism is also voiced in a diametrically opposite direction—the argument being that in effect the mandatory limit is tantamount to the adoption of a 1:1 "gearing ratio" between the Bank's capital and reserves on the one hand, and the aggregate of the loans and guarantees on the other, and is therefore, unduly conservative having regard to normal banking practice.[6] The validity of this argument may be questioned on the ground that the World Bank is not typical of most commercial banks, which adopt a higher leverage for their capital base, as only a fraction of the capital is paid in, the percentage having fallen from the original 20% to the current figure of 3% and the paid in portion alone is available to the Bank for its normal operations.

The fourth Section lays down the conditions which the IBRD should fulfil when making or guaranteeing loans, and these conditions call for further comment, as they determine the manner in which the Bank discharges its primary function of lending money to its borrowers, or of guaranteeing loans by other investors. The first condition seeks to involve the member either directly as the borrower, or as the guarantor if the loan is to some other entity in the territory of the member. Thus, an essential condition attached to all loans or guarantees by the World Bank, is that the concerned Government or the Central Bank, or some other comparable agency acceptable to the Bank, must assume responsibility for the repayment of the principal, and the payment of interest and other charges, as these fall due. Loans, etc. can be given to the concerned Government directly, or to any political sub-division, or to any business, or enterprise, industrial or agricultural, in the territory of the member, subject to the foregoing safeguard. Consequently, when loans are sanctioned for organisations located, say in India, such as the National Thermal Power Corporation, the Indian Iron and Steel Co., the National Bank for Agricultural Development, the Industrial Credit and Investment Corporation of India, or a quasi-municipal body such as the Calcutta Metropolitan Development Authority, the legal documentation is completed in several parts, obligating each of the parties involved, but invariably there is a legal document obligating the Government of India. The second condition stipulates that the Bank has to be satisfied that in the prevailing market conditions, the borrower would otherwise be unable to obtain the loan on reasonable terms. To avoid any dispute, the Articles specify that the opinion of the Bank will determine the reasonableness or otherwise of the terms. This condition is a re-affirmation of the principle laid down in Article I and referred to earlier, though now spelt out in more specific terms. These provisions are said to make the Bank a lender of last resort. The third condition is that a committee (known as the Loan Committee) should have submitted a written report recommending the project after a careful study of the merits of the proposal. This Committee is to include an expert selected by the Governor representing the member in whose territory the project is located. Normally, the Senior Vice President (Operations) of the Bank chairs this Committee. For India, the 'expert' selected is the Minister (Economic) attached to the Embassy in Washington. In practice, the recommendation made to the Executive Directors by the President of the Bank, goes through so many reviews and revisions before finalisation, that the Loan Committee's recommendation is often a formality. If the World Bank is to be at all faulted, it is for its many-tiered examination of a project from diverse angles, and the protracted nature of the review process adopted by it prior to consideration by the mandatory Loan Committee. The next two conditions seek to ensure the economic viability of the project, and the fulfillment of the repayment and servicing obligations of the borrower, or the guarantor, as the case may be. The Bank has to see that the interest and other charges levied, and the repayment schedule are appropriate for the project in question. Further, the Bank is enjoined to pay due regard to the prospects that the borrower, or the guarantor, would be in a position to meet their obligations under the loan. Finally, the Bank is directed to act prudently, in a dual role viz. in the interests of the particular member in whose territory the project is situated, and also in the interests of the members collectively. The sixth condition enjoins that when the Bank guarantees a loan, it is suitably compensated for the risk undertaken. The final condition stipulates that the loan made by the Bank, or guaranteed by it, will be for the purpose of specific projects of reconstruction or development, though exceptions may be made in special circumstances. This condition has led to some discussion, as the term 'project' has not been defined. Views have oscillated over a wide range from time to time.

Sometimes, projects have been defined narrowly to mean a particular construction project such as a multi-purpose dam, or a power station, and at other times it has been argued that the only pre-requisite is that the project must have a productive purpose. Instead of invoking the 'special circumstances' clause, it is argued by the proponents of the latter view that loans given for structural adjustment, and for imports of particular items in short supply, the lack of which is inhibiting the development of the full productive potential of the borrower, would also qualify under this clause in the normal course. There are precedents in support of such a view. Thus Mason and Asher in their book 'The World Bank since Bretton Woods' lists 26 programme loans or credits which were approved till 1971.[7] These include four reconstruction loans to France, Netherlands, Denmark and Luxembourg approved during 1946-48. The French loan was for the import of specific commodities, and at the meeting of the Board of Executive Directors, the Chairman thought that the project contemplated by the French application was the "Monet Plan". The sense of the Executive Directors seems to have been that countries want to import goods—sometimes for building bridges or railways, but sometimes to make their industries work—and this could be treated as a "general project". An essential feature, however, was that control of the loan vested in the Bank, and not in the borrower.

Section 5 specifies certain conditions with regard to the use of loans made or guaranteed by the IBRD. A vital safeguard is introduced which benefits the borrowers, viz. that the Bank is prohibited from imposing conditions requiring that the proceeds of any such loan are to be spent in the territories of any member or members. It further specifies that the proceeds of any such loan will be used exclusively for the purposes for which the loan was made. The Articles require that due attention be paid to considerations of economy and efficiency, but political or other non-economic considerations and influences be eschewed. An account is to be opened in the name of the borrower, and the amount of the loan, with particulars of the currency, credited to this account. The borrower can draw on this account only to meet expenses on the project, as these are incurred. These provisions distinguish lending by an international multilateral institution such as the IBRD, from bilateral lending. Not only is the loan untied, but also, owing to the stress on economy and efficiency, the Bank has adopted a system of open international competitive bidding for purchase of plant and equipment and award of contracts for civil works, etc. However, in the interests of the developing countries, which now constitute an overwhelming proportion of the borrowers, local supplies and contractors are given a marginal price preference. The reference to political and non-economic influences is presumably introduced to ensure that contracts and purchases generally are awarded or finalised on strictly economic considerations. Not infrequently particular Executive Directors canvass for contracts or orders going to suppliers, etc. from the countries they represent. However, these provisions in the Articles of Agreement ensure a degree of fairness and give credibility to the system of open competitive bidding. They act as a salutary check not only on the developed countries, but also on the developing countries, which are mostly buying countries, and ensure that the borrowers receive full value from the loans made, as the Bank management is better able to resist undesirable pressure owing to the existence of these provisions. The one feature which can operate somewhat harshly is that unlike loans from commercial banks, loans from the IBRD normally can be drawn down as expenditure is incurred, which usually means on a reimbursement basis, after the expenditure has been incurred, and fully vouched for, and hence only after a considerable time-lag. However, relaxations have been made for programme loans, etc.

The final Section under this Article is an amendment introduced in December 1965, which authorises loans to the International Finance Corporation (IFC) set up to participate in the equity of private companies and to make loans to them, without the involvement of the concerned Government. There are some consequential exceptions in favour of the IFC, and a limit on the total indebtedness of that body, equivalent to 4 times its unimpaired subscribed capital.

ARTICLE IV deals with the operations of the IBRD. Section 1 empowers the Bank to lend money directly, or to participate in loans *first* out of its own funds, i.e. its unimpaired paid-up capital, its surplus, and its reserves (subject to a special reserve being held in liquid form), and *secondly* out of funds which are raised in the market of a member, or are otherwise borrowed by the Bank. The Bank is also empowered to guarantee loans made by private investors through the usual investment channels. The operations of the Bank have now reached a stage where it has to borrow in the financial markets of the world, various currencies aggregating to around $ 12 billion per annum. The Section expressly provides that the Bank can borrow funds only with the approval of the member in whose markets the funds are raised, and only if the member agrees that the proceeds may be exchanged for other currencies without restrictions. Consequently, only markets of member countries with freely convertible currencies are open to the Bank for raising funds, and its access to those markets also is dependent on the approval of the member concerned. As a result, countries such as the USA, Germany, and Japan can exercise considerable influence on the *Bank's* policies, etc. as their financial markets are important sources of borrowed funds, which the Bank thereafter re-lends. Similarly, the Bank can guarantee only those loans made by private investors where the loan is denominated in a convertible currency and the concerned member has approved. Though the framers of the Articles had envisaged considerable use of Bank guarantees, in practice the Bank has mostly lent directly. Recently, the Bank's Board has emphasised the guarantee option especially for financing infrastructure projects through private sector funds in a dramatic deviation from past practice (Annual Report, 1995).[8] Also, for some years the Bank has encouraged co-financing with other parties. It is noteworthy that so long as the capital base is adequate, additional Bank lending need not be a *direct* drain on the resources of the member Governments as such, since the Bank can fund such additional activities by re-lending funds raised from the market. It can be argued, of course, that additional World Bank borrowing in a member's financial markets, crowds out other domestic borrowers. Members normally impose limits on the World Bank borrowings to eliminate the possibility of any such adverse effects. A fascinating paper written by the former World Bank Vice-President and Treasurer, Mr. Eugene Rotberg, who headed the organisation responsible for raising resources from the global financial markets for the World Bank, and published as part of the report of the Bretton Woods Commission, gives a graphic account of the difficulties that can be created by the member, in whose territory, the financial market being tapped, is located. Access could be curtailed in unpredictable ways, and he states that by 1982, the Bank's access to markets in virtually all non-dollar currencies was limited to a programme well below what the Bank was required to borrow. These constraints were due not only to domestic economic conditions, but also because of a perceived weak foreign exchange position. The host Government was fully aware that the currency borrowed by the Bank would be immediately convertible, and put further pressure on their currency. He also cites instances where access was constrained because of disagreement with the Bank management on lending to particular sectors of the developing world, which were deemed to be potentially 'competitive'. Access could also be affected because of 'geopolitical' differences with the countries to whom the Bank was lending. Owing to reasons of 'burden-sharing', the Bank's access to markets for certain currencies was explicitly conditioned by access to markets in other countries.[9] Fortunately, the position has improved greatly in recent years (vide Chapter 6).

Section 2 imposes further conditions on the IBRD with regard to the availability and transferability of currencies, and is designed to strengthen the hands of the member-Governments in minimizing any strain on their currencies because of the operations of the Bank, and its borrowers. The paid-in portion of the capital can only be loaned by the Bank with the prior approval of the concerned member. As an extension of this condition, it is also provided that currencies which are received by the Bank in repayment of the principal of such a loan from the borrower or the guarantor, can be re-loaned or converted into other currencies only with the approval of the concerned member. However, in both cases, these restrictions do not apply where the entire capital has been called up and the monies are required for meeting the obligations of the Bank, and this provision thus constitutes a safeguard for the Bank's creditors. Use of borrowed funds is less restricted in certain cases viz., *first*, repayments by the borrowers or the guarantors of the principal of loans financed out of funds that are borrowed by the Bank can be used without restriction for the purposes of amortisation or for repurchase of the Banks' obligations, *secondly*, currencies obtained from the market, or otherwise borrowed, interest payments received as well as other charges on account of all loans, guarantees, commissions, etc. as also proceeds from the sale of gold, can be used or exchanged for other currencies or for gold, if required for the Bank's operations, without restrictions, and *thirdly*, currencies re-used in the market by borrowers against guarantees by the Bank can be similarly used or exchanged without restrictions.

Section 3 lays down conditions on the type of expenditure that direct World Bank loans can finance, irrespective of whether these loans are met out of the Bank's own funds, or out of borrowed funds. The Bank is authorised to furnish currencies of those members (other than that of the member where the project is located), as are needed for the expenditure in their territories to carry out the purposes of the loan. It is, therefore, obligatory for the Bank to finance the foreign exchange required for purchase of plant and equipment from other countries, as well as to finance expenditure in foreign exchange directly required for consultancy services, works contracts etc. By general usage, this clause also covers some indirect requirements of foreign exchange which are directly traceable to the concerned project. Thus if a domestic producer of equipment for a Bank financed project requires imported material to produce this equipment, then the foreign exchange needed would also qualify under this provision.[10] There is a provision for expenditure in local currency to be financed in exceptional circumstances, but this provision is not frequently used as members are usually able to raise internal resources or to print more local currency to meet requirements. Clause (c) of this Section, which also applies to all direct loans, reads as follows:

> "The Bank, if the project gives rise indirectly to an increased need for foreign exchange by the member in whose territories the project is located may in exceptional circumstances provide the borrower as part of the loan with an appropriate amount of gold or foreign exchange not in excess of the borrower's local expenditure in connection with the purposes of the loan."

It is reproduced as its application, and evolution of Bank policy in this regard has been controversial. The Bank has been liberal and broadened its interpretation from time to time, so that local expenditure can also be financed by loans in foreign exchange in most cases where the Bank is convinced that the borrower has a suitable programme of development, and is making an adequate development effort. One consideration in favour of a broader interpretation is that many high priority projects may have relatively low foreign exchange requirements, and otherwise would not be posed for Bank financing, as borrowers are often chronically short of foreign exchange and would normally propose projects with a high foreign exchange component for such financing. Often domestic suppliers of equipment or works contractors are competitive, and the Bank would like to encourage them by covering the total cost in foreign exchange. It is also a consideration if the borrower has an overall development programme which is acceptable to the Bank, but does not have the resources, whether in foreign exchange or in local currency to finance such a programme, without disrupting the economy, owing to inflation or otherwise. The Bank may even be prepared to finance a project which appears desirable on all grounds, except that it has too small a foreign exchange component, by supplementing its lending through financing some local costs.[11] From time to time, financing of local costs has shaded into programme lending, and credits for the import of required raw materials and equipment. Later still, this clause has provided the vehicle for advancing Structural Adjustment Loans with heavy emphasis on policy dialogue, and the imposition of conditions requiring major shifts in economic policy on the part of the borrower. There is a further provision, that in exceptional circumstances and upon request the Bank may repurchase a part of a member's currency in whose territory a portion of a Bank loan has been spent. This provision too has been infrequently used in recent years.

Section 4 provides for the servicing of direct loans made by the World Bank. The terms and conditions of the loan are to be determined by the Bank, i.e. the maturity of the loan, the rate of interest, as well as the terms and conditions of the commission to be charged. For loans out of borrowed funds, the Section stipulates that for the first ten years the Bank has to charge a commission between 1% and 1½% of the amount of the loan outstanding, which is credited to a special reserve. However, beyond this period the

World Bank can alter the rate of the commission depending upon the reserves. Because the IBRD has to deal in various currencies, there are special provisions to minimize the currency risk to which it is exposed, owing to volatility of the currencies in which it has to transact business. All loan contracts have to stipulate the currency or currencies in which payments have to be made under them by the borrower to the Bank. For loans made out of the Bank's own funds, the loan contracts shall provide that payments to the Bank of interest, other charges and amortisation shall be made in the currency loaned. However, an exception has been allowed where the member whose currency is loaned, agrees that payment may be made in some other specified currency, or currencies. These payments are to be equivalent in value to the contractual payments at the time the loans were made, and expressed in terms of a single currency specified by the Bank by a three-fourth majority. However, this stipulation may be waived if there is a uniform proportionate change in the par values of the currencies of all members under the aegis of the IMF. On the other hand, for loans made out of funds borrowed by the World Bank, the Section imposes a limit that the total amount outstanding and payable to the Bank in any particular currency is not to exceed the total amount borrowed by the Bank in that currency. The section further provides a theoretical option to the borrower, to repay in gold or in another currency of a member, to which the Bank agrees. The Section provides for a situation where the borrowing or guaranteeing member faces an acute exchange stringency and is unable to fulfil its obligation in the stipulated manner. The IBRD may then agree to some relaxation if such a course is found to be in the interest of the particular member, of the Bank and of the members as a whole. The relaxation may be on two counts, viz. to accept the member's currency for a period not exceeding three years, subject to safeguards about maintenance of its value, or in the alternative, to extend the period of the loan. As a matter of general policy, in recent years the World Bank has decided against re-scheduling any of its loans, and there have been no significant long term defaults.

Section 5 empowers the Bank to guarantee loans and to determine the commission and other conditions for their issue. Similar to the conditions imposed with regard to direct loans made out of borrowed funds, the commission is to be fixed in the range of 1% to 1½% during the initial ten years and discretion to alter this rate as deemed fit has been allowed both during and after this period. In case of default, the Bank is authorised to offer to purchase the bonds, etc. guaranteed by it upon which its interest liability will cease. During previous years, guarantees issued by the Bank, except for co-financing arrangements have been infrequent, though this position may now change consequent upon the decision of the Board referred to earlier to mainstream Bank guarantees as an operational tool.

Section 6 constituted a Special Reserve where the commission stipulated by the preceding two Sections was to be set aside. This Section had laid down a period of ten years, after which the Bank was empowered to reduce the commission if the accumulated reserves were considered adequate. Since 1964 no further amounts have been credited to the special reserve. The Bank does maintain a general reserve, however, which is part of the Retained Earnings.

The next Section (Sec. 7) outlines the steps to be taken in the event of default in loans made or guaranteed by the IBRD. Since the Bank has been empowered to borrow funds in the market and from elsewhere, for re-lending to its borrowers, massive defaults by the latter could affect the position of the Bank itself and hence provision has been made for such a contingency, should it arise. Though never invoked, these explicit provisions provide considerable re-assurance to the Bank's creditors and facilitate the task of raising large sums from the financial markets of the world on very favourable terms. In the event of a default, the Bank is empowered to adjust the obligations, and also to re-schedule the loan, or even accept payment in local currency for a period not exceeding three years, in the manner already referred to above. Adjustment of the obligations, in respect of which default has occurred, can be carried out in several ways; one that readily comes to mind is that the borrower may be entitled to reimbursement of expenditure under the concerned loan, or some other World Bank loan, and the Bank could adjust these payments due to the borrower against such obligations. Clearly also, in the event of a borrower with several World Bank loans, default in one loan, would affect transactions under both preceding and succeeding loans.

The Bank's liabilities under its own borrowings or arising from guarantees issued by it, if not otherwise cleared, should first be met out of the special reserve, and if this does not suffice, then out of other reserves, the Bank's surplus, and its paid-in capital. However, should contractual liabilities of the Bank still remain because of its borrowings, or because of its guarantees, then an appropriate amount could be called from the unpaid capital of the Bank, to be subscribed by the members (i.e. out of the balance of the 20%, and if required, the 80% unpaid capital). If it is anticipated that the default would continue for a protracted period, the Bank is authorised to make calls on the unpaid capital not exceeding 1% in any one year of the member's subscription for the purpose of either reducing all or part of the principal of any loan guaranteed by it, or repurchasing all or part of its own outstanding borrowings.

Section 8 incorporates some miscellaneous provisions, which give the World Bank the needed authority and flexibility to buy and sell securities either issued or guaranteed by it, or in which it has invested, but only with the approval of the concerned member. An additional stipulation with regard to investment of the special reserve, is that the securities have to be approved by a three-fourth's majority. The Bank is also authorised to borrow currency but again with the approval of the concerned member.

Section 9 contains a stipulation that securities issued or guaranteed by the Bank must bear a conspicuous endorsement that it is not an obligation of any Government (unless of course, this is expressly the case). The intention clearly is to distance the Bank's financial transactions from those of any member Government, so that there is no confusion in the public mind on this score, and the liability of any member Government is strictly limited to its shareholding (excluding, of course, liabilities incurred on account of loans or guarantees taken from the Bank as a client).

Section 10 is noteworthy as it is an express direction requiring the World Bank and its officers to desist from interfering in the political affairs of any member, and not to be influenced in its decisions by the political character of any member. It is not unlikely that this provision was introduced having the Soviet Union in mind. This provision results in the Bank having to tread a thin line, especially at its Washington, D.C. Headquarters, since the U.S.

Congress appropriates funds and the USA is still the biggest shareholder, and the distinction between educational and clarificatory activities on Capitol Hill on the one hand, and lobbying with Congress on the other, can be tenuous in the extreme. Similarly, the free enterprise and market philosophy of the Bank can lead to complications when dealing with Socialist countries—but there has been admirable accommodation on both sides. This Section also contains a general direction that only economic considerations would be relevant in arriving at decisions. This provision, thus, reinforces a similar direction in Article III, Section 5, which it will be recalled, stresses that the proceeds of a Bank loan will be used with due attention to considerations of economy and efficiency, and eschews political or other non-economic considerations. Further, the Section adds that the economic considerations will be weighed impartially in order to achieve the purposes outlined in Article I, to which attention has been drawn earlier. The further re-affirmation in this Section of the purposes actuating the World Bank, despite the basic directive already incorporated in Article 1 itself, viz., that "the Bank shall be guided in all its decisions by the purposes set forth above", strongly suggests that the framers attached great importance to this aspect, and desired that these purposes should remain inviolate. This Section, therefore, is unusual in harking back to two distinct ideas which have already been incorporated in the Articles and reinforcing them. The Articles of Agreement are a meticulously drafted document by a body of experts, and each Section has been skilfully crafted, hence the repetition of the above mentioned twin ideas can only be assumed to have been deliberate, so as to serve as a constant and powerful reminder to the Bank and its Board of Governors, when overseeing the activities of the Bank.

ARTICLE V deals with the World Bank's organisation and management. Section 1 defines the basic structure, which is to comprise a Board of Governors, a number of Executive Directors, a President together with "such other officers and staff to perform such duties as the Bank may determine". Section 2 elaborates the powers and functions of the Board of Governors, which is the supreme authority. All the powers of the Bank are vested in the Board of Governors. Each member can appoint a Governor, and an alternate Governor to function in his absence. The Board of Governors will select one of the Governors as a Chairman.

The Board of Governors is authorised to delegate all its powers to the Executive Directors excluding certain powers which it alone can exercise. The list of 'reserved' powers makes interesting reading —one group deals with the admission of new members, and the conditions of their admission, and the suspension of a member. Another group of reserved powers deals with changes in the capital stock, distribution of the net income of the Bank, the permanent suspension of the operations of the Bank and distribution of its assets. Logically, appeals against interpretations of the Article given by the Executive Directors has to be decided by the Board of Governors. The Board of Governors alone can make arrangements to cooperate with other international organisations except where these arrangements are informal and of a temporary or administrative nature. Finally, the Board of Governors can fix the remuneration of the Executive Directors, and the salary as well as the terms of the contract with the President. The Articles require an annual meeting of the Board of Governors to be held. The requirements for holding other meetings of the Board of Governors have been laid down. Other procedural matters such as the quorum, and obtaining a vote on any question arising, *without* holding a meeting of the Board have been covered, and call for no further comment. Though the Board of Governors is the supreme authority, genuine power is vested in the Executive Directors and the President, as all the Board's powers have been delegated, excepting the reserved powers. Further, the Board of Governors is an unwieldy body with around 178 members,[12] all of whom hold highly responsible offices in their respective Governments; normally it is the Finance or Economic Affairs Minister or his equivalent, who represents a member country as its Governor on the Board. It is customary for the Board as such to meet only once a year, because of the pre-occupations of the Governors in their home countries, and other time constraints. Decisions are to be generally decided by a majority of votes cast, though there are important exceptions, which require not only a specified majority (3/4 or 4/5) of votes, but also a majority in the numbers of the Governors. All members have 250 votes, and in addition, one vote for each share of stock held. While this system of weighted voting enormously strengthens the hands of the major industrial countries, yet care has been taken to ensure that the developing countries are not steam-rollered in all cases. Both the allotment of 250 votes to each member and also the requirement to have a majority of the Governors voting in favour, when certain important issues come for decision, seek to redress the balance to some extent.

Initially, there were 12 Executive Directors but as provided in the Articles, when the membership increased, the number of Executive Directors also increased, and currently stands at 24. Of these, one each is appointed by the five largest shareholders, viz., USA, Japan, U.K., France and Germany. The remaining 19 are selected in the manner laid down by the Articles, and except in the cases of China and Russia, the Executive Director is representing a group of countries, rather than a single country. Some of the groups are quite large, e.g. those comprising the African countries, and may not even be homogeneous. Thus even amongst countries represented by a single Executive Director, divergent views on particular issues may be held by the member-Governments. The Articles, however, require that the Executive Director will cast his vote as a unit, comprising the total of all the votes of the countries in the group. If there are irreconcilable views on an issue amongst the members of the group, then a piquant situation can arise. Sometimes, fairness necessitates that the concerned Executive Director abstain, should such an issue come up for a vote. Executive Directors are appointed for a two years term, though the same person may be re-appointed or re-elected for a further term or terms. Each Executive Director is required to appoint an alternate. If an elected Executive Director resigns or his office otherwise becomes vacant, with ninety days or more remaining before his term would normally end, then a re-election takes place.

Executive Directors are responsible for the general conduct of the operations of the Bank and for the exercise of the powers delegated by the Board of Governors. The Articles require the Executive Directors to select the President, who is also their Chairman. The President will cease to hold office when the Executive Directors so decide. The President shall be Chief of the operating staff of the Bank and shall conduct the ordinary business of the Bank under the direction of the Executive Directors. The President is responsible for the organisation, appointment and dismissal of the officers and staff of the Bank. The impression that may be left by this brief outline of the relevant provisions in the Articles, is that the Executive Directors wield enormous powers while the President is relegated to a subordinate role, especially since he has no vote except in the event of a tie. In practice, however, this is not the case. The Executive Directors necessarily have to abide by the directions of the Government or Governments they represent and often lack cohesion, as they may not be able to speak in one voice, mirroring the often conflicting views of the various nation-states. The power of selection of the President vested in the Executive Directors is largely theoretical, as a convention has developed since the early days when the USA was providing most of the funds, that the President would be a U.S. national (and for balance the Managing Director of the I.M.F. would be a European). His selection is made initially at a very high level within the U.S. administration, and the Executive Directors merely ratify it, though for forms sake a committee of Executive Directors meets the prospective candidate, and discusses the terms and conditions of his appointment prior to the ratification. Because of the lack of progress under the first President, Mr. Eugene Mayer, his successor, President McCloy accepted his assignment only on the understanding that, by convention, the President would initiate a proposal, and it was the prerogative of the Executive Directors to either accept it, with or without modification, or to reject it.[13] Thus, with the initiative passing to the President, the role of the Executive Directors has diminished somewhat from what was envisaged in the Articles. Nevertheless, since the Executive Directors function in continuous session at the Bank's Headquarters, and meet as often as is required, normally at least once a week, they collectively play a crucial role. Not only is the size of the Board of Executive Directors manageable, but also they speak with the authority of the Governments they represent, and their deliberations covering a wide spectrum of views, have a profound influence on the policies of the Bank, as well as on the attitude of the Bank's staff. Their authority to oversee the various activities of the Bank, including the approval of loans, and its borrowings from the financial markets or through private placements, as well as the detailed scrutiny of the budget by the Executive Directors, ensure that the Bank's functioning is closely monitored, and necessary correctives can be applied, as and when required. The Articles empower the appointment of Committees of the Executive Directors. One such, viz., the Joint Audit Committee, carries out a *post facto* evaluation of projects which have been executed with the help of Bank loans and is serviced by the Director-General, Operations Evaluation and his staff. The Executive Directors and this Committee can ensure that lessons are learned from the execution of past schemes and applied with necessary modifications to future projects, despite the wide variations that prevail between conditions in one country and another, and the enormous differences that exist in the formulation and execution of projects located in a multitude of countries, at different stages of development.

The outline, as given above, of the role of the President, envisaged in the Articles needs some elaboration. Besides being the Chairman of the Executive Directors, he is authorised to participate in the meetings of the Board of Governors, though he has no vote. This provides him with a unique opportunity of addressing the Governors, reporting on developments, as well as outlining the future policies and programmes of the Bank. Since the annual meetings of the World Bank and the I.M.F. are held simultaneously, it is a glittering function, usually addressed by the President of the USA, if held in Washington. It attracts the attention of the mass media, and is well attended by economic journalists. Most Presidents take full advantage of the opportunity to focus world attention on the activities of the Bank. Section 5 of this Article lays down that the President, officers, and staff of the Bank, in the discharge of their offices, owe their duty entirely to the Bank and to no other authority. Corresponding to this direction, a parallel direction requires each member of the Bank to respect the international character of this duty, and to refrain from all attempts to influence the President or any of the Bank staff in the discharge of their duties. Finally, the last clause of this Section requires the President in appointing officers and staff to pay due regard to the importance of recruiting personnel on as wide a geographical basis as possible; this provision is subject to the paramount importance of securing the highest standards of efficiency, and of technical competence.

Reference has been made already to the direction given to the Bank to ensure that when using loan-proceeds due attention should be paid to considerations of economy and efficiency. This direction, coupled with the further direction that in recruiting personnel paramount importance has to be attached to securing the highest standards of efficiency and of technical competence, is indicative of the importance given by the framers of the Articles to the efficient functioning of the World Bank. These expectations have not been belied, and the Bank functions as an efficient, if prudent and conservative, organisation, though perhaps somewhat slow-moving. Earlier, attention has been drawn also to the directions given to the *Bank* regarding non-interference in the political affairs of members and the avoidance of political considerations in using loan funds. This direction is reinforced by the equally significant parallel direction in this Section calling upon the *members* in this case, to respect the international character of the duties of the Bank staff, and to desist from influencing them in the discharge of their duties. This set of far-reaching general directions has had a salutary effect on the functioning of the Bank, and ensures high standards of equity and fairness in such matters as procurement, award of contracts, and recruitment of staff. Whatever success has been achieved by the Bank, and its high standing in financial markets can be ascribed in large measure, to the wisdom of the framers of the Articles in categorically setting down these basic tenets, and to the firm adherence by the Bank's management and by successive generations of its Executive Directors, to the letter and spirit of these provisions in the Articles ever since its inception.

Section 6 of this Articles deals with the Advisory Council. Section 7 deals with the Loan Committee, and its provisions have been earlier considered in connection with the conditions on which the Bank can make loans (Article III, Section 4). Section 8 outlines the relationship with other international organisations and while cooperation is stressed, the Section is clear that such cooperation can only occur within the terms of the Articles of Agreement. To ensure that there is no misunderstanding, it also provides that if any cooperation sought for would involve a modification of the Articles, then it can only proceed *after* the Bank's Articles have been suitably amended. International Organisations have been grouped into general organisations and those with specialised responsibilities; in both cases, however, when deciding on applications for loans and guarantees relating to matters directly within the competence of the international organisations, the Bank is only required to give consideration to the views and recommendations of the former. The Bank is, therefore, given adequate latitude to function as it deems fit. During its early years, the question of the World Bank's relationship with the U.N. did arise and it was resolved without unduly fettering the Bank's freedom of action, as it agreed only to give consideration to the views of the U.N. In retrospect, it is perhaps fortunate that the World Bank was early on able to get out of the embrace of the U.N. The Bank is an international organisation which is financially well placed, and does not depend on contributions from the member-Governments for its administrative and other needs. Even loans are financed largely by borrowings from the market, etc. It has, therefore, been able to grow and develop to its present stature. Further, the World Bank is mercifully insulated somewhat from the main political currents and the sometimes acrimonious debates that occur in the U.N. While politics plays an important role in the Bank also, it is in a somewhat attenuated and benign form. Though the World Bank is a member of the U.N. family, it is nevertheless acknowledged to be a very special member. A formal agreement was negotiated with the U.N. where it was recognised that by virtue of its Articles, the Bank is and is required to function as an independent international organisation. Further, it was recognised by the U.N. that the action to the taken by the Bank on any loan is a matter to be determined by the independent exercise of the Bank's own judgement.[14] However, there is considerable liaison between the Bank and specialised agencies such as UNCTAD and GATT for trade matters, IFAD for agricultural development and research, WHO in health matters as the Bank has programmes for health and sanitation, and also assists in medical research relating to certain diseases endemic in the developing countries. The World Bank also maintains contacts with the regional Banks such as the Inter-American Development Bank, the Asian Development Bank and the African Development Bank and co-financing with some of them has occurred. The closest cooperation, however, is with the other member of the Bretton Woods "Twins", viz., the I.M.F. and this subject will be dealt with in greater detail later on.

Section 9 provides for the location of the Bank's Headquarters. The Section lays down that its principal office shall be located in the territory of the member holding the greatest number of shares and this was clearly the USA. There was some difference of opinion between the USA and the U.K. as to the precise city which should be selected—the U.K. favouring New York, as it was the financial capital, and also the headquarters of the U.N. Another argument adduced by the U.K. was that the World Bank should be autonomous, and therefore, should be insulated to the extent possible from the pressures of the Government. On the other hand, the USA favoured Washington, D.C., for the diametrically opposite reason, viz., that since it was providing the bulk of the funds, the U.S. Government needed to have close liaison with its Executive Director, and he should be constantly available to their Treasury. Moreover, the U.S. view was that both the IBRD and the IMF were cooperative institutions of the member-Governments and not mere financial institutions. Washington would be a more suitable location as all member Governments have adequate representatives there.[15] Needless to say, the U.S. view prevailed. Section 9 also provides for the establishment of agencies or branch offices in the territories of any member.

Section 10 provides for the establishment of regional offices and regional councils. These provisions have been frequently used and several offices established in various countries, both developing and developed. Section 11 deals with 'depositories' where the World Bank can keep its assets including gold. Being mainly procedural, further comment is unnecessary, except to mention in passing that the five largest shareholders have been given a preferential status, particularly the shareholder in whose territory the Bank's headquarters are located, as at least one half of the Bank's gold is to be kept in a depository designated by it.

Section 12, incorporates a gesture to the developing countries. The Bank is authorised to accept in lieu of a member's currency, a note or similar obligation issued by the member-Government, or a Central Bank or comparable organisation. These notes are non-interest-bearing, and non-negotiable. Since the currencies of developing countries are oft n non-convertible, and there are relatively few demands on such currencies, as compared with convertible currencies, the Bank may not have any need for such currencies immediately, and can therefore safely accommodate the member by accepting a note, and thereby obviating the need for making an immediate cash payment.

Section 13 requires an annual report and quarterly summary statements of the Bank's financial position, as well as its profit and loss statement, to be prepared and circulated to the members. In addition, the Bank has been allowed the latitude to prepare other reports as it deems desirable for carrying out its purposes. Two such which deserve mention are the World Development Report, and the Debt Tables of member countries.

Section 14 deals with the allocation of net income, which is the prerogative of the Board of Governors, though of course, it is advised by the President and the Executive Directors. The first requirement is to provide for the reserves, as deemed fit. Thereafter, the balance can be allocated to surplus or distributed to the shareholders. For the latter, the articles provide that a first charge on the amount to be distributed will be up to 2% on the basis of the members currency lent out from the Bank's own funds, and outstanding. The balance to be distributed would be according to the respective shareholdings of the members. It is not customary for the World Bank to distribute any part of its net income to its shareholders, although this point does come up from time to time, particularly with a view to create a favourable opinion in the territories of the major industrial countries, as the amounts distributable to them would be larger than those distributable to the developing countries. On the other hand, it has been customary in recent years to transfer varying amounts out of the World Bank's net income (ranging from $ 650 millions to over $ 1.6 billion) to the International Development Agency (IDA), the affiliate lending funds to the poorest countries on highly concessional terms and to other funds and purposes.

ARTICLE VI deals with the withdrawal and suspension of membership, and the suspension of operations of the IBRD. It also deals in considerable detail with the settlement of accounts, and the settlement of obligations, should these eventualities occur. Since the World Bank is a lusty organisation, no such event occurred during the period covered by this book, and there is little prospect of the IBRD winding up its operations in the foreseeable future, further comments on this Article are perhaps unnecessary.

ARTICLE VII deals with the status, immunities and privileges of the IBRD and its personnel. These provisions are necessary if it is to function as an international organisation. While action can be brought against the Bank in a Court of competent jurisdiction, no action can be brought against the Bank by members, or persons acting for or deriving claims from members (Section 3). The Bank's property is immune from search, etc. and seizure by executive or legislative action (Section 4). Similarly, its property and assets are free from restriction, regulation, control, etc. The Bank, its property, income, and transactions authorised by the Articles, are immune from all taxation and from customs duties. No taxes are to be levied in respect of salaries and emoluments paid by the Bank to its Executive Directors, officials, employees, etc. who are not local citizens or local nationals (Section 9). Section 10 requires each member to take such action as is necessary to make the principles set forth in the Articles effective in its territory, and to inform the Bank of the action taken.

ARTICLE VIII deals with amendments to the Articles. Any amendment to be accepted requires a three-fifth majority of the members, as well as a four-fifth majority of the voting power. Further, certain basic provisions such as the right to withdraw from the Bank, the pre-emptive right to subscribe to certain shares, when there is a capital increase, and the limitation on the liability of members, requires unanimity before any changes can be made. The stringent provisions laid down in the Articles for compliance before they can be amended, call for an overwhelming measure of agreement amongst both the developed and developing members; this feature explains why very few amendments have been made in the last 50 years. Perhaps, the latent apprehension that once an amendment is proposed, it would open the floodgates to a spate of further proposals, which could adversely affect the character and efficient functioning of the Bank, has also inhibited changes being proposed.

ARTICLE IX deals with interpretation of the Articles. In the first instance, the power is left to the Executive Directors. Any member, if dissatisfied by their decision, can have the matter referred to the Board of Governors, whose decision is final, though pending the appeal, the Bank can act on the basis of the decision of the Executive Directors, so far as it deems necessary. If there is a disagreement between the Bank and a country, which has ceased to be a member, or if there is a disagreement between the Bank and a member during the permanent suspension of the operations of the Bank, then this disagreement can be submitted to arbitration. Earlier in this Chapter, it has been mentioned that reliance was placed on the interpretative powers of the Board of Executive Directors to resolve the issue of the common standard of value necessary for operating under the provisions of Section 9 of Article II (i.e maintenance of value of certain currency holdings). The rigidities imposed by Article VIII with regard to amendments of the Articles, can be circumvented to some extent by recourse to Article IX. This device makes for flexibility, and allows considerable scope to the management and the Executive Directors to create conditions conducive to the smooth and efficient functioning of the Bank.

ARTICLE X is a procedural provision to facilitate the functioning of the IBRD. Except with regard to proposed amendments, the approval of a member can be deemed to have been given, unless the member objects within such reasonable period as may be fixed by the Bank, when notifying the member.

ARTICLE XI contains transitional provisions for bringing the articles into force, for their signature and the inauguration of the IBRD, and needs no further comment.

Notes and References

1. The World Bank since Bretton Woods, Mason & Asher, p. 15.
2. I am indebted to 'The World Bank since Bretton Woods' by Mason and Asher for some of the material.
3. 1 billion = 1000 million.
4. The World Bank since Bretton Woods, Mason & Asher, p. 171.
5. Factual data were obtained from the report of the Ad hoc Committee, dated July 23rd 1986, and the summary of the Board discussions on Oct. 14th 1986.
6. Cp. Report of Brandt Commission.
7. P. 264, footnote 7.
8. Annual Report 1995, pp. 17 and 30.
9. Bretton Woods Commission Report, p. c-195.
10. The World Bank since Bretton Woods, Mason & Asher, p. 263, footnote 4.
11. I am indebted to 'The World Bank since Bretton Woods', Mason & Asher for a detailed account of the development of Bank Policy in this regard, vide page 264, footnote 43 in particular.
12. List on, p. 190, World Banks' Annual Report 1995.
13. Page 50/63, The World Bank Since Bretton Woods, Mason and Asher.
14. The World Bank since Bretton Woods, Mason & Asher, p. 58. This book contains a fascinating account of the negotiations between the Bank and the U.N.
15. The World Bank since Bretton Woods, Mason & Asher, p. 58.

CHAPTER 2

WORLD BANK LENDING

The term World Bank (or even Bank for short) is being used collectively to refer both to the International Bank for Reconstruction and Development (IBRD) and to its soft lending affiliate, the International Development Association (IDA). Under the Articles of Agreement, as mentioned in Chapter 1, supreme authority over the IBRD (and *mutatis mutandis*, the IDA) vests in the Board of Governors, but almost all powers have been delegated to the Board of Executive Directors, except a few (including those reserved under the Articles themselves). This latter Board currently comprises 24 Executive Directors,[1] five of whom are appointed respectively by the five largest shareholders, while the rest are elected by the other member-Governments, many of which are grouped into various "constituencies" comprising more than one country. This Board is chaired by the President of the World Bank, who also heads the large staff of the Bank, collectively referred to as the Management. The President and the Management are responsible for conducting the ordinary business of the Bank, under the overall direction of the Executive Directors. The Board deals with policy issues, and also finally approves loans or credits recommended by the President to various borrowers. IBRD loans may be given to the member-Governments themselves or to institutions under them, in which case the guarantee of the concerned Government is required. IDA credits may be given to member-Governments, to be passed on, if required, to other entities. The Executive Directors serve on a whole-time basis and meetings of the Board can be convened at short notice. The World Bank is a premier developmental institution, and its lending operations have generally grown over the years. The loans approved by the IBRD during 1979 totalled about $ 6.99

billion[2] and climbed steadily to $ 14.76 billion in 1988. There was a further increase to $ 16.43 billion in 1989, but subsequently, some stagnancy was discernible, as the 1989 figure was surpassed only in FY 1993, when commitments reached the high watermark of $ 16.94 billion. In FY 1994, commitments declined to $ 14.2 billion, the lowest figure for the last several years. The flow of funds is determined by the gross disbursements rather than by the commitments, as the borrowers have to comply with certain conditions before they can draw the loan funds, and most projects financed by the Bank have to first incur expenditure, and then claim reimbursement. The disbursement head figures follow a similar pattern. There is a steady growth in disbursements from $ 3.6 billion in 1979 to $ 11.6 billion in 1988. Thereafter, the trend is somewhat mixed. After falling in 1989 to $ 11.3 billion, disbursements peaked at $ 13.86 billion in 1990. During FY 1993, disbursements have been put at $ 12.9 billion. There was a further decline to $ 10.45 billion in FY 1994 but disbursements picked up to $ 12.67 billion in FY 1995. If note is taken of the secular rising price trend, the stagnancy in real terms apparent from these figures is a cause for concern especially if the additional number of members, and their requirements are taken into account, though some qualification on this score may be needed, as the requirements of the former members of the Soviet Union are yet to be determined, and it may be somewhat premature for the full impact to be felt. As a corollary, total loans have been burgeoning; in 1988, the cumulative figure stood at $ 155 billion, and has increased to $ 235 billion in 1993 and to $ 249 billion in FY 1994.

The figures for IDA lending display a somewhat different trend. The total credits given in 1979 were $ 3.02 billion. There was a sharp rise to $ 3.8 billion in 1980, but thereafter the figure fell, reaching a low of $ 2.69 billion in 1982, reflecting the squeeze during the Reagan years. This aspect is considered in detail in Part A of Chapter 4. The 1980 figure of credits approved was only surpassed in 1988 ($ 4.46 billion). Thereafter, there has been a welcome increase, and IDA credits have steadily increased to $ 6.75 billion in FY 1993, only to decline to $ 5.67 billion in FY 1995.

IDA credits are given on highly concessional terms, with a long maturity period (35-50 years), and only a small service charge is levied. These credits are meant for the poor countries. It is noteworthy that the net disbursements during 1993 (i.e. after taking into account capital repayments) are higher from IDA credits ($ 4.58 billion), than from IBRD loans ($ 2.3 billion) even though the commitments by the latter are over 2½ times that of the former. The contrast is more glaring in FY 1994 in that IBRD net disbursements are *negative* (minus $ 731 million), while IDA net disbursements show an increase to a *positive* $ 5.1 billion.

Since lending is one of the major activities of the Bank, it is proposed to consider it in somewhat greater detail. While the Bank's first three loans[3] were made in the late 1940s to France, the Netherlands and Denmark, for general reconstruction, subsequent lending has been predominantly to the developing countries for their further development. Probably the Marshall Plan triggered this trend, as it was directly concerned with post-war reconstruction, and the role of the IBRD consequently got circumscribed. Over the years, the Bank has devised an array of lending instruments to further its objectives, and to meet the needs of the borrowers.

Though the bulk of Bank lending (both IBRD and IDA) is for specific projects, the proportion under various heads changes over the years. Funds are allocated also for programme loans, and for structural adjustment loans, which are meant to finance activities such as bulk imports, essentially required for the borrower's industries to work at or near optimal capacity, or to enable far-reaching policy reforms to be undertaken by the borrower, so as to achieve a viable position, both internally and externally. The proportion of resources allocated to the different functions varies, and is driven by the needs and requirements at a given time, as well as the dates of receipt and the pace of processing of the proposals.

The following table shows the percentages of total lending accounted for by certain broad categories of loans during 1988 and 1990. Investment loans, whether for specific projects or for a sector, account for the bulk of the lending (57.22% and 68.29% for these two years respectively) and have shown a tendency to revert to the earlier pattern, with a moderate rise in the later year. While programme lending and structural adjustment lending have also increased, the allied category of sector adjustment loans has declined sharply, with the result that overall these non-project loans have

Table

Types of loans	Percentages	
	1988	1990
Specific investment loans	39.02	49.17
Sector investment loans	18.20	19.12
Total	57.22	68.29
Programme lending and Structural Adj. lending	5.20	6.92
Sector Adj. loans	19.77	12.29
Total	24.97	19.21
Financial Intermediary	10.92	4.25

declined during 1990 as compared to 1988 (from 24.97% to 19.21%). Variability in lending is also indicated by the sharp decrease during 1990 under the head Financial Intermediary Loans. A new category of Debt Reduction loans to cope with the problems of the severely indebted countries was introduced, and accounted for 7.65% of total lending during 1990. Lending for projects and for investment *per se* falls squarely within the substantive provisions of the Articles, which enjoin that loans shall be for the purpose of specific projects "except in special circumstances". To the credit of the World Bank, it has been pragmatic and flexible in interpreting the term "projects", which has not been precisely defined. The concept has evolved over the years to include a wide range of productive activities, involving not only capital investment in civil works, equipment, etc., but also a series of investment programmes in the railways, highways, and telecommunication enterprises, as well as in a country's agricultural, extension, health and water-supply services.

Frequently loans are made to financial intermediaries such as the Industrial Development Bank of India, and the Industrial Credit and Investment Corporation of India, which in turn lend out smaller amounts to various individual enterprises. By operating through such apex bodies, the World Bank is relieved of much detailed work, and the borrowing country enjoys greater flexibility. Loans, known as Program Loans, have also been made for financing imports, etc. by the borrowing country, which it otherwise would not have been able to buy because of the scarcity of foreign exchange. During the early 1980s, a series of Structural Adjustment Loans (SALs) were given with the specific objective of enabling the borrowing country to embark upon a series of far reaching "adjustments" and reforms in macro-economic policies. These loans were usually fast disbursing, and were meant to support the balance of payments during the period of adjustment. The loans were preceded by a period of intense policy dialogue, and a written assurance was sought at the highest political level, that certain reforms and adjustments including changes in macro-economic policies, would be carried out within a prescribed time-frame. To ensure adherence, these loans were 'tranched', and releases were dependent on the fulfillment of the assurances. These loans raise extraordinarily difficult questions about coordination with the IMF, and the effect of the Bank's policy dialogue on the sovereignty of the borrowing Government. The adjustment process can also prove to be protracted, calling for long term commitment by the Bank. It is therefore, interesting that the 1988 Annual Report mentions:[4]

> "The characteristics of Bank-supported adjustment lending have changed. While Structural Adjustment loans predominated early on, in the past four years Sector Adjustment loans have come to form the majority of adjustment lending".

With more Structural Adjustment lending, Sectoral Adjustment loans also came into being after a short time-lag. These loans are claimed to involve a widening and deepening of the adjustment process to enable more sharply focussed attention to be devoted to particular sectors of the economy. Often such loans are provided for countries where economic adjustment is well underway. Another category of related loans are 'hybrid' loans, which are investment-oriented, with a sharper focus on in-depth restructuring of sectoral investment programmes. "The hybrid operation establishes a sector-wise policy framework and a consistent set of investment priorities, some of whose components may be financed by a subsequent series of investment operations that are approved only if the whole sector program remains on track" (Annual Report, 1988, p. 67). There is thus a continuum with structural adjustment loans at one end, moving over to sector adjustment loans and finally to hybrid loans at the other. Sector adjustment loans have been given for a variety of purposes, including trade liberalisation, elimination of controls, (Mexico, Argentina, etc.), export development (Pakistan), educational reform (Ghana), rationalisation of public sector enterprises (Morocco), agriculture, promotion of financial institutions, and development of energy (Turkey).[5] Where a country is not prepared to embark on a comprehensive structural adjustment programme eligible for a SAL, it can still be eligible for a sector adjustment loan—a factor which may partially explain the greater acceptability of the latter. Structural Adjustment lending and its implications will be considered in greater detail subsequently (Chapter 6).

It is usually accepted that the World Bank over its life has developed great strength in project lending, and this is a tribute to the systematic and meticulous manner in which it has undertaken this task. Every project financed by the Bank is required to pass through various stages of a well-established project cycle.[6] The first stage is the identification of the project. This initial step, though apparently simple, can be crucial for the eventual success or failure of the project. Clearly, the proposal must constitute a high priority use of resources, which are usually scarce. The objectives of the proposed project should command wide support, and should be compatible with the long term coherent development strategy that the country has in view. The World Bank usually collects much data about a borrowing country's economy, and analyses the data with a view to assessing the 'creditworthiness' of the country, particularly for IBRD loans, as required by the Articles, and for use during a continuing dialogue with its Government regarding an appropriate development strategy. This usually enables the Bank to arrive at tentative conclusions regarding the level of lending to the country for the next few years. The proposal has to fit in reasonably well with these general considerations. There is a multiplicity of ways in which a proposal gets considered for World Bank financing, e.g. the line agencies may have a project which has to be financed, other bilateral donors may be exploring possibilities of working with the Bank, or even private entrepreneurs may be eager to get a project started and the Bank officials may express their interest in a proposal. In a situation where the borrower has already embarked on a long term development plan, and is ready with a number of projects, a centralised agency, e.g. the Finance Ministry, may sponsor some schemes for World Bank financing, leaving others to be financed by bilateral or other multilateral aid agencies. An essential pre-requisite is a pre-feasibility report concerning the proposal, which considers different alternatives. Such a report is usually worked up into a project brief by the Bank. For convenience and economy in time and effort, the process moves in tandem, the number of project ideas getting narrowed down and simultaneously the surviving ones, getting sharpened with the project proposals being worked out in more detail and with greater precision. Consideration of the various alternatives is not only to show that the project proposals are feasible, and are sound enough to be deserving of support, but also to establish, within the limitations to which such exercises are subject, that the proposal put forward is the best one for achieving the developmental goals. In a planned regime, much of this preliminary work has already been carried out by the Government, and there is usually a shelf of projects from which to select those that are to be sponsored for World Bank financing.

This stage merges into the next stage, viz., preparation of the project. Various aspects of the project have to be worked out in considerable detail, e.g. the technical, financial and economic aspects as well as the institutional aspect. Some further elaboration may be required. For any of the traditional infrastructural and industrial projects, the technical aspects would involve surveys, preliminary engineering, preparation of cost estimates, and selection of the optimum product-mix, the most appropriate process technology, and estimation of the demand for, as also the realisation anticipated from the sale of the products. For some of the newer projects, where human and socio-economic factors come into play, the benefits may not be accurately quantifiable, and the institutional aspects will call for closer examination. The financial aspects call for fairly precise cost estimates and an overall financing plan, together with estimates of the likely returns. For traditional projects, the financial viability of the project has to be demonstrated. The economic aspects call for an examination of the pricing policies, and the overall policy framework within which the project will be operating. The shadow pricing of foreign exchange, and of labour, as well as the duties and taxes levied would come under scrutiny to determine the overall impact on the economy, and the resources generated. The institutional aspect may be of crucial importance in the more recent genre of projects dealing with socio-economic aspects of development, and involving large numbers of beneficiaries. For the more traditional projects, over the years, fairly competent organisations have evolved in most countries, which can handle engineering and industrial issues professionally, and can be relied upon to both plan and implement such projects. The usual requirement is the preparation of a feasibility report on the project, giving its objectives and also detailing the various items mentioned above, particularly the cost estimates based upon surveys and preliminary engineering. The report should establish the financial viability, estimate the financial and economic rates of return and detail the institutional arrangements for its implementation. Some idea of the time-frame for the completion of the project also should be given. Indian experience shows that once funds are committed for a feasibility report, and more so for a detailed project report, the project in question will get sanctioned sooner or later, and eventually will be implemented, with or without modifications, though the manner of financing and the costs incurred may differ greatly from the initial estimates.

The World Bank maintains the formal position that the borrower is responsible for the preparation of the project to be financed by the former, including the drawing up of the feasibility report, and for furnishing all the data that may be required from time to time. However, where the institutional arrangements available to the borrower are inadequate, the Bank is usually prepared to help by providing additional funds for the purpose, by enlisting the support of other agencies such as the UNDP, and in extreme cases, even doing some of the preparatory work itself. Nevertheless, the World Bank prefers to keep its role as financier and banker distinct, and to exercise its right to oversee the project, as prepared by the borrower. By this means, the full commitment of the borrower and its involvement in project preparation, leading to successful implementation are achieved.

The next step in the project cycle is the appraisal by the Bank of the project. This responsibility rests solely on the Bank staff, assisted, if necessary, by Consultants, and calls for one or more visits to the field. The technical, financial, economic and institutional aspects are re-traversed, but this time from the Bank's own angle. Technical review during the appraisal phase of a project has sometimes resulted in considerable modifications of the original proposal. Indian projects, particularly of the traditional type, are generally well conceived, and documented, but even so, in the case of a major new port, during appraisal, the number of berths originally proposed, had to be reduced, consequent on certain queries raised by the appraisal mission. This instance is cited to show that appraisal is a comprehensive exercise undertaken professionally. Another aspect that the mission is frequently concerned with is the procurement of the equipment, and the award of the works and service contracts. This concern stems from the firm policy of the Bank to purchase major items of equipment, and to award works contracts on the basis of international competitive bidding, except where this procedure is clearly infeasible owing to the dispersed nature of the work, the relatively small sums involved, or the accent on use of local material and labour, which would preclude bidding by international firms. Procurement is an issue which is of interest to most member-Governments, because they are vitally concerned that their nationals should be able to compete on fair terms for the large and lucrative contracts generated by World Bank projects. This aspect is further considered at Chapter 6.

During the economic appraisal, the project is studied in its sectoral setting, and key government policies are examined. The principle seems to be that even a sound project cannot succeed, if the policy environment in which it is to operate is not conducive to efficient functioning. This results in the pricing, subsidy and tax policies relevant to the sector being closely examined, and often suggestions are put forward for increasing prices, reducing subsidies, etc. as pre-requisites for the loan being approved (e.g. for power projects and fertiliser projects). The financial review involves projections of the cash flow, balance-sheets, profit and loss accounts, etc. for the next several years, to ensure the financial viability of the project, and its capacity to pay back the loan. The plan for financing the project also comes under scrutiny, as the Bank attempts to gain the most leverage from its participation. The Bank as a rule does not finance the entire cost, and the borrower is expected to raise the balance either from its own resources or otherwise. Earlier, the Bank would be reluctant to finance the local costs, being content merely to meet the foreign exchange costs, either wholly or partly. This reluctance over the years has been somewhat softened and even local costs qualify for Bank lending as mentioned earlier. On the other hand, there is renewed emphasis on co-financing, with either bilateral or other multilateral aid agencies, or with commercial banks. The appraisal report by the mission is subjected to an elaborate procedure of internal review. The report on the project is drafted and re-drafted repeatedly (with covers in different colours for each re-draft) and finally cleared by the management for negotiations with the borrower. As discussed subsequently, the Staff Appraisal Reports produced in recent years have come in for criticism by the Wapenhans Task Force.

The proposals made by the World Bank, and the conditions suggested by them, financial and otherwise, are then discussed with a team from the borrowing country. There is considerable scope for give and take in these negotiations, which can be quite intensive. The conditions suggested by the Bank often prove onerous, and frequently have political overtones, e.g. reduction in subsidies for fertilisers used by farmers, where a fertiliser plant is proposed to be set up; raising of the tariff for electricity supplied, where a power project is being negotiated; more stringent measures for collection of overdues from beneficiaries, where loans for agricultural credit are under negotiation; raising prices of petroleum products where the Bank has been approached for financing an oil field exploration and development project. The Bank's proposals often transcend the scope of the particular project, and impinge on macro-economic policies. Particularly under a democratic Government, there can be considerable resistance to unpopular measures or those with a high social cost and likely to cause hardship to the under-privileged. In the Indian context, conditions imposed may create difficulties in Centre-State relations, either directly or by their impact on State agencies, e.g. the State Electricity Boards. There have been occasions when negotiations have had to be suspended because the differences could not be bridged. The Executive Director concerned is usually called upon to mediate, and in the vast majority of cases, agreement is reached. Considerable flexibility and pragmatism have been displayed by the Bank management in arriving at an acceptable arrangement, having regard to the difficulties of the borrower, and the harsh realities on the ground. Conversely, the borrowers respect the experience of the Bank's management spanning countries worldwide, as well as their professional competence. Further, there is a realisation that the suggestions made are for the benefit of the project, and its success—issues which are of vital importance to the borrower. Basically, the borrower has approached the Bank because of a shortage of resources, and *a fortiori*, this shortage may be even more acute with regard to foreign exchange, which the Bank would be able to provide. Consequently, borrowers are often prepared to acquiesce in conditions stipulated by the Bank, except where their vital interests are affected. Large countries which depend upon the World Bank for a relatively small percentage of their requirements for development, are in a stronger bargaining position, as compared with other countries relying more heavily on the Bank.

This step is followed by presentation to the Board of Executive Directors, and after approval, formal loan documents are signed—putting the seal on the commitments by the Bank to provide the funds, and the obligations of the borrower to complete the project on the agreed basis, and to fulfil the conditions stipulated in the loan and supplementary agreements. Board procedures may be of some interest and are dealt with somewhat more elaborately later on. At this stage it will be convenient to consider the further stages of the project cycle.

The next stage in the cycle is the implementation of the project. The responsibility for this rests squarely on the borrower, but unlike the practice normally followed by commercial banks when financing projects, the World Bank continues to be closely involved with the implementation of the project even after approval. A partial explanation for such involvement can be found in the Articles. As already mentioned,[7] Article III, Sec. 5 of the IBRD Articles enjoins that the proceeds of any loan granted by the Bank are to be used only for the purposes for which it was granted, and the Bank is required to make arrangements to ensure compliance. In addition, the same Article requires the IBRD to also ensure that the proceeds are used "with due attention to economy and efficiency". There are parallel provisions in the Articles of IDA. Even at the prior stage of making the loan, the Articles stipulate that the IBRD is to pay due regard to the prospects of the borrower being in a position to meet its obligations, and is required to act prudently in the interests both of the concerned member, as also of all the members collectively. These provisions oblige the Bank to see that the money is well spent, and the benefits from the project, both financial and otherwise, are commensurate with the costs, and approximate those estimated when the loan was made. Since the normal practice (except for start-up, etc.) is to reimburse the borrower for the expenditure already incurred on the project, and full documentation is required, the Bank is in a strong position to enforce these provisions, particularly if several missions are despatched from Washington periodically to inspect conditions in the field.

Besides this 'watchdog' function, another reason for the Bank's close involvement is to profit from the experience gained in the execution of a project, so that the lessons learned can be used both when preparing and appraising other projects, and also in implementing similar projects. Undoubtedly, the Bank deals with an extremely wide range of projects, which are being executed under highly disparate conditions. As such, the experience of one project may not be fully applicable to another, separated both in time, and also geographically, though both these may belong to the same type. Nevertheless, there are several valuable lessons which can be learnt particularly with regard to prior preparation, management and institutional arrangements, performance of contractors, suppliers, and consultants, and these lessons are readily transferable from one project to another, though implemented under different circumstances.

Yet another reason for the close involvement of the Bank is that projects seldom proceed smoothly, or as planned. Technical, organisational, or financial problems often arise. The accumulated experience of the Bank, and the underpinning provided by its expert technical staff and consultants often help in collective solution of these problems as they arise. Frequently, project authorities use the special relationship that the Bank has developed with many borrowers because of an almost steady stream of projects financed in the past, or likely to come up soon, to get internal problems solved with their higher authorities, or with other connected ministries. This special relationship allows Bank officials easy access to the corridors of power, and the project authorities are not above occasionally taking advantage of this factor. Funding of projects, especially when resources are exiguous, can lead to delays. Bank-assisted projects have an inherent advantage in that reimbursement is usually in foreign exchange, and most Governments in the developing countries are short of this resource. As such, Bank-assisted projects are often accorded priority by the Finance Ministries of the borrowers.

The Bank's penchant for international competitive bidding mentioned earlier, entails considerable work and requires its close involvement. The stance of all members is that equity and fair play should be ensured both in procurement of equipment, etc. and in the award of works contracts. Procurement of equipment and supplies, or award of works contracts have to conform to the relevant regulations laid down by the Bank. The Bank management is therefore associated at the various stages such as finalisation of the designs, drawing up the specifications, scrutiny of the bids received, and their evaluation so as to put them on a comparable basis. This last stage is necessary as the bids may differ on some of the terms and conditions, and the characteristics of the equipment offered, or of the civil works, and their design may vary, requiring monetary values to be assigned to these variations. This procedure calls for the exercise of judgement by experts. The appropriateness of the procedure followed, and the Bank's role, may be tested, as a particular Executive Director may be called upon to intervene, should a grievance, real or imagined, be voiced sufficiently strongly regarding the consideration given to the bid of a supplier or contractor from his constituency, or concerning the final award of the contract. Thereafter, it would be up to the Management, in conjunction with the borrower, to establish the fairness of the decision reached, or to take remedial action. There have been instances, where after the Board has approved a loan, it has had to be cancelled because of differences with the borrower concerning the award of a contract. During the implementation of a major project, missions are sent out from Washington periodically to inspect work in the field. Besides a stream of reports from the project authorities is required, thus ensuring close monitoring. Having been associated also with a project which was being assisted by the World Bank, the reaction of the field engineers could be ascertained informally. These engineers, felt that the additional workload imposed by the Bank was substantial, but they seemed to appreciate that the Bank's involvement kept them on their toes, and also helped to keep the project on course. The Bank attaches considerable weight to these supervisory functions, which ensure that loans and credits are used effectively, and also provide valuable 'feedback' on project execution experience. Bank documents estimate that supervision represents an essential and significant part of operational staff work equivalent to approximately two-thirds of lending work input.

The last stage of the project cycle is evaluation after the completion of the project. One of the grounds for the Bank's continued involvement with a project even after loan approval was earlier mentioned to be the need to profit from the lessons learned. This was institutionalised during Mr. Robert McNamara's term as President, when the Operations Evaluation Department (OED) was created. This is an independent organisation headed by a Director General which reports directly to the President and to the Executive Directors. The World Bank can justifiably claim credit for being the first multilateral aid agency to create such a body, and to publish its reports. The evaluation reports have not hesitated to be critical, where justified, and on balance, the existence of such a body, has enhanced the standing and image of the Bank in financial markets and amongst member-Governments, because of its genuine desire to ensure economy and efficiency, by having its successes and shortcomings judged by an independent organisation, which publishes its findings. The procedure normally followed is for a project completion report to be prepared soon after the project is finished. The costs and benefits as then ascertained and updated, can be compared with the corresponding figures when the project was approved. While there is some finality with regard to the direct costs, the benefits may not be fully determinable immediately upon physical completion, as in many projects, e.g. irrigation and power, the benefits start flowing in full measure only with a time-lag, because agronomic practices have to be altered, on-farm improvements have to be undertaken, and for power-projects, the load has to develop with new units coming up. Maintenance and operating costs also build up over a period. Nevertheless, upon completion a more accurate estimate of the likely benefits becomes available than what was available at commencement. The shortcomings and successes can be highlighted, and improvements suggested. The operational staff have an opportunity of recording their views, and since they are directly involved, these views are authentic and of great value. The practice is to get the completion reports prepared by the borrower, though the Bank staff may assist them by suggesting a standard proforma, or even more directly, by highlighting certain aspects. Previously, the Bank staff would prepare most completion reports, but more responsibility was thrust on to borrowers, as it was thought that the exercise would help to build up experience within the country, which could be readily drawn upon in future.

A project completion report is required for every Bank-assisted project. Previously, the OED would audit each report. However, with the increasing project load, a decision was taken in the early 1980s to be selective, and to use the limited manpower resources of the OED more effectively. Currently, of the approximately 250 completion reports generated annually, about one-half are selected for a detailed performance audit by OED staff.[8] In selecting reports for this further scrutiny, several criteria are adopted, e.g. those which invite further enquiry owing to poor performance, groups may be formed of projects which lend themselves to eventual cross-country comparison owing to similarities, projects which are first of their type in a country. Some further projects (about 10%) are selected at random to correct for any bias in the selection process. While sometimes the audit may be confined to a desk review, and a study of all previous papers, in other cases, the audit involves visits to the field, and study of both the physical achievements and the local documents. These studies lead to a document detailing the Project Performance Audit Results (PPAR) for each project audited. The OED thereupon carries out an Annual Review of the Project Performance Audit Results, which is discussed in detail by the Executive Directors at a Board meeting. Borrowers are also invited to comment on the findings of the OED, and these comments are made available to the Board. In addition, the work of OED is overseen by a Committee of the Board (The Joint Audit Committee), which not only reviews the work programme of the Department, but also reviews and identifies reports with policy implications, with a view to bringing major issues to the notice of the Board as a whole. Further, a Sub-Committee usually comprising the Alternate Directors, reviews a number of PPARs and gives its findings for the consideration of the Committee, and eventually of the Board.

Attention has already been drawn to the time-lag between the physical completion of a project, and the flow of the benefits from it at full potential. Similarly, operating costs will not be accurately known till the project has stabilised. For these reasons, an 'Impact evaluation study' for a number of carefully selected projects is carried out after a period of five years or so from completion. Such studies can be revealing, as many strengths and weaknesses become apparent in the fullness of time and as a result, the final assessments may differ from those made upon the physical completion of the project. Studies are also made of groups of projects (e.g. loans to development finance companies), or covering particular sectors. These comparative studies serve to provide valuable insights for planning and implementing similar projects in future. Recently the OED has launched some further studies. Country Assistance Reviews were introduced in fiscal year 1994 to assess the suitability of the Bank's assistance strategy in particular countries, and the effectiveness of the instruments chosen. These reviews are geared to assessments of lending and non-lending services, and they offer lessons and recommendations for the Bank's regional staff. The noteworthy feature is that these findings are then used when carrying out country-portfolio performances reviews (vide Chapter 6), and in designing suitable country assistance strategies. The OED also conducts sector Reviews, and studies include the social impact of adjustment programmes, irrigation projects, industrial restructuring etc.[9]

The findings of the OED provide material to assess whether the project cycle laid down by the Bank, and the constant supervision and monitoring carried out by it, are justified by the results achieved. The OED found that of the 87 projects audited and commented upon in the Seventh Annual Review (which was discussed by the Board in November 1981), an overwhelming number were successful. Some 1014 projects representing about $ 22 billion in Bank loans, and about $ 67 billion in total investment were evaluated *ex post*. Of this total, 86% of the projects by number, and more than 90% by value of Bank lending are claimed to have achieved their major objectives, and were adjudged to have been worthwhile. For those projects for which an economic rate of return was calculated, the re-estimated rate of return averaged 18%.[10] The Annual Report for 1988 mentions that of the 246 projects covered by the 1986 review, some 85% were characterised as having achieved satisfactory results. The Report also mentions that these evaluated projects were approved in the latter half of the 1970s, and were completed during the first half of the 1980s. Consequent on the emphasis placed by the then President, Mr. McNamara, on the alleviation of absolute poverty,[11] a new thrust was given to projects for rural development, and for other projects with a people orientation, e.g. education, health, water supply and urban development. Not only are these projects more difficult to implement successfully, but also the results achieved are hard to capture in precise monetary terms, compared with the traditional projects, which predominantly concerned the Bank during its earlier years. Moreover, the rural development programme was launched deliberately without having clear answers to many issues related to technology, and organisation, and in the knowledge that risks were being taken because of the urgency to alleviate some of the hardships of the absolute poor. It was clarified that the Bank hoped to learn from failures. The Bank's experience has been that though the strategy was successful in some ways, yet many problems had surfaced. Amongst these were the sustainability of some of the programmes, and the longer time-frame required for area-based rural development projects. During this period, several Structural Adjustment Loans were approved, and though quick disbursing, the success or otherwise of these loans cannot be readily and unambiguously established, especially by using the usual macroeconomic indicators. To further complicate the picture, sudden oil-price increases in 1979-80, a recession soon thereafter, and volatile interest rates, all led to economic turbulence. The success rate of

85% achieved despite these many uncertainties, which could not have been reasonably anticipated when the loans were made, must be judged to be highly creditable.

Another study comparing the effectiveness of IBRD-financed projects, with those financed by IDA, provides some insight into the successes achieved by these two organisations, which though almost inseparable, yet are distinct entities, with very different terms for lending, and serving dissimilar clientele. The study[12] considered 273 completed IBRD projects, and 183 IDA projects, and used the rate of return for making comparisons. The financial rate of return obviously has many limitations, especially when considering projects with a high social content, and it under-estimates the true return to the country as a whole. The average rate of return was found to be 17% for IBRD loans, and 17.9% for IDA credits. Not only are these returns high, but what is surprising is that IDA credits which are given to the poorer developing countries lacking in credit-worthiness, on 'soft' terms should achieve a marginally higher rate of return than the IBRD loans made at market-related rates. The average rates mask the differences that occur from sector to sector, and from region to region. For IDA projects, the study shows that the average return postulated at the time of appraisal was 20.6% but on completion, the figure fell to 17.9%, which is by no means a disappointing figure, when the many imponderables are recalled. There was considerable variability from one project to another, and the re-estimated rate of return was in the range of 12% to 30%. Further analysis shows that of all the IDA projects audited, only some 8.7% showed negative rates after completion, and judged solely by this criterion, must be considered failures. Almost two-thirds of the projects achieved rates of return ranging from 10% to 29%, which has to be considered commendable. A little more than 15% of these projects achieved a rate of return in excess of 30%. The bulk of the projects yielding negative returns were located in East and West Africa, while in South Asia there were no such projects, though the numbers of IDA projects studied in each of these regions were broadly comparable. The effectiveness of Structural Adjustment Loans will be considered elsewhere (vide Chapter 6).

Rigid adherence to the project cycle, and the attention paid by the expert staff of the Bank at all stages of the project, have resulted in the high success rate as established by repeated studies covering long periods. However, this statement needs qualification in the light of the findings of the Wapenhans task-force appointed by the Bank, which commented on the deterioration in project performance revealed in recent years. The Bank is seized of this development, and, doubtless, appropriate action will be taken. The issue has been considered in Chapter 6. What is noteworthy is that the effort put in by the Bank in identification, preparation, and supervision of a project has not been motivated primarily by a desire to ensure the safety of the funds loaned out. The security of the funds loaned out by the World Bank rests largely on the credit and the guarantees of the sovereign borrowing Governments. Experience shows that member-Governments would be loathe to default in their dues to the World Bank or the IMF, because of the severe repercussions. Not only would future loans, and payments on existing loans, by these bodies be suspended, but also credit from commercial banks and other sources would dry up, and international trade and commerce would be severely hit, with all the attendant political consequences. The measures constantly adopted by the Bank to ensure the economic viability of the assisted project, and to achieve high levels of productivity with the resources invested, are designed rather with the long term objectives of strengthening the economy of the borrower, and imparting a greater degree of resilience to it. Indirectly, of course, the resources generated by sound projects make it less onerous to service the debt incurred, and hence enhance the credit-worthiness of the borrower.

By systematically cataloguing its experience with various projects, and installing an efficient retrieval system, the Bank is in a position to utilise this experience when new projects are designed or taken up for funding. The feedback derived from the Bank's experience benefits not only the Bank itself, but also other borrowers, by avoiding likely pitfalls, and adopting techniques and practices which have proved their worth. The Bank has also adopted the policy of lending late[13] and to this policy can be attributed in part the high success rates achieved in Bank-financed projects. Adequate project preparation greatly helps in the smooth implementation of the project. Further, with much of the engineering work completed, the cost estimates are comparatively firm, and the difficult start-up phase is usually well under control. In turn, the priority accorded to Bank-financed projects in funding, as already mentioned, coupled with the reliability of the estimates, confers an advantage in the allocation of funds, resulting in steady progress, with consequently less time and cost over-runs.

Certain characteristics can be identified which increase the probability of a project being successfully implemented. The commitment of the borrower is an essential pre-requisite, as it alone would ensure that the policy environment, and the price and tax structure would remain conducive to success. Sustained support is required to ensure the orderly flow of funds, the building up of an efficient team for the execution of the project, and the completion of the myriad other tasks which have to be undertaken in time, for the work on the main project to proceed smoothly, e.g. land acquisition, re-settlement of displaced persons, creation of road and rail links, and linking up power-lines. The above comment is reinforced by the findings of the Wapenhans task-force, and the issue has been further considered in Chapter 6. Efficient management is another factor which can make all the difference between success and failure. Despite the attention devoted to the project by the Bank's staff, and repeated missions, experience shows that unless the organisation employed by the borrower is intrinsically strong, achievements may be indifferent. Commenting on rates of return achieved by IDA projects, the Bank writes "IDA's rates of return also vary widely between regions. They are decidedly lower in Africa than anywhere else: the average rate of return on 88 IDA projects in Africa was about 14%, compared with about 22% on 40 projects in South Asia. This contrast underscores the difficulties of operating in Africa, which is relatively less developed, and where IDA's involvement and experience has been less extensive."[14] The position does not appear to have changed much subsequently, because the Annual Report for 1988, while mentioning that the 1986 review by the OED had found that some 85% of the projects had achieved satisfactory results added: "The percentage was lower, however, for projects in sub-Saharan Africa, where performance continued to be disappointing."

A visit to some road projects under construction in East Africa which we were privileged to make was revealing. Expatriates had been entrusted with the construction of a highway project, which to all appearances, looked impressive. Alongside some rural roads had also been 'improved' under the project, but the only tangible result was the spreading of some road metal on the dirt-track, and that too not of uniform size. When asked whether the metal would not be consolidated and fixed in place by road-rollers, and at least water-bound, the answer was that the traffic using the road would in due course look after the consolidation! Project design and execution should also be suited to the prevailing conditions in the borrowing country. Some difficult questions can arise in this regard, as choices have to be made between modern practice on the one hand, and simplicity demanded by local conditions on the other. During the same trip to East Africa, we had the privilege of visiting a power station under construction located near a coal mine. Though quite large, the boilers and turbo-generators had not been fitted with reheat facilities, a standard feature for units of this capacity under Indian conditions, as it achieves quite significant gains in heat efficiency. The project head was a UK expatriate, and he had recruited operating staff from India. There was no mistaking the difficulties he was encountering in implementing the project, and the sharp contrast between the facilities available in the U.K., and those in East Africa, as well as the problems faced in building a cohesive and dedicated team from workmen of different nationalities, and varying backgrounds. Having regard to these factors, and to the cheapness and abundance of the poor quality coal at the mine-head, the trade-off between efficiency and simplicity was perhaps justified. These illustrations will serve to highlight the disparate conditions under which Bank-assisted projects are implemented, and the major role that the local organisations, engineering and otherwise, can and do play. The African projects are no less monitored or supervised than elsewhere, and the lower success rate of the former, can be reasonably ascribed to the local conditions, including the organisational set-up there.

It is natural to expect that, as happens in the generality of cases, there should be some shortcomings in Bank-assisted projects, and even failures. These include the usual ones of results not coming up to the expectations, particularly in projects involving livestock, cost and time over-runs, and inadequate attention to ecological damage. There are other more understandable and excusable lapses, where infrastructure projects have been taken up without paying due attention to the dynamic aspects of growth, and by extrapolating demand mechanistically according to past trends. Because of such inadequate attention to future traffic growth, and to the demand for power, crippling shortages recur in transportation and power sectors,[15] fairly soon after the project is completed. It is easy to be critical of demand projections in the light of hind-sight, but making accurate demand projections at the time of planning a project can be hazardous, and the limitations under which the project staff work should be appreciated. What is commendable, however, is the consistently high success rate achieved overall till recently by Bank-assisted projects. Even more heartening is that agricultural projects were known to have achieved better results than were anticipated at the time of appraisal; small decentralised groundwater development projects were completed at costs lower than estimated and the profits to the farmer were good.

It might be of some interest to consider what transpires at Board meetings when the Executive Directors (E.Ds) discuss and approve project loans. Each proposal comes to the Board with the recommendation of the President after approval by the loan committees. The final Board paper is a comprehensive document, and the culmination of many months of intensive effort, during which it has been redrafted several times, and polished and crafted to near perfection. Besides the description of the project, details are given of the total cost, the quantum of World Bank financing, the expected pattern of financing, the likely foreign exchange costs and the benefits both monetary and otherwise. The rates of return, both financial and economic, are worked out, and the assumptions stated. Frequently, there is a sensitivity analysis, showing how the rate of return will vary, depending upon changes in some of the more significant factors characterising the project, where such an analysis would be appropriate. However, it should be clarified that this aspect has come in for adverse comments in the report of the Wapenhans task-force, and further particulars are given in Chapter 6. Wherever necessary, the report mentions about the likely procurement of equipment, and the award of contracts. The question of international competitive bidding, and its appropriateness in the special circumstances of the project are also examined. An overwhelming majority of the projects placed before the E.Ds are approved. Outright rejection is almost unknown, though infrequently, a project may have been sent back for reconsideration. Projects require only a simple majority for approval, and cases occur where a project has been opposed even by important members such as the USA, but has nevertheless been approved by the Board. Sometimes members oppose a project, or merely record their abstention for reasons other than those stemming directly from the project, e.g. record of the borrower with regard to violation of human rights.

Borrowers are almost invariably the developing countries, and because they would like to cultivate the goodwill of their peers and ask for their support in case of need, a tacit understanding has evolved amongst developing countries, to support one another's projects, and not to criticise a project concerning another developing country. Critical comments concerning a project have usually come to be the prerogative of the developed countries. The USA, in particular during the Reagan years, was quite vociferous in demanding that IBRD should be the lender of last resort. The exploration for oil, and development of known oilfields, was considered by them to be inappropriate for World Bank financing, the argument being that commercial banks would be prepared to finance such projects, particularly where the returns were likely to be high. The argument was further developed by adding that World Bank lending in such circumstances displaced commercial lending, and therefore, the total external lending available to the borrower got reduced, since commercial banks, unlike the World Bank, would not finance marginal projects, or socially-oriented projects. The counter-argument was unassailable, viz., the total number of projects needing financing and the amount required were far in excess of what the commercial banks, and the multilateral financial institutions together were able to finance. Moreover, developing countries, especially those importing oil, were eager to develop marginal oilfields, including even small ones in remote and unpromising locations, because of their dire need. Commercial bank financing was unlikely to be forthcoming in these conditions, and would be more expensive, even if available, compared to World Bank financing. There was thus no basis for the apprehension that World Bank financing would displace commercial bank lending. The USA was also opposed to repetitive projects, i.e. the same organisation receiving repeated loans, albeit for different schemes. Though *prima facie* plausible on grounds of equity, this approach overlooked some positive advantages of repetitive loans. These included the building up and reinforcement of a long term relationship between the Bank and the project authorities to the mutual advantage of both. The Bank's advice was likely to be heeded more because of the likely continuance of assistance. Again, both sides could profit from their experience with the same or allied projects over a longer term, and make necessary adjustments both in the on-going schemes, and in future projects. The longer time horizon also permitted more comprehensive planning, and therefore more efficient use of funds. The experience with loans to the Indian Railways, the Oil and Natural Gas Commission, and the National Thermal Power Corporation also in India (which have all received more than one loan from the World Bank) on the whole strengthens the argument in favour of continued support over a longer term. This view is buttressed by the findings of Prof. Cassen entrusted to study aid-effectiveness, where he argues for regularity and continuity in lending. The study has been referred to in Part D of Chapter 4 (Development Committee).

On more than one occasion, Indian projects for exploration and development of oilfields were approved by the Board, in the teeth of determined opposition by the USA on these grounds. There were prior indications of the U.S. stand. During the writer's tenure, there was a healthy convention that the E.D. concerned would not intervene when a project from his constituency came up before the Board for consideration. Accordingly, I was relieved of the responsibility of directly supporting such a project at the meeting itself. I felt it to be my duty, however, to canvass support from my other colleagues on the Board, as their views being disinterested, could be expected to sway opinion in favour of the project much more powerfully and effectively than any special pleading on my part in defiance of the convention. The French and the Nordic countries fully appreciated the force of the arguments marshalled by the Management in favour of these projects, and were not averse to openly supporting them, and to question the suggestion that the World Bank should be required to take up the less profitable projects, while the more profitable ones were left to the commercial banks to finance. The British were also in favour of these Indian projects, despite their special relationship with the USA, and one got the feeling that there was a sympathetic response from them to any genuine pleas from India. Perhaps the old links, and the recollection that India was once the jewel in the Crown, were still cherished. The Germans fully appreciated the arguments in favour of the project, and assured us that they would not support the USA in this case, but indicated their reluctance to speak out openly against the U.S. stand. During the cold war era, the Germans, despite their growing economic strength, were painfully aware that their ultimate security rested with the Nato alliance, and the U.S. nuclear umbrella. Needless to add, India could always depend upon the support of other developing countries.

It is not uncommon for the Board to be called upon to deal with several projects, besides other proposals involving borrowings, etc. at a single meeting. Sometimes projects get taken up with other proposals involving policy issues. Normally, the staff are called upon to make a presentation about the project under consideration, and thereafter, the paper is thrown open for discussion—with different views expressed, some in favour, and some rather critical. Depending upon the project, the discussion may be pedestrian, or it may be lively, and not infrequently, a project just sails through because of its inherent merit, without any discussion. E.Ds as a rule keep their constituencies fully informed of the discussion at Board meetings, and the stands taken by each of their colleagues who may elect to speak. I recollect an Indian fertiliser project which was being constructed to utilise the vast quantities of gas produced from the Bombay High oilfield, and neighbouring gasfields. Surprisingly, the Japanese E.D. made rather critical comments, pointing out that the cost of production of Indian fertilisers was high in comparison with international prices, and there was considerable inefficiency in the operation of some Indian fertiliser units. His suggestion was that India would do well to import fertilisers rather than put up high cost fertiliser plants. Perhaps it was overlooked that with oil production rising, the associated gas had to be profitably utilised,

India did not have the foreign exchange to import fertilisers to meet all her growing requirements, and a measure of self-reliance was desirable in a strategic commodity such as fertilisers which were essential if India were to be in a position to continue to feed her burgeoning population. While there were admittedly some inefficient fertiliser units, the project in question related to a new unit with considerable economies of scale, and an energy-efficient cycle. My colleague, perhaps, had not realised how inopportune his comments were, as the Japanese had recently agreed to assist the Indian fertiliser industry, and the Japanese Government had also made some laudatory references. These discussions seem to have got reported, and my colleague was good enough to ruefully admit later that Tokyo had not been favourably impressed!

As long ago as 1973, it had been accepted that the Board should operate so as to be in a position to devote adequate time and attention when deliberating on policy issues, and a special procedure had accordingly been devised for dealing with the growing number of projects coming to the Board for approval, so as to conserve its time. For relatively minor projects involving not more than $ 25 million, the normal full documentation, and its circulation to the Board would continue, but presentation of the project by the staff at the Board meeting was dispensed with, and the Board approved the project without discussion. However, some safeguards were built into the procedure. Any E.D. had the inherent right to discuss any such project, but should he decide to do so, he was expected to give prior notice, so that the staff could come prepared. Even for projects falling below the monetary threshold, the special procedure was not followed in any of the following circumstances: The project was the first one for the country; the project related to a new sector; or, the project had some special features.

In late 1981, the management put forward proposals to lighten the load on the Board, which had to cope with an increasing number of projects, and other complex issues such as Structural Adjustment Loans. The monetary threshold was proposed to be raised from $ 25 million to $ 35 million. In addition, the Management suggested that under special circumstances, the special procedure could be applied to projects in the range of $ 35-75 million. Surprisingly, there was some dissent even with the modest proposal of raising the threshold from $ 25 million fixed in 1973 to $ 35 million, with some E.Ds suggesting a limit of $ 30 million. Most E.Ds were averse to the additional relaxation covering projects in the range of $ 35-75 million. The upshot was that the Board approved raising the threshold to $ 35 million for the special procedure to be applied, but decided to defer consideration of the second tier approach covering the range of $ 35 to $ 75 million to the future, after experience had been gained with the working of the enhanced threshold level. This debate gives an indication of the Board's desire to zealously protect its own supervisory functions in relation to the management, and the importance it attaches to project lending.

On the other hand, there was perhaps imperfect appreciation of the need to be selective, and to thus make efficient use of the time that the Board can devote for consideration of projects after dealing with policy issues, which necessarily are accorded priority because of their inherent importance. The position is further compounded by the uneven flow of projects to the Board. Over the years, there is a trend for the flow to slow down during the beginning of the year, and to speed up thereafter, rising to a peak in the fourth quarter. During F.Y. 1985 it was estimated that only 46% of all projects approved were cleared during the first three quarters, and the remaining 54% were approved in the fourth quarter alone. In the last month of June, for some years 18% of the projects were approved, though pro-rata only some 8.33% should have been presented to the Board for approval. It is perhaps understandable that because of the discipline imposed by the close of the fiscal year, there should be a peak in the fourth quarter, and the Board should accept the reality.

Recently (December 1992), the pressure of events has resulted in further streamlining of project approval procedures at the Board level. The Bank's Annual Report 1993 states as follows (p. 23):

> "In the light of increased Board attention to policy formulation and implementation, and the initiation of country-assistance strategy discussions for all Bank borrowers, the Board has expanded the use of streamlined project-approval procedures. Under these procedures, lending operations would normally be approved without Board discussion on the basis of a prior Board discussion of a country-assistance strategy. Adjustment, debt-reduction,

and lending operations deemed by Bank management to have particular policy interest, special features, or which significantly deviate from a previously discussed country-assistance strategy framework are approved under existing regular procedures. Although Executive Directors retain the right to request that any item be considered under regular procedures, all other lending operations are intended to be taken up under streamlined procedures allowing for their approval without Board discussion."

The result is that most routine projects would be approved almost automatically, on the basis of the country-assistance strategy previously formulated. The role of the management is thus substantially augmented with respect to projects.

Since the recommendations of the Management are almost invariably accepted by the Board, when lending for projects is considered, the question arises whether Board approval and discussion serve a useful purpose. Since lending is one of the major functions of the World Bank, it is of prime importance that final approval be accorded by the Board, so as to exercise a salutary check, and also to preserve its own authority by overseeing the functioning of the Management. Even if Management's recommendations are almost invariably accepted, the requirements that there should be a detailed analysis of both the project, and the general economic and policy environment, and that the Management should go on record with their recommendations, ensure that the operational and project staff will perform efficiently, as their work will be scrutinised, and perhaps commented upon by the Board. That the staff can be called upon to make a presentation of the project before the Board provides some stimulus and encouragement to the staff who are directly involved. Consideration of a project by the Board, allows an opportunity to the interested E.Ds to focus on country and sector policy issues. Further, discussions at the Board provide strong signals to the Management about current thinking on particular issues, and these serve as guidelines both when formulating fresh proposals for approval, and also when implementing current projects. When comments by influential E.Ds, whether from the developed or the developing countries, find support from others also, and there are indications of a consensus crystallising, the Management necessarily has to pay close attention, and comply with these guidelines. The greater emphasis on policy dialogue, and co-financing, as well as the high social costs of some of the conditions involved in structural adjustment, and in reduction of subsidies, etc. together with possible steps to reduce these costs, are instances where Board discussions have had an impact on the functioning of the Bank, especially with regard to its lending activities.

It may be appropriate to end this chapter with a brief appraisal of the project lending activities of the World Bank. The crowning achievement of the organisation is the massive volume of funds transferred to the borrowers over the years for a large number of diverse projects, and the commendably high success rate achieved overall. This performance is all the more remarkable because of the disparate conditions under which these projects are implemented, and the enormous range covered. There can be little doubt that the Bank has succeeded in developing great strength in its operational branches, and has provided much needed managerial, technical and financial underpinning to the field staff of the borrowers. This wide-ranging experience is available to other borrowers also, both for formulating new projects, and for implementing ongoing ones. Though interest charged on IBRD loans is market-related, some financial benefits accrue to borrowers because these charges are somewhat more favourable than those available elsewhere, owing to the cost-free monies it can use (e.g. subscribed capital and reserves). Even more important is the much longer maturity period associated with IBRD loans, as compared with the usual commercial borrowings. IDA credits are provided at highly concessional rates, and the grant element at one stage was estimated at over 80%. Further intangible benefits are derived from the Bank's association with a project. The higher priority automatically accorded to such projects has already been mentioned. In addition, political and other extraneous or undesirable influences are somewhat contained, because of the supervision exercised by the Bank, particularly with regard to procurement and award of contracts. The Bank's influence with regard to prices, rates charged for supplies and services, tariffs, and recoupment of monies advanced, though it may be resented at the time, does help to improve the financial and economic viability of the project, and therefore, serves to create a more favourable environment for the replication of more such projects.

One possible criticism of the Bank's procedures is the protracted period that usually elapses between the identification of a project, and the eventual making of the loan, as the various stages of the project cycle are slowly traversed. It can be argued that the very success achieved by the Bank is because of its meticulous adherence to the project cycle, and its striving for perfection. While by no means discounting this claim, one could reasonably plead for a somewhat more realistic balance. By and large, the Bank necessarily has to depend for much of the engineering and other data on the borrower and its agencies, and has to content itself with some spot checks. The quality of the data collected by the borrower may not always be of a consistently high order, and any amount of subsequent analysis will not remove the imperfection. In most projects, there are many imponderables, and circumstances may change dramatically between the time a project is conceived, and the time it is fully complete and operational, and this period could well range from 5 to 15 years. Having regard to these factors, perhaps prudence would suggest greater reliance on the judgement and experience of persons in the borrowing countries, who have handled such projects in the past, rather than meticulous and time-consuming analysis by theoreticians based in Washington. While undoubtedly such analysis cannot be dispensed with, there is a case for speeding it up, and confining it to essentials, bearing in mind the inadequacies of the data, and the many uncertainties lying ahead. After all, the cost of the delay is borne by the borrower, quite frequently a very poor country. This cost can take many forms, of which two are worth highlighting. Because of the secular trend of rising prices, which is more pronounced in the developing countries, with delay, the cost of the project is likely to rise steeply. Even more telling is the cost incurred by the borrower because of the denial or the deferment of the benefits from the project, available only on completion. Delay occurs not only in the approval of a project, but also in its implementation. While the latter is primarily the borrower's responsibility, the Bank can do much to expedite matters, as it holds the purse-strings, and its missions are continuously in the field. Interestingly, the OED once reported[16] that project appraisal and loan presentation activities often received priority over supervision of existing projects. While this was disputed by the Management, the OEDs comments are worth pursuing so that a more purposeful approach is adopted by the Bank to speed up both the approval of projects and their proper implementation. That the OED's earlier comments were valid is fully borne out by the subsequent finding of the task-force under Mr. Wapenhans, which found that there was inadequate supervision, resulting in poor performance, owing to the Banks' pre-occupation with new lending, and its involvement during the preparatory stage (vide Chapter 6).

As with most bureaucratic organisations, there is a tendency on the part of the World Bank to treat all countries and all projects on par to the extent possible. There are exceptions of course, but by and large, existing procedures and practices do not differentiate as much as would be justified by the present inter-country differences, and the wide range of the projects currently financed. Some borrowers have built up their own engineering, technical, financial and managerial institutions, and have on their own successfully completed projects similar to the ones being proposed for World Bank financing. Of the total investments made in the public sector, the bulk may be financed out of domestic resources, while only a relatively small percentage (may be less than 10%) is coming from several external sources including the World Bank. On the other hand, another category of borrowers may not have the requisite institutional strength, or adequate experience of formulating and implementing large projects. External resources may constitute a larger percentage of the total investments in the second category as compared to the first. Amongst projects also, there might be a case for distinguishing between relatively routine projects such as installing a power-station, and another category, e.g. rural development, with a high social content, and involving activities that are widely dispersed over the countryside where organisational, institutional, and supervisory problems may be formidable. For the second category, the techniques, and the set-up may still be somewhat experimental. The suggestion is that the World Bank should be more selective in its approach, and depend to the extent feasible upon the borrower's organisations and institutions, rather than on repeated missions sent out from Washington, for the better equipped countries and for projects of the first category. Perhaps it would be appreciated by some borrowers if the World Bank were to assume less responsibility, and squarely place added responsibilities upon the former. For the other category, continued assistance and supervision may not only be required, but may have to be strengthened. The Bank's own experience referred to earlier, shows that there is a significant difference between the performance in South Asia, and that in East and West Africa, or in sub-Saharan Africa. Better use of manpower and resources would perhaps result if a freer rein were to be given to those countries, and projects, where performance can be reasonably expected to be good in the light of experience, and tighter supervision exercised where performance has been disappointing in the past. In the ultimate analysis, it is the borrowing member-Government that is responsible for repaying the loans and the credits given to it by the Bank.

A related issue concerns fuller utilisation of Resident Missions of the World Bank. A Sub-Committee on PPAR's functioning under the Joint Audit Committee recommended in September 1981 that more authority should be delegated to the Resident Missions to deal with procurement issues, and the possibility of shifting more of the supervisory functions to these Missions should be examined. If needed, local professionals could be engaged for the purpose. It appears that Mr. McNamara, the then President, had also mentioned this approach to the Board in April 1981. These suggestions seem attractive, and should help in reducing costs and in speeding up implementation, as problems could be resolved on the spot. It is significant that these suggestions have been reiterated by the task-force under Mr. Wapenhans' Chairmanship. This issue is dealt with in greater detail in Chapter 6.

The Bank's documents are replete with tables, and charts showing the loans and credits made to countries classified by income-groups, or by regions, and also of such commitments by sectors, e.g. agriculture, energy, industry, transportation. These tables attract considerable attention. Inter-country allocations serve a useful purpose in ensuring equitable distribution of the available funds, in the light of the concepts weighing with the Board. On the other hand, discussions of the allocations amongst various sectors are somewhat pointless, because these present a fragmentary view, and also for the reasons outlined in Chapter 3 under "Budget".

Notes and References

1. World Bank Annual Report, 1995.
2. Billion = 1000 million or 10^9.
3. Investing in Development by Baum & Tolbert, p. 7.
4. Annual Report for 1988, p. 66.
5. Special Report, World Bank News, April 1988.
6. The Project Cycle, by Warren Baum. I am indebted to this booklet for some of the material in this chapter.
7. Chapter 1.
8. Investing in Development by Baum & Tolbert, p. 384.
9. Annual Report, 1994, p. 155.
10. Investing in Development by Baum & Tolbert, p. 366.
11. Speech by Mr. Robert McNamara to the Board of Governors at Nairobi (Sept. 1973).
12. IDA in Retrospect, Ch. 5.
13. Investing in Development by Baum & Tolbert, p. 350.
14. IDA in Retrospect, p. 63.
15. Seventh Annual Review of Project Performance Audit Results.
16. Seventh Annual Review of PPARs.

CHAPTER 3

FINANCING THE OPERATIONS OF THE INTERNATIONAL BANK FOR RECONSTRUCTION & DEVELOPMENT AND THE BUDGET OF THE BANK GROUP

Taking into account the General Capital Increase (GCI) approved by the Board of Governors in April 1988, and amounting to $ 74.8 billion, the IBRD's total authorised capital stands at $ 184.05 billion. However, subscription to the GCI (or other capital increase) is a slow process. The 1993 Annual Report mentions that during financial year 1993, subscriptions to this GCI proceeded smoothly. As on June 30th, 1994 the total subscribed capital of the IBRD was $ 170.0 billion or 92% of the authorised capital. The corresponding subscribed capital as on June 30th, 1995 was $ 176.4 billion or 96% of the authorised capital. The increase was on account of 20 countries subscribing an aggregate of $ 6.4 billion. At the end of fiscal year 1995, the permissible increase of net disbursements ("headroom") was $ 75.3 billion, thus implying that though for the present, the Bank's capital would not be a constraint there was no room for complacency as the outstanding loans and callable guarantees have risen from 57% of the statutory lending limit to 62% during FY 1993-95, despite the influx of fresh subscribed capital. This influx is likely to cease shortly, as the subscribed capital is already 96% of the authorised capital, and the 'headroom' for additional outstanding loans may be eroded quite rapidly. As already mentioned, the Articles themselves provide that 80% of the subscribed capital shall be subject to call *only* when required to meet obligations of the Bank, e.g. to repay market borrowings, or to fulfil guarantees. Because of the inherent strength of the Bank, the possibility of such calls is remote. For the 1988 GCI by a Resolution of the Board of Governors, only 3% is required to be paid in. The paid-in portion has varied for earlier capital increases, but over the years it has progressively gone down. As on June 30th, 1995, though the subscribed capital stood at $ 176.4 billion approximately, the uncalled portion of the subscriptions was about $ 166 billion, and the paid-in portion was some $ 10.86 billion.[1] This sum represents the *aggregate* cash contributions of both the developed and developing countries over 50 years, to the IBRD, and must be adjudged modest. To place these figures in perspective, it has to be recalled that the Central Government's expenditure in the U.S.A., the largest shareholder, was about $ 1490 trillion at 23.8% of G.D.P. during 1993. Defence expenditure alone, after the end of the cold war, was estimated at 19.3% of Central Government expenditure, or about $ 288 trillion that year. On the other hand, the *total* paid-in subscription to the IBRD's capital ever since its inception by the U.S.A. was $ 1.964 billion. (*Source:* WDR and Annual Report 1995). The U.S.A.'s capital contribution to the IBRD, therefore, constitutes a minuscule proportion of its total Governmental expenditure. Over the years, the Bank has accumulated substantial reserves. The Special Reserve amounts to some $ 293 million and has been created pursuant to Art. IV, Sec. 6. It can be used only for the purpose of meeting the liabilities of the IBRD on its borrowings and guarantees in the event of defaults in loans made, participated in, or guaranteed by the IBRD. Since 1964 allocations to the Special Reserve have been discontinued with respect to the subsequent loans, and there has been no further accretion. The bulk of the income generated by the IBRD is now allocated to the General Reserve, which stands at about $ 13.629 billion. The aggregate of the paid-in capital and the reserves is therefore of the order of $ 24.5 billion. On the other hand, the IBRD is committed to provide loans amounting to approximately $ 179 billion. Of these loans, the undisbursed amounts to be paid to the borrowers (the member-Governments and their agencies) approximate $ 44 billion. During FY 1995, the Bank has entered into new commitments with its borrowers to provide $ 16.85 billion, an improvement over the FY

1994 figure, but still slightly below the FY 1993 figures. From these figures and the scale of the operations undertaken by the IBRD, it is clear that the IBRD does not rely solely on its paid-in capital and its reserves. Instead, for operational purposes, the Bank relies in great measure upon the financial market, from where it borrows funds, and re-lends to its own borrowers. During FY 1993 and FY 1995 it borrowed $ 12.6 billion and $ 9.0 billion respectively from various financial centres, and the total disbursements to its own borrowers were $ 12.9 billion and $ 12.67 billion respectively. One of the most significant roles played by the IBRD is that of financial intermediation, by which money borrowed from the financial markets of the world at exceptionally favourable rates are re-lent to the developing countries. Developing countries on their own would find it well-nigh impossible to tap these markets, and even harder to secure the favourable rates and the long maturities at which the IBRD lends to them.

A digression at this stage may be in order. Mention has already been made of the provision in the Articles which limits the total amount outstanding of guarantees, participation in loans and direct loans to the aggregate of the subscribed capital, reserves and surplus of the Bank. This has been construed as a "gearing ratio" of 1:1, and suggestions have been made from time to time to increase this ratio so as to permit more loans to be made, even by bodies as eminent as the Brandt Commission. Judging from the 1988 GCI, where the paid-in portion is a mere 3% of the subscribed capital, when assessing the leverage effectively obtained by the IBRD in its lending operations, it would be more appropriate to proceed on the basis of the paid-in portion, which alone is available to the Bank for its current operations. Perhaps, with a paid-in portion of about $ 10.86 billion, and a General Reserve of $ 13.63 billion, aggregate loans of $ 179 billion approximately constitute a reasonable proportion. The Annual Report for 1995 mentions that the retained earnings (which includes the Special and General Reserves, the surplus and the unallocated net income) totalled $ 15.5 billion. If, to this are added the paid-in capital and some minor amounts, the total equity comes to about $ 30.46 billion. The effective gearing ratio is thus of the order of 5.88:1. Perhaps no further upward revision would be desirable. There is also considerable force in the Management's contention that when issuing its prospectus for borrowing in the financial markets, the Bank has stressed the limits laid down in the Articles, and any dilution, particularly one having retrospective effect, would not be appreciated by the Bank's creditors, and may adversely affect market sentiment. Mr. Rotberg in his article published as a part of the Bretton Woods Commission report (p. c. 205) refers to this aspect and mentions that any deviations from the one-to-one basis would give rise to the likelihood—indeed the certainty—that a bondholder would bring suit against the Bank for a false and misleading prospectus—having bought bonds on that assumption.

According to the Balance sheet, as on June 30th, 1995, medium and long term borrowings of the IBRD stood at $ 104.5 billion approximately, while short term borrowings were of the order of $ 3.9 billion, with total borrowings standing at $ 108.4 billion approximately. The Bank provides a break-up of the various currencies which have been borrowed, and the preponderance of certain currencies is striking. After 'swaps', which will be referred to later, about 96% of the total effective borrowings as on that date were in only 4 major currencies, viz. Japanese yen, U.S. dollar, Deutsche mark, and the Swiss franc.[2] Many types of financial instruments are used to tap the financial markets. It may not be out of place to refer to one instrument, viz the zero-coupon bonds. These are recorded in the Balance sheet at their discounted values, and since they will have to be repaid on maturity at their face value, which is higher, there is an element of underestimation, which should not cause concern, however, as the magnitudes are relatively small, and the period of maturity may be substantial. By way of illustration, a reference may be made to the zero-coupon borrowings in U.S. dollars, which is the currency most used for such borrowings. While the discounted value was $ 591 million approximately, the face value was $ 2.83 billion approximately. Since interest charges are merged into the face value, and the IBRD in fact pays no more than it otherwise would with a more conventional borrowing instrument, a difference of this order, when viewed against total borrowings in the range of $ 100 billion, should not cause any qualms.

It might be of some interest to compare the maturity structure of the loans made by the IBRD to its various borrowers, with the maturity structure of its borrowings from various creditors. During each of the fiscal years 1996, 1997, 1998, 1999 and 2000, the Bank's loans due to mature range around $ 12 to $ 14 billion. Correspondingly, during each of the same years, the Bank's medium and long term borrowings falling due for redemption vary from a minimum of $ 8.2 billion to a maximum of $ 15.6 billion, the latter figure being for fiscal year 2000. The aggregates for these five years show that the Bank's loans maturing exceed the Bank's debt falling due for redemption ($ 66.4 billion vs. $ 63.5 billion). During the next five years, i.e. upto fiscal year 2005, the same pattern persists ($ 40.7 billion vs. $ 30.7 billion). Thus, this analysis shows that the Bank has carefully ensured that no mismatch occurs, and it has been conservative in its borrowing and lending operations. Major borrowings by the IBRD have to be approved by the Board, and frequently the staff mention how the period of the particular borrowing has been negotiated to achieve a certain degree of smoothness, and to avoid the sudden bunching of commitments during particular years.

Prior to July 1982, the lending rate, adopted by the IBRD for loans made by it, was a fixed rate, so that the borrower had to pay this rate on all outstanding amounts till the loan was repaid, i.e. over a period of 15 to 20 years. Though this rate itself was market-related, in the sense that the Bank fixed its lending rate on the basis of the cost of its borrowings plus a spread, it had a great advantage from the borrowers' point of view, as it made for certainty, and the borrower could estimate precisely what interest payments would have to be made till the maturity of the loan. This precision also facilitated a more accurate estimation of a project's financial viability.

During 1981 and 1982, there was considerable volatility in interest rates, and turmoil in the financial markets, which had its repercussions on the operations of the IBRD. In late 1981, and early 1982, the Bank's management drew attention to the undesirable risks that the IBRD was exposing itself to by entering into fixed rate commitments with its borrowers, when making loans. These loans were usually disbursed over a fairly long period, particularly in the case of project loans, and if the gestation period were lengthy, 7 to 10 years may elapse before the full amount was disbursed.

During a period of rising interest rates the Bank could suffer a loss, because of this time-lag, as the rate at which it borrowed from the market to fulfil its commitments may be significantly higher than the rate committed to its borrower when making the loan. Initially, the Management put forward two alternatives, viz. a full-fledged pool-based variable interest rate, or a rate for each loan based upon the Bank's borrowing costs during the disbursement of the loan. From the beginning, the Management favoured a full-fledged variable interest rate, and the other option was not pursued. The Management marshalled yet another even more powerful argument for a change in the lending rate policy. Because of turmoil in the financial markets, they argued that the availability of long and medium term funds was dwindling, and it may not be possible to attain the programmed lending levels, far less to expand them, if the Bank did not change its borrowing instruments, and also tapped the short term funds at variable interest rates. The Bank would not be justified in doing so, unless the interest rate risk was simultaneously passed on to its borrowers. They were also averse to getting locked on to the prevailing high interest rates by excessive long and medium term borrowings.

Thereafter followed a succession of seminars, and luncheon meetings with small groups of Executive Directors, elaborating the undesirable exposure that the IBRD was letting itself into under the present system, and generally educating the Board on the functioning of the financial markets. The borrowers, who were *ex hypothesi* poor and in need of funds at reasonable rates, argued that they were already bearing the full currency risk, and were now being asked in addition to shoulder the interest risk. In the process, they were being exposed to a high degree of uncertainty because of variable interest rates, over which they had no control. Since they did not have the resilience generally to cope with this new challenge, they should be shielded by the Bank, which had vast resources. It could augment these resources, if needed, by building in a cushion in the interest rate structure by way of insurance. The Management countered by arguing that the pool-based variable interest rate alternative was the most efficient and the cheapest. On the basis of certain prior assumptions, they estimated that the alternative based on the Bank's costs during the period of disbursement would require a higher spread of 0.6% as compared to the variable interest rate they proposed. Continuance of the present system, they said, would require that the spread would have to be 3.6% above the spread under the pool-based variable interest rate alternative, in order to cover the exposure of the Bank adequately. The then President, Mr. Clausen, was himself a professional banker of great experience, and therefore, well aware of the problems facing the IBRD. The Management were convinced of the need to strengthen the Bank's financial position and its standing, by moving over to variable interest rates, and they spared no pains in preparing graphs, charts, and statements, when putting forward their point of view, and answering queries raised by the Board members.

The Management, feeling that they had done all that was feasible to explain their proposals, and to wear down the opposition, brought forward a detailed paper on the subject in early June of 1982, and the issue was discussed by the Board on July Ist. All the preceding points were set forth, and it was further proposed that the lending rate should be determined every six months by adding a spread of 0.5% to the average cost of the 'pool'. The 'pool' would consist of all outstanding borrowings made by the IBRD after the date when the new lending rate policy was introduced. However, in order to ensure stability, and as a transitional measure for the first three years, there would be the addition of a proxy, namely, the average cost of IBRD borrowings settled during FY 1982. The lending rate fixed for a six-monthly period would apply for all future loans after the due date, and would, therefore, vary for each such loan during its life, i.e. till maturity and redemption. Though this introduced a large element of uncertainty, and made budgeting for the service charges, as also the provisioning of foreign exchange for the purpose, a daunting task for the borrowers, it was claimed that the new policy introduced a measure of equity as between the borrowers, in that loans by the IBRD can often be lumpy, and fortuitously some borrowers could profit from low interest rates, while others could be penalised by high rates depending upon when they got the loan under the old system.

Surprisingly, the discussions revealed considerable differences of opinion, and the divide was not along the familiar industrial countries, and developing countries groupings. While the U.S.A., the U.K. and the Nordic countries were fully supportive of the Management, Germany, France and to a lesser extent, Japan, were less than enthusiastic about the Management's proposals. There was also a schism among the developing countries. While the African and Arab countries supported the Management's proposals, other developing countries had their reservations. There was a general agreement that the position should be reviewed soon, and that nothing should be done to make the proposed change irreversible.

Amongst those of us in the developing countries who had reservations about the proposals, one of the concerns expressed related to the image of the IBRD, and its functioning as the world's premier developmental institution. It was thought that the change to variable interest rates was symptomatic of a shift from development to commercial banking, and did not fully appreciate the formidable difficulties faced by most developing countries in making adequate provision in scarce foreign exchange for servicing their debts. However, Mr. Clausen himself intervened promptly to assure the Board that there was no intention of changing the developmental character of the IBRD.

Another aspect of the new policy which attracted comment was the addition of the proxy as a transitional measure for three years to achieve a degree of stability in the lending rate. Since it was based upon the average cost of IBRD borrowings during 1982, when interest rates were prevailing at historically high levels, some of us thought that an unjustifiably high bias had been imparted to the lending rates, to the detriment of the borrowers. However, even a suggestion to fix the proxy on the basis of the borrowing costs for both 1981 and 1982 did not find favour. This aspect was, however, not dropped by the developing countries, and was to be raised more than once at the Board whenever a suitable opportunity presented itself. Eventually, the proxy was dropped one year before the due date, showing that persistence pays, and both the Management and the Board cannot long remain impervious to a plea grounded on sound reasons.

The Management's proposals were eventually agreed to by the Board, and the changeover to pool-based variable interest rates was approved, though with reluctance on the part of some members. As a counter to the Managements' plea that without the flexibility of variable interest rates, even the programmed lending levels would not be attained, some of us optimistically suggested that a *quid pro quo* for the adoption of variable interest-rates should be an expansion of Bank lending. A factor which influenced the decision, was put succinctly by a representative of some African countries, when he told me informally that the IBRD had no existence beyond its members, and if the financial position of the Bank were to be improved, albeit at the cost of some of the borrowers, in the long run the members would themselves stand to gain. The short term borrowings of the IBRD got off to a good start, and lowered the cost of borrowing compared to what it otherwise would have been. There was also an interesting debate on the investment of the short term funds borrowed by the IBRD, as such investments were made with the commercial banks. Having regard to the international banking situation and the difficult conditions through which the commercial banks were passing, certain limits were imposed to safeguard the IBRD's interests. In retrospect, the IBRD has not performed badly, and the interests of the borrowers have been borne in mind, as the variable lending rate has steadily declined from its initial level of 11.43% (July 1, 1982) to 7.72% on January 1, 1988. On July 1, 1988, the rate was reduced further to 7.59%. Though the IBRD lending rates under the new policy are market related, these rates follow the market only with a time-lag because of the pool. Thus, while the former rates are relatively stable, yet it is not inconceivable that the IBRD rates may turn out to be higher at particular periods than what is prevailing in the markets of particular countries for comparable loans.

The Annual Report of the Bank for 1989 mentions that two changes have been made subsequently in the lending rate system, viz.

(a) the borrowings funding investments will be excluded in calculating the currency-by-currency cost of borrowing, and
(b) the currency weights applied to each currency's costs will be the share of each currency outstanding in the loan currency pool during the past semester.

The new rates are to apply to all loans where the invitations to negotiate have been issued after May 18th, 1989 (referred to as VLR 1989).

Borrowers can opt to adopt the VLR 1989 rates for their previous loans also, but in the absence of any such request, the old lending rates (VLR 1982) would apply to the previous loans. The changes made are thus not fundamental, but try to ensure that the pool costs reflect only the costs incurred for borrowing funds which are lent out and not invested as part of the liquid reserves. The ostensible purpose is to facilitate interest risk management.

Table

Fiscal year		Lending rates/percentages First semester	Second semester
1995	VLR 89	7.0	7.09
	VLR 82	7.11	7.13
1994	VLR 89	7.43	7.27
	VLR 82	7.42	7.25
1993	VLR 89	7.60	7.43
	VLR 82	7.58	7.40
1992	VLR 89	7.73	7.73
	VLR 82	7.71	7.72
1991	VLR 89	7.72	7.73
	VLR 82	7.70	7.70
1990	VLR 89	7.74	7.75
	VLR 82	7.73	7.75

Source : Various Annual Reports.

The above table shows the lending rates for various subsequent years under both the old and the new formulae. It will be noticed that the two formulae yield rates which differ by only a few basis points. The Bank strives for perfection, and this may be an instance where the refinements introduced, doubtless on ostensibly rational grounds, have produced insignificant practical results, and that too, often to the detriment of the borrowers. It could perhaps be asked whether the refinement introduced is worth the additional cost and labour involved in allocating the available funds by purpose, viz., investment or lending, and further by weighing each currency according to the outstandings in the loan currency pool. Not only has the Board spent much time and effort in approving the new formula, but also it will require effort every time the rates are fixed, and borrowers will have to decide their best course when opting for the formula of their choice in respect of pre-1989 loans. Most borrowers would perhaps prefer to have greater access to Bank funds, so that they can implement much needed projects, rather than be given a reduction of a few basis points in the interest rate. One can be pardoned for wondering whether these man-hours could not have been put to better use, e.g. by supervising performance of projects, as suggested by the Wapenhans report, or by raising additional resources.

A further twist to the determination of lending rates is mentioned in the Bank's Annual Report, 1995. Doubtless the existence of these dual variable lending rates was proving inconvenient, and the Board decided in December 1994, that as an incentive to the borrowers they have been offered a one-time waiver of 10 basis points in the annual interest, spread over two interest periods, if they opt for the VLR 89. At the end of FY 1995, conversions following this initiative amounted to $ 28 billion approximately, or 73% of the unconverted volume outstanding on December 31st, 1994.

A further refinement introduced, albeit on a pilot basis, in February 1993 was to offer eligible borrowers a choice of currencies on their loans as an alternative to the existing standard loan product. The new loan programme offers U.S. dollars, Japanese yen, Deutsche mark, French francs, and pounds sterling or a combination of these currencies. The interest rate is tied to the six-month LIBOR rate or to the PIBOR rate for French francs. During the pilot phase, the facility was offered only to borrowers managed autonomously of their Governments, and expected to service IBRD debt from their own revenues in the same currency as the loan. The advantage foreseen was that these borrowers would be able to cope better with the currency and interest rate risks under this option, as they could take note of their earnings in various currencies, and distribute their debt servicing burden accordingly. In May 1995, this pilot programme was reviewed, and liberalised. The eligibility was widened, and Governments on their own were also entitled to borrow in the currency of their choice. It was now made permissible to borrow in currencies other than those mentioned above, provided that the Bank was able to borrow efficiently in those currencies. Besides the variable rate option, fixed rate loans were also now permissible. Borrowers thus had the following options:

(i) selected currency loans at variable rates
(ii) selected currency loans at fixed rates, and
(iii) the previous standard, a variable rate, currency pool loan.

Subject to review, these options are conditional upon:

(a) borrowers opting for VLR 89 for outstanding loans, and
(b) a maximum of selected currency loans of $ 100 million *or* 50% of the annual borrowing programme for a borrower, whichever is higher.

The Bank has thus made a genuine effort to allow borrowers a wide choice of loans, which could be matched to the prevailing conditions and the foreign exchange earning capacity of the borrower. However, the Bank will now have to be even more circumspect in managing its affairs, so as to minimise the currency and interest rate risks that it will have to bear consequent upon the choices of the borrowers. Borrowers, too, will be required to take agonising decisions. Time alone will tell whether these deviations from the standard currency pool system, which moderates and distributes risks, are fully justified. The fact remains that currencies and interest rates are notoriously volatile, and the available options cast an onerous burden upon the borrowers to make the right choice. Even with access to information world-wide, and after sophisticated analysis it may not always be possible to make the right choice particularly over a relatively long period of 10-15 years.

It may be worthwhile at this stage to refer to some comments of Mr. Rotberg in his paper published as a part of the Bretton Woods Commission Report, and mentioned earlier also.[3] Referring to the borrowing programme of the Bank during the early 1980s, he states that the Bank's financial staff was on auto-pilot, and found it more convenient to have scores of bond issues in Germany, Switzerland and Japan, rather than borrow in dollars in the USA owing to the hassle of gaining access to the US market. The implicit assumption was that the German, Swiss and Japanese currencies would not *re-value* to the extent of offsetting the interest differential over the period of the bond maturity (i.e. 10 to 15 years). What actually transpired was that the deutsche mark, yen and Swiss franc did not revalue, but *devalued* vis-a-vis the dollar, producing not only interest savings, but extraordinary exchange rate gains through February 1985. Mr. Rotberg laments that though some calls were made by senior financial staff to capture the revaluation gains, nothing was done. These gains were lost, and when these other currencies *revalued* against the U.S. dollar, the currency losses substantially exceeded the savings in interest over what would have been the notional rate in U.S. dollars. This comment illustrates the difficulties that the borrowers would be experiencing when making a choice. Even the Bank's staff could go wrong despite their experience, and the information and the communication and computing facilities that the Bank possesses. There is, therefore, something to be said for simplicity and a pooling system to moderate risks.

The World Development Report for 1989 makes an interesting comment when dealing with the debt problem, and it is reproduced below:

> "One lesson of the debt crisis is that commercial bank lending at floating rates is not the ideal form of financing for long term development. It exposes the borrower to interest rate and exchange rate fluctuations, and it does not tie the borrower's payments to the outcome of the investment" (page 23).

These were the precise difficulties that the borrowing countries apprehended when the pool-based variable interest rate proposal was considered by the Board in the early 1980s, and the WDR comment would show that there is belated recognition of the validity of this aspect even amongst the top management in the Bank.

A digression may be in order at this stage. The Annual Report for 1989 states that the Directors had approved a one year reduction in the commitment fee, effective July 1st, 1989, which would save the borrowers about $ 200 million during the year. This fee used to be levied at 0.75% on the undisbursed balance of a sanctioned loan, and conventional wisdom justified it on two grounds, viz. *first* making good the cost to the Bank of carrying the liquidity necessitated by its contractual commitment to the borrower to pay the loan amount in the appropriate tranches, and *secondly* to encourage speedy disbursement of the loan, which is usually linked to the expeditious completion of the project. The reasons given for the reduction, consistent with the maintenance of the reserves to loans ratio at the stipulated figure, were *first,* the decline in the funding risk for the loans consequent on the adoption of the pool-based variable interest rate, and *secondly*, the inequitable incidence of the commitment fee on slow disbursing projects. These loans may have been made to finance high priority schemes with long gestation periods, and the commitment fee would bear heavily on these projects, even if they were implemented according to the schedule envisaged at the time when the loan was approved.

It is worth recalling that in late 1981, proposals were put forward by the Management, when Mr. Clausen was the President, to introduce a front-end fee of 1% on new IBRD commitments, and to also raise the commitment fee of ¾% to 1%. The ground advanced for the suggested increases was that the projections of the Bank's income made by the Management showed disturbing trends, and against the required $ 500 million, the income was projected to fall to around $ 350 million in FY 1985 and 1986. The discussions at the Board meeting held on January 5th, 1982 were interesting. The borrowing countries were naturally exercised at the higher costs imposed on them, and showed that the IBRD's charges compared unfavourably with those of other multilateral institutions such as the Asian Development Bank and the Inter American Development Bank. It was also suggested that these imposts ill-befitted the image of the IBRD as a premier developmental institution, and in any case the projections of income made by the Management were unduly conservative. Some of us thought that against the desired level of $ 500 million, the Bank's income might rise to $ 1 billion by FY 1988 for various reasons, including the yield from these new levies, and as such we felt that the Management had provided a considerable cushion in their estimates, at a time when the borrowing countries were hard pressed. Incidentally, hindsight shows that our anticipations were proved correct, and the IBRD's income did rise to the $ 1 billion level. Criticism of the proposed increase in the commitment fee was more severe than that of the introduction of the front-end fee for several reasons. There was a feeling that the Management was over-reacting to a temporary difficulty, and the measures introduced should, therefore, be easily reversible upon review. While this condition was satisfied by the front-end fee, an enhanced commitment fee would presumably have to be continued till the loan in question was fully disbursed, and this process could take several years. Some of us also pointed to the disadvantage of a higher commitment fee bearing heavily on long gestation and slow disbursing projects—a point that seems to have touched a responsive chord in the IBRD in 1989, resulting in the current reduction, but which was ignored when the Management formulated its proposals for these increases in late 1981.

The Management's proposals received full support of the major industrial countries such as the USA, UK, Japan and France. Some other Part I countries were lukewarm, e.g. Germany, the Nordic countries and Spain objected to the over-emphasis given to the Bank's net income and to the attempt to pass on all burdens to the borrowers. Even the Dutch opposed an increase in the commitment fee, and suggested instead a front-end fee of 1.5%. It was noteworthy that throughout the discussions there was universal recognition of the need to keep the IBRD as a strong and vibrant institution, and the cooperative nature of its functioning was stressed. The developing countries fully appreciated the need for maintaining the Bank's high financial standing in their own interest.

Mr. Clausen sensed the genuineness of the grievances voiced by the prospective borrowers, and instead of forcing through the Managements' proposals with the brute majority of the Part I countries, he displayed commendable flexibility. He seized on the Dutch proposal, and offered a compromise under which a front-end fee would be levied at 1.5%, subject to continuous review, and the commitment fee would remain unchanged. This compromise was eventually accepted, and is one of the rare instance where the Management's considered proposals were modified by the Board.

The subsequent developments with regard to the front-end fee may be of some interest. Towards the end of 1982, the Management put forward proposals to reduce this fee from 1.5% to 1% because the Bank's income had shown a welcome spurt. The Group of Nine

(G-9) developing countries thought that the front-end fee could now be abolished, but were prudent enough to hold informal discussions with the industrial countries, meeting with them collectively. It was possible to arrive at an informal understanding acceptable to both groups that the fee should be halved to 0.75%. In the result, the formal Board meeting held on December 7th, 1982 was rather uneventful, as the Management had no option but to accept the consensus, though Japan continued to support the Management. For the second time, therefore, the Management's proposal regarding the front-end fee was modified by the Board. The further history of the fee is that it was reduced to 0.25% (though on merits it could have been abolished) in March 1983. At the Board meeting some industrialised countries pressed for a smaller reduction to 0.5% even though the Management now estimated the Bank's income at $ 810 million, and the overhang of past commitments of fixed rate loans was diminishing. They preferred to retain a nominal fee of 0.25%, which could be raised if circumstances so warranted, rather than its complete abolition, which would have removed an important weapon from their armoury. Eventually the levy of this fee has been discontinued[4] from FY 1986. It is noteworthy that the Annual Report for 1993 mentions that during fiscal year 1993, the IBRD waived 35 basis points of the semester interest rate on loans, provided that the borrowers had made all loan-service payments within 30 days of their due date. This waiver was in addition to the continuation during the year of the reduction of the IBRD's commitment fee on undisbursed balances from 75 to 25 basis points. The report adds that the incentive for timely repayments has been effective, as approximately 80% of IBRD's total volume of outstanding loans is currently eligible for the waiver. The same trend continued in FY 1995, as the Annual Report 1995 mentions a one year interest waiver of 25 basis points on disbursed and outstanding loans for all eligible borrowers. The waiver of 50 basis points in the commitment fee is also continued. Reference has been made earlier to the 10 basis points interest waiver given as an incentive to convert outstanding loans from VLR 82 to VLR 89. The total of these waivers comes to $ 251 million, but even thereafter, the net income of the IBRD for FY 1995 was a high $ 1354 million.

The issue of the front-end and the commitment fee has been

considered in some detail as it provides interesting insights into the functioning of the Bank. There is first the contrast in styles between Mr. Clausen, the banker, and Mr. Conable, the politician, during their respective stewardships of the World Bank. Mr. Clausen was aware of the possible difficulties that the IBRD would be facing in the turbulent days ahead, and of the chinks in its financial armour. Hence his drive to improve the finances of the Bank by introducing variable interest rates, new instruments, swaps, etc. He also forced through the front-end fee, though with some modification by the Board. Mr. Conable could rely on the eminently sound financial position of the Bank, further strengthened by Mr. Clausen, and could afford to pay heed to the susceptibilities of the borrowing countries, and reduce the commitment fee. The next Chairman, Mr. Preston, also seems to have utilised the strengths developed by the Bank to make concessions. The Management, like most bureaucracies, can marshal plausible arguments to support stands adopted by the ultimate policy makers—though over the years, some inconsistencies can surface, as for example, the inequitable incidence of the commitment fee on slow-disbursing loans, and the gradual dissolution of the overhang of fixed rate commitments after the adoption of the pool-based variable interest rate, which nevertheless did not preclude proposals for sharp increases in Bank charges at one stage. The innate conservatism of the Bank in its projections, and the unquestioning support lent by the major industrial countries in this regard also come to light. The Board, if it so desires, can play a decisive role, and assert its authority over the Management. Usually, the developed and developing countries hold divergent views, but given valid grounds and the establishment of the right personal equations, the Board can play an assertive, and beneficial role, especially if both the Part I and Part II countries have convergent views.

The intermediation role of the IBRD has been referred to earlier. For the efficient discharge of this role, the Bank has developed a funding strategy over the years. Clearly the first objective of this strategy is to ensure availability of funds as and when required by the IBRD to meet its commitments. When entering into a loan agreement with a borrower, the IBRD makes a firm commitment to provide the borrower with the contracted amount. Particularly for project loans, the IBRD normally disburses the funds against expenditure incurred by the borrower in connection with the project, and these disbursements take place over the period of its execution. The IBRD has to be in a position to meet all these commitments to its different borrowers, which extend for several years beyond the dates of execution of the loan agreements, and depend upon the gestation period of the projects. Some other loans, e.g. S.A.L.'s, and programme loans, are relatively quick disbursing, and the committed funds have to be disbursed as required. To place itself in funds the IBRD taps diverse financial markets located in various industrial countries, particularly the U.S.A, Japan, Switzerland and Germany. However, it can do so only if the Governments of these countries permit it. Most Governments have been extremely accommodating to the IBRD so far, with regard to access to their financial markets, mainly because of the reputation and the standing built up by the IBRD over the years, and the belief that the IBRD will always repay its creditors. This belief is grounded not only on its own enormous financial strength, but also on the direct involvement of the member-Governments, and the share capital contributed by them, including the major industrial countries. Access to major financial markets is a highly sensitive question as far as the Management and the Board are conçerned, as any prolonged denial could disrupt the operations of the IBRD, and the concerned Governments are fully aware of this position. Grant or denial of access to their financial markets are at the complete discretion of these industrial country Governments, and it is always open to them to say that their own domestic credit requirements preclude any further borrowings by an international organisation such as the IBRD. The consequence is that these particular Governments are in a position to exercise considerable influence over the IBRD by the use of this lever, whether subtly or blatantly.

To provide itself with an adequate cushion, the IBRD maintains liquid assets amounting to 40 to 45% of its net cash requirements over the next three years or so (this aspect is elaborated upon later). In addition, it has endeavoured to diversify its borrowings by currency, market, types of investors, and borrowing techniques. Besides tapping the well known markets in the U.S.A., Japan, Switzerland and Germany, the Bank has borrowed many other currencies also, e.g. pound sterling, Italian lire, Canadian and Australian dollars, Spanish pesetas. It has also recently tapped the Hong Kong market. The IBRD is concerned with maintaining a long term position in the market, and it tries to ensure that no market nears saturation at any time.

A second objective is to minimise the cost of the borrowing. The IBRD contrives to achieve this objective by increasing its borrowings in currencies with low nominal interest rates, though attention is simultaneously paid to the possibility that likely movements in exchange rates will offset, if not reverse, the anticipated savings in nominal interest rates. The timing of the proposed borrowings is also important for bringing down the costs. A third objective is to moderate the variability of the rates charged to the borrower. This has been achieved to a large extent by linking the charged rate to the cost incurred by the IBRD on its total borrowings, as mentioned when considering the pool-based variable interest rate. A fourth objective is to provide the borrower with an appropriate degree of 'maturity transformation'. This expression means that the lender enables itself to lend at somewhat longer maturities than those at which it itself borrows. Care has to be taken to ensure that broadly there is no unacceptable mismatch between the averages of the borrowing maturity and the lending maturity, as was discussed earlier, when the IBRD's maturity structure for both its loans and its borrowings was found to be sound. The IBRD often borrows short term funds in order to lower costs, but after coming into the pool, the monies lent out to the member-Governments (or their agents) are on fairly long term maturities, usually better than the maturities offered by the commercial banks.

Even Mr. McNamara, probably the most dynamic and effective President the World Bank has had and who transformed the institution, encountered some difficulty towards the end of his long stewardship, in raising funds from the market at reasonable rates. His successor, Mr. Clausen was a distinguished professional banker of long experience and introduced a number of innovations, based upon his intimate knowledge of banking. One such was the adoption of 'Swaps' by the IBRD. Though this was a well known technique in banking circles, the Bank had not used it previously. It came before the Board at a seminar in August 1981, fairly soon after Mr.

Clausen had taken over as President. The rather wide interest differentials prevailing in different countries made this technique attractive for the IBRD. Illustratively, the transaction involved the Bank borrowing medium or long term funds in U.S. dollars. Thereafter another party was located who had borrowed, say Swiss francs. An exchange was agreed to whereby the other party took over the Bank's liabilities to repay the principal and interest in U.S. dollars for the first loan, and as a *quid pro quo* the Bank took over the other party's liabilities in respect of the loan in Swiss francs. These transactions were possible because of different perceptions of the likely currency movements in future. Also, certain U.S. companies were keen on exchanging their foreign currency liabilities for dollar liabilities, or they wanted to lock in their profits in dollars. From the IBRD's viewpoint, there were two advantages, viz., first, since the Swiss nominal interest rates were substantially lower than the U.S. rates for the corresponding maturity, the 'Swap' transaction resulted in a distinct lowering of the overall cost of borrowing, and therefore, of the lending rate payable by the borrowers; second, because of the turmoil in the financial markets and the volatile interest rates, certain Governments were discouraging borrowings by the IBRD in their financial markets, and imposing limits. By these 'Swap' transactions, the IBRD was, in effect, being able to tap these markets in excess of the limits. Without such a facility, the IBRD would have had to borrow further amounts in the high cost U.S. market. The Annual Report for 1985[5] mentions that during that year 50 such transactions took place aggregating $ 1,360 million. These transactions are claimed to have reduced the IBRD's borrowing cost for the $ 1,360 million by 5.56%. The cost of total borrowings ($ 11,086 million) was reduced by 68 basis points. In the four years, 1982 to 1985, the IBRD has engaged in Swap transactions that aggregate $ 5,147 million. The Annual Report for 1989[6] mentions that 29 currency Swap transactions were settled in 1989, aggregating $ 2,570 million. On the other hand, the nature of the transactions were different. While in previous years, the IBRD was moving out of U.S. dollar liabilities, during 1989 it exchanged Japanese yen, Deutsche mark, and other currency liabilities into U.S. dollars and Swiss francs.

Since the introduction of Swap transaction in the early 1980s there have been further refinements. Besides exchanging currencies, the device has been used to change fixed interest rate borrowings into floating rate borrowings. In recent years, Swaps out of non-dollar vehicle currencies into fixed rate dollar liabilities have been accomplished through a two-step process, first, a cross-currency swap into floating rate dollars, and second, one or more U.S. dollar interest-rate swaps that produced the desired fixed rate funding. Sometimes the sequence can be reversed, and it is claimed that delinking the two steps allows the IBRD to take advantage of attractive cross-currency arbitrage. During fiscal year 1993, the IBRD borrowed about $ 12.68 billion. Swaps totalling $ 3.6 billion of currency swaps and $ 3.8 billion of interest-rate swaps were undertaken, and resulted in the following significant changes:

(a) Before swaps, Deutsche mark borrowings constituted only 6% of the total, but after swaps, these rose to 34%. Per contra, U.S. dollar holdings fell from 33% to 26% after swaps.
(b) Other currencies fell from 25% of holdings to 3% after swaps. The principal vehicle currencies used for swaps into the Deutsche mark were the Canadian dollar, pounds sterling, and the Italian lire.
(c) After these swaps, all the year's borrowings were *fixed rate* liabilities, and shows the Bank's own preference for certainty, though borrowers are obliged to take loans on floating rates, thus safeguarding its own position.
(d) After swaps, the maturity remained the same (9.3 years) though the average cost was 5.97%. As initially borrowed, some of the funds were expensive, e.g. 7-year DM bonds due in the year 2000 at 9%, 5-year Spanish bonds due in 1998 at 12.45%, 5-year Italian notes due in 1997 at 12.125%, 10-year notes due in 2002 in Switzerland at 6.75%. Also large amounts were initially borrowed at floating rates.

The overall position as on June 30th, 1993 taking into account previous transactions shows the Bank's borrowings to be about $ 92.49 billion with a weighted average cost of 7.32%. However, after swaps, the average cost went down to 6.9%. The other noteworthy changes resulting from the swaps is that the Deutsche mark liabilities went up from $ 9.13 billion to $ 19.21 billion, and the Swiss franc liabilities from $ 5.69 billion to $ 10.37 billion.[7]

Because of the volatility of exchange rates and the rapid changes which occur in nominal interest rates, the final outcome till redemption of the borrowings may be somewhat problematic. While in the short term, the lower nominal interest rate achieved by the swap transaction may be a decided advantage for the borrower, currency changes involving a sharp appreciation of the currency into which the swap has occurred, may offset the gain from lower interest rates. The nature of these transactions and the impact that they could have on the Bank's borrowers, requires that the IBRD should develop the best and most sophisticated expertise to safeguard itself and its clientele from the adverse effects of gyrations in the currency markets. One positive advantage that cannot be gainsaid is that swap transactions permit the IBRD to tap other currencies and markets which it otherwise would not have, and also these transactions permit the IBRD to by-pass ceilings that may be imposed on its borrowings in certain preferred currencies by the host Government.

Besides 'Swap' transactions, some other innovative borrowing techniques were introduced, e.g. floating rate notes. Serious efforts were also made to tap the short term market, and discount notes were introduced. Further, attractive instruments were devised, tailored to the special requirements of the Central banks of the member-Governments. To take advantage of the demand for securities, Bank securities were made available as collateral and other devices were adopted to earn a neat profit for the Bank. Again, the IBRD initiated a short term borrowing programme in Swiss francs with maturities up to one year termed 'Continuously offered payment rights' (COPS). The IBRD has also introduced a programme of 'continuously offered longer term securities' (COLTS) which operates in the U.S. medium term note market. The Annual Report for 1989 mentions that this programme was expanded during that year. The securities were sold through a group of 14 U.S. regional agents, and 3 Canadian agents, as well as 5 primary agents based in New York. COLTS transactions totalled $ 833 million.

Major borrowing transactions have to be approved by the Board. In practice, however, the transactions are put through by the Management, and the Board approves the proposals with few, if any, modifications. The time factor is also crucial, and though the Board meets weekly, or more frequently if required, there is much delegation to the Finance wing. To borrow annually sums of the order of $ 10 billion continuously over several years calls for a high degree of competence, a detailed knowledge of the world's financial markets, and establishment of favourable personal equations with the large business houses and operators on these markets. The IBRD has been well served by its staff in this department. One recalls with considerable admiration the part played by the then Vice President, Mr. Eugene Rotberg, during this formative stage, and the convincing presentations he would make to the Board urging acceptance of the proposals. He was also a past master at marshalling facts and statistics to prove that the transactions undertaken at his instance, including 'Swaps' were in the best interests of the IBRD and of the borrowers. To single him out may not be entirely fair, as he was very ably assisted by middle level staff. That he is no longer with the Bank shows that the organisation was able to groom successors in time.

The IBRD enjoys a triple 'A' rating, and is justifiably proud of its standing. The Management makes no secret of its assessment that the IBRD's present standing is in no small measure because of the direct involvement of the large industrial countries as its major shareholders, and the powerful influence they exercise in its operation. It is natural that the financial markets should set considerable store by the Governments of the countries where they are themselves located. The fact remains, however, that *all* member-Governments are shareholders, and are therefore, collectively responsible for the IBRD's operations, and have pledged their resources to meet the obligations of the Bank. Their contribution to the financial strength of the IBRD should not, therefore, be minimised, especially since the largest shareholder is currently perhaps the largest debtor country. Publications released during the Bank's 50th anniversary, however, have shifted the emphasis somewhat and claimed that the triple 'A' rating was in part attributable to shareholders' guarantees, but for the *most part* was *earned* by prudent Management (vide Chapter 7). The Management is generally at pains to emphasise the 'market perception' of the IBRD, and to caution that any deterioration in this perception may affect the flow of borrowings. As a consequence, steps are taken to ensure a reasonable income from the Bank's activities, the maintenance of appropriate reserves, the making of sound loans, and the careful appraisal of projects, as well as the exercise of due supervision over the implementation of IBRD-financed projects. This aspect is also highlighted when considering changes in the interest rate policy, the liquidity policy, and the allocation of the net income of the Bank.

As mentioned earlier, the IBRD has firm commitments to its borrowers to provide funds as specified in the loan agreements. Similarly, it has commitments to its creditors and bond-holders which have to be fully honored. As long ago as 1978, a "Liquidity Policy" had crystallised, which was designed to protect the IBRD against possible interruptions in cash flow, and shortfalls in borrowings. This specified that the IBRD should maintain its liquidity at 40% of its estimated net cash requirements during the next three years. In early 1983, it was deemed necessary to review this policy in the light of subsequent developments, some of which could pose difficulties, while others were favourable. There were several uncertainties confronting the Bank, interest rates were volatile, debt problems had begun to surface and the Bank's exposure had also grown rapidly with the greatly enhanced scale of operations. Bank borrowers had increasingly gone deeper into debt, and were themselves facing financial difficulties, which could be reflected in possible defaults. On the other hand, a positive development was the adoption of a pool-based variable interest rate by the IBRD for its loans. All these aspects were considered in detail by the Management and a comprehensive paper prepared for Board consideration, making concrete proposals. While the basic objective of the liquidity policy was endorsed, some of the provisions were further strengthened. In formulating the proposals, several scenarios were considered, and the possible responses of the IBRD to a crisis were outlined. It was thought that the 'threshold' liquidity level should not be allowed to fall below $ 6 billion, i.e. to maintain confidence in the financial markets, this amount should always be available. In the event of a crisis, the IBRD would stop commitments for 6 months, followed by a period of 18 months, when commitments would be resumed but only at 50% of the earlier planned level. Thereafter, commitments could be increased to 75% of the planned level. When borrowing countries found this response harsh, Mr. Clausen, the then President, was quick to assure them that the IBRD's commitment levels would not be reduced, and every endeavour would be made to protect the interests of the borrowing countries.

In computing the estimated cash requirements for the next three years, it was decided that, in addition to the net outgo to its own borrowers, the full repayment obligation of the IBRD's discount note programme should be taken into account, besides the outstanding debt maturing in the next three years. Further, the 40% figure was adopted as the minimum, and the IBRD's liquidity should fall in the range of 40 to 45% of the net cash requirements during the next three years, the higher figure being reached whenever the capital market conditions permitted. It was decided that year's borrowings should be increased by a further $ 1 billion, so as to achieve total borrowings of $ 10.8 billion. Some flexibility was also allowed in the 'threshold' figure of $ 6 billion, so that commitments to borrowers could be respected.

The discussion of the IBRD's liquidity policy would show the enormous pains that the institution took to ensure that its lending programme was not disrupted owing to shortfalls in borrowings, which as already stated, were subject to access being permitted by the major industrial countries to their financial markets. Despite the discretionary factor involved, the massive liquidity built up by the IBRD gave it great staying power, and it could ride out market vagaries with relative ease. At the end of 1993, and 1994 the IBRD's liquidity totaled $ 18.5 billion, and $ 19 billion respectively, equivalent to about 45% of anticipated net cash requirements over the next three fiscal years. These funds are invested and during fiscal year 1993, the return on its portfolio was 6.09%, but fell to 3.56% in 1994. The low returns in FY 1994 are ascribed by the Annual Report for that year to the combination of the absolute low level of short term interest rates and capital losses due to increase in rates since the middle of the year. There has been a welcome improvement in the return on investments during FY 1995, when it rose to 5.71%. This figure may be compared with the cost incurred by the IBRD during FY 1995 on its borrowings (after swaps) viz. 6.32%. The long term planning of the Bank's strategy, which proceeded on conservative lines, with pessimistic scenarios and sound management of its finances, has helped its borrowers by ensuring that committed funds are available without interruption and at favourable rates. It has also built up an enviable reputation in the financial markets, which assures a continuous flow of funds to the IBRD from investors. Because of this policy, the IBRD is relatively insulated from pressures being exerted by interested operators, and can bide its time to borrow on favourable terms.

It might be instructive to examine the rate at which the IBRD borrows and lends, and the margins it retains. The Annual Report for 1989 publishes certain figures which throw light on the IBRD's functioning, and are referred to, as the same format is not repeated for subsequent years. Its total outstanding medium and long term borrowings (or debt) as on 30th June 1989[8] cost on an average 7.72%. After swaps, the cost came down to 7.24%, i.e. the swaps had the effect of bringing down the cost by almost ½%. Taking into account short term borrowings the average overall cost was 7.38%. However, the IBRD has at its disposal, its capital, reserves and accumulated net income. Taking these into account, but only the *usable* capital, (as the capital subscribed by some members may not be generally acceptable), the overall cost comes to 6.31%. Per contra, the average return on loans disbursed and outstanding during FY 1989 came to 7.86%, i.e. the margin available to the IBRD between the overall cost it was incurring on account of its borrowings, and the return it was getting from the loans it had made was 0.48%, i.e. close to the ½% spread adopted for determining the pool-based variable lending interest rate, and the earlier lending rate. It will be recalled that the IBRD maintains a high degree of liquidity in order to meet its commitments despite the vagaries of the market, and the uncertainties about market access. These funds and other resources are invested suitably, and the return from the liquid investments during FY 1989 was 8.20%, i.e. higher than the overall borrowing cost of 7.38%. At least during some years, the IBRD has contrived to earn more from these liquid investments, than it has had to pay its lenders. Thus one of the conventional grounds adduced for levying a commitment fee on loans, viz. the cost of carrying high liquidity, is not borne out by the facts as presented by the Bank. The IBRD has also secured an average overall return of 8.20% on its total earning assets during FY 1989. The overall profitability of the IBRD is determined by the spread available to it between the average returns it is able to secure from its total earning assets, interest from loans made, and returns from liquid investments on the one hand, and the average *costs* incurred on its total funds (debt and equity) i.e. 8.20% minus 6.31% or 1.89%. The capital contributed by the members, and the reserves built up over the years, are also part of the funds available to the IBRD for its operations, and being 'cost-free' nominally, help to swell its profitability. The ratio of outstanding loans to equity for FY 1989 is put at 5.30:1. Equity is defined as usable paid-in capital, reserves and accumulated net income, and is an indication of the effective gearing ratio adopted by the IBRD.

The Annual Report for 1993, though not using the earlier format provides more up-to-date information, and gives the following rates:

	percentages
Weighted average costs of medium and long term borrowings	7.32
Weighted average costs of above (after swaps)	6.90
Weighted average costs of short term borrowings	3.58
Borrowing costs after swaps	5.97
Financial returns on investment portfolio	6.09

These figures could be compared with the corresponding lending rates, which, of course, vary every six months:

First semester	7.60
Second semester	7.43

The earlier pattern is, therefore, repeated with the lending rate holding well above the borrowing cost. Also, the financial return from the investment portfolio continues to be above the borrowing costs. The magnitudes of these flows may also be of interest. The income from interest on loans came to about $ 7.96 billion. The income from investments was about $ 1.36 billion. The interest paid on borrowings came to $ 6.65 billion approximately, i.e. it was well below the interest income from loans. Administrative expenses, including retirement charges, were $ 679 million, or about 8% of total expenses. After taking account of other minor items of income and expenditure, the year ended with a significant income of $ 1.13 billion, despite provision of $ 578 million for possible losses. These figures provide evidence of the financial strength of the Bank, and the care with which its operations are conducted.

THE BUDGET

For the numerous and somewhat complex transactions involved in the operations of the World Bank, to successfully achieve their objectives, these necessarily have to be comprehensively considered and meticulously planned in advance. The Management prepares annually a comprehensive document entitled "Review of World Bank Programs and FY Budgets" which is briefly referred to as the 'Budget' in the rest of this Chapter. This document covers the operations of the IBRD and IDA and provides detailed information *inter-alia* about the lending operations, the likely disbursements, the borrowing programme, the net income of the IBRD and the allocation by sector and country-group. The staffing of each department is considered in detail, as well as the expenses likely to be incurred on travelling, and the overheads on account of the Board of Governors, and the Executive Board. The Budget contains much data and analysis. As such, it is a mine of valuable information. The Bank has a good record of fairly close adherence to the estimates it prepares in advance, despite the many uncertainties that have to be faced and the volatility in world financial markets. The drill followed earlier in obtaining the Board's approval usually was to have one or two preliminary 'Seminars' with the Executive Directors meeting informally, where the salient features of the Budget were outlined, and various queries raised were answered by the Management and the staff of the Budget division. These Seminars were then followed by a formal meeting of the Board, when approval was accorded.

The fiscal budget 1994, however, was the first budget to be prepared under a revised system, which was designed to reduce complexity, while increasing transparency, and cost-consciousness. The procedure involved the following steps: (a) preparation of a Planning Directions Paper, with indicative three-year planning and provisional resource guidelines, for review in February by the Committee of the Whole; (b) the preparation in February and March by units of detailed three-year business plans, including proposed budget's for the coming fiscal year, consistent with the provisional guidelines; (c) the preparation of the Bank-wide budget proposal for the new fiscal year, formulated within the three-year business-planning framework, presented to the Executive Directors for consideration in June; and (d) the Bank-wide application of dollar budgets to enhance individual managers' ability to make effective resource trade-offs.

Till 1986, the position regarding the Bank's functioning remained similar to that described by Mason and Asher when it started business, viz. the Management would actually manage the institution and the Directors would play the usual role of general supervision without interference in the conduct of the business. The same authors go on to state that the Board has concerned itself primarily with the problems that the President chooses to put before it.[9] The Budget is prepared by the Management, and the President usually gives it the thrust in the desired direction, as evidenced by the phenomenal increase in the activities of the Bank during the stewardship of Mr. Robert McNamara. The input from the Executive Directors during the preparation stage was not significant, though their deliberations at the Seminars and the formal Board meeting did have an effect on the formulation of subsequent budgets. The Executive Directors, particularly those representing the industrial countries, chafed at not being able to influence the Budget adequately during formulation, and repeatedly asked for the constitution of a Budget Committee. On the other hand, the views of the developing countries, which are the main borrowers, were somewhat mixed. While the logic of the position adopted by the developed countries was appreciated, some misgivings surfaced. There was a feeling that such a Committee of the Board would be influenced disproportionately by the views of the major industrial countries, not only because of their voting strength, but also because of their inherent right to curtail access to their financial markets. Some developing countries thought that their borrowing programmes, and the resultant allocation of funds for lending, would receive fairer treatment from the Bank Management untrammelled by the views of a Budget Committee. The Annual Report for 1989 mentions that a Committee of the Board on Cost Effectiveness and Budget practices was established in November 1986. It was to primarily examine certain aspects of the Bank's business processes, administrative policies, standards and budget practices that significantly affect the cost-effectiveness of the Bank's operations. This Committee, according to the information available, not only looked at travel costs, but also discharged a responsible task entrusted to it, viz. reviewed the planning directions paper, which as indicated above, is the first document discussed by the Executive Directors in the course of the budget cycle, and conducted a mid-year review. Its influence on the budget is thus significant, and presumably its labours cut short discussions at the Board proper. The Management's role to initiate proposals is perhaps not constrained, but the Committee's overview may lead to closer scrutiny of these proposals.

When formulating the proposals for the particular year, not only have the updated estimates of the immediately preceding year got to be taken into account, but also projections made for the given year, as well as for two or more years ahead. A relatively long term view has perforce to be taken, because of the way the Bank is organised. The project cycle is such that a period of about 12 months or more normally elapses from the time a project is identified till the Board's approval is obtained, though there may be fluctuations in this period depending upon the nature of the proposal, e.g. a S.A.L. or other quick disbursing loan as opposed to a traditional project loan, for say a power scheme, and the urgency of the situation. Depending upon the project, execution may take several years, and since most project loans involve reimbursement of expenditure incurred by the borrower, the Bank's staff are required to both supervise the execution of the project, keep a watch on procurement procedures, and also disburse loans on completion of necessary checks and documentation. The evaluation stage is still further in the future. The lending in a particular year thus depends upon economic and sector work on the country, the drawing up of a programme, the identification and appraisal of particular projects, which all entail considerable work preceding the year when that project finds a place in the budget. Conversely, the approval of a project creates a substantial work load in subsequent years. Staff strength is thus driven by all these considerations, and since the skills required call for previous training and knowledge, a certain degree of continuity is called for, as effective personnel cannot be easily recruited and deployed straightaway.

There are several uncertainties when drawing up the Bank's lending programme for a given year. The borrower is required to pose a project for lending by the Bank, and though there is close interaction between the borrower's staff and the Bank's, and the latter often express an interest in financing particular projects, in the final analysis the decision has to be taken by the borrower. The issues posed are often complex, particularly because the Bank is usually prepared to finance only a part of the total cost of the project, and even if there happens to be co-financing with other bodies or agencies, the major portion of the required resources has to be provided by the borrower in most cases. Indeed, the concept of 'leveraging' has this objective in view. Though loans by the Bank and other similar institutions provide most of the foreign exchange that may be required, other 'local costs', which may be heavy, have to be borne. Further, the project has to be dovetailed into the overall long term programme of the borrowing country, especially in cases where a country has adopted a Five Year Plan, or some system of planned development. There is also the question of providing the required finances till completion, and making the requisite budgetary appropriations by the borrower, in face of competing demands, and budgetary constraints. Most Bank-financed projects are large, and some are quite major, and hence their approval calls for detailed consultation between the concerned departments or Ministries, such as Finance, and the one directly responsible for the execution of the project, as well as with the Planning agency. Clearance from the environmental angle has added a new dimension, and can involve difficult decisions, raising sensitive issues. Not only can these stages be time consuming, but also they can lead to considerable uncertainty. It has happened, e.g. in FY 1984 and again more recently in FY 1993 that the Bank has not been able to fulfil its lending programme for a particular year because the prospective borrowers were unable to provide the requisite funds, or otherwise could not undertake the project posed for World Bank financing.

These uncertainties have resulted in some modification in the practice adopted when framing the budget. Thus in the budget for FY 1983, the commitments for the IBRD were put down at a definite figure, viz $ 11.2 billion. In the budget for FY 1990, however, IBRD commitments were estimated in the context of three scenarios, viz. a high case ($ 19 billion), a base case ($ 17 billion), and a low case ($ 15 billion). The base case represents the most likely outcome, and is the basic reference point for determining budget requirements. The budget document mentions that the high case will be able to accommodate the IBRD commitments including additional commitments undertaken in relation to credit enhancement, extended co-financing and debt reduction in pursuance of the Bank's strategy for dealing with the heavily indebted countries. All the three scenarios are projected in the FY 1990 budget till FY 1993. The budget for FY 1994 similarly projects a range for IBRD commitments viz $ 17.0 to $ 19.5 billion, and also indicates the best estimate of $ 18 billion used to calculate the growth rate for IBRD commitments. As earlier mentioned,[10] the IBRD's Articles impose a limit on the quantum of lending by the Bank, and in the interest of maintaining stability and continuity, this mandatory limit has given rise to the concept of the 'sustainable level of lending' (S.L.L) which can be continued indefinitely with a given capital base. An added reason for projecting the Bank's likely commitments during the ensuing few years is to cover this aspect also. The FY 1990 budget indicates that under the base case scenario, the planned commitments during the financial years 1989 to 1993 would fall within the sustainable level of lending implied by the projected capital of the Bank, while commitments in the high case would exceed that level in the final year of the planning period. Such projections serve to alert the Board to take the necessary measures well in advance so that there is no disruption in the flow of commitments (e.g. make arrangements for a further increase in the capital). During discussion of the budget proposals, developing countries are generally wont to press for higher levels of lending, while conversely, developed countries call for restraint. At one stage, a limit of $ 60 billion lending in the aggregate over the next five years was imposed, and the developing countries had to argue hard to ensure that this artificial limit did not adversely affect the quantum of Bank loans, which were desperately required to meet genuine needs. The S.L.L also provided a convenient instrument to the developed countries for restraining Bank lending, while the developing countries would argue that the real purpose of this concept was to activate the Board to initiate steps for a general capital increase, rather than to restrain lending at a premature stage, particularly when the S.L.L. was sensitive to many factors, which could be controlled to some extent by the Bank itself. The funds required for additional lending could be mobilised from the financial markets of the world, and therefore such lending would not directly impact on the budgets of the member-Governments. Nevertheless, the developed countries took a long term view, and called for restraint, because higher lending levels would accelerate the next general capital increase, and as principal shareholders, their contributions would be higher.

The budget document analyses the commitments made by country groups and by sectors. Such data are naturally scrutinised by the Executive Directors with care, especially by those representing the borrowing countries, as they would like to ensure that their constituencies are getting their due shares, particularly of the IDA funds, which are offered on generous terms, and therefore have a high grant element. In more recent times, with the priority given to sub-Saharan African countries, the spotlight has fallen on them, and also on the least developed countries, to the detriment of the populous countries such as India and Pakistan and to some extent, China. The issue was agitated during the discussion of the budget for FY 1983, when the trend became pronounced. The South Asian share of IDA funds during 1977 to 1981 was 59.2% of the total, and was initially projected to increase to 63.5% during financial years 1982 to 1986. In the budget document for FY 1983, however, the share was brought down to 53.5%. Considerable lobbying takes place with regard to country allocations, and the industrial countries also take a hand in trying to improve the shares of those countries with which they have particularly friendly relations. It is still true to say that France, in particular, maintains close ties with its former colonies and possessions abroad, and exerts its influence in favour of the African countries. The African caucus has succeeded in drawing the attention of the industrialised countries to their needs, and the World Bank has also played its part by providing the necessary intellectual underpinning, and carried out some excellent studies. The net result has been the creation of a favourable climate for siphoning more funds to the countries of sub-Saharan Africa, particularly IDA resources. This became apparent quite early, as during these budget discussions, the allocation of IDA funds initially suggested for South Asia was 55.8%, but in the final proposal, as already stated it was cut to 53.5%. Subsequent years have witnessed a further deterioration, particularly for countries such as India and China. Previously, India alone was privileged to receive 40% of IDA funds, and mainland China, not being a member, did not qualify. The aggregate share of both India and China fell below 40%, and that of sub-Saharan Africa, rose to 45% during financial years 1987-1989. The IDA credits approved for Africa, China and India respectively out of the total IDA commitments of $ 6,751 million during fiscal year 1993 are as follows:

	$ (mill.)	% of total
Africa	2,770.3	41.03
China	1,017.0	15.06
India	1,532.7	22.70

For financial year 1994, the budget provides $ 3.2 billion for Africa out of a total of $ 7.2 billion or about 44.4%. The size of countries such as India and China militates against a fair and equitable consideration of their genuine requirements. A rational basis for judging the fairness of the allocations would be to consider the *per capita* allocation of IDA resources for each region. As far back as FY 1982, when India's share was still quite high, and therefore got reflected in the South Asian figure, the comparable per capita figures were: South Asia, $ 1.98; East Africa, $ 4.74; West Africa, $ 5.19; Europe, Middle East and North Africa, $ 6.11; Latin

America, $ 5.54. While African countries deserve every sympathy, and suffer considerable disadvantages such as lack of infrastructure, and an efficient administrative machine, a stage may have been reached when the balance should be righted in favour of the populous Asian countries. The pressure of population, and their inferior natural endowments, actually make their problems even more intractable than those of sub-Saharan Africa. Finally, the bulk of the really poor reside in South Asia, not in Africa. This issue has also been dealt with in some detail in Part A of Chapter 4 dealing with IDA.

The analysis of Bank commitments by sectors used to provoke some debate, and there were pleas for raising the shares of lending for agriculture, transport, etc. From the Bank's perspective, such issues have a certain relevance, as the shareholders should be satisfied that resources are being used in accordance with a pattern of priorities adjudged to be suitable. From the view point of the borrower, however, the debate is somewhat pointless, as the borrower has its own priorities, and the Bank normally finances only a small portion of the total developmental expenditure. Posing a particular project for Bank financing may often be decided by extraneous factors, and by mutual convenience. Other bilateral donors and multilateral institutions may have expressed preferences for particular projects, and it is often somewhat fortuitous that a particular project is posed to the World Bank for financing. Consequently, the priorities on the ground for a particular country may be different from those worked out by the Bank for its purposes and for public dissemination and one may not influence the other. In any case, the Bank has been flexible, and the shares have changed over the years, presumably in the light of ground realities, and experience with the execution of projects. During FY 1977-81, agriculture and rural development accounted for as much as 32% of the Bank's commitment. Its share fell to 18% during FY 1987-89 and further to 16.2% during FY 1991-93. The budget for FY 1994 postulates an increase to 20.6%. There is a view that in developing countries, where unemployment is a problem, there should be added emphasis on the development of agriculture because of its capacity to absorb a large workforce, at a comparatively lower per capita investment. Industry, particularly large scale industry, is highly capital-intensive, and its employment potential has fallen sharply. Despite these considerations, Bank lending for industry, DFCs, small scale industries, etc. had risen from 16% during FY 1977-84 to 22% during FY 1987-89. The FY 1994 budget, on the contrary, shows a downward trend. Thus the allocations for both IBRD and IDA lending shows that while 'Industry and Finance' claimed 12.2% of the total during FY 1991-93, this figure fell to 11% during FY 1994, and is projected to fall further to 10.1% during FY 1994-96. These figures suggest that the above mentioned view is gaining acceptance. A significant development has been the rise in the allocation to 'urbanisation' from 3% in FY 1977-81 to 8% during FY 1987-89, and suggests a continued shift in the Bank's thinking from financing infrastructure and allied projects, to assisting in schemes which have a social impact, and directly improve living conditions. The percentage allocations for urban development during FY 1991-93 (6.8%), and FY 1994-96 (projected at 7.7%) broadly conform to the same pattern. Perhaps the Bank should pay more heed to the expressed requirements of the borrowers, and be prepared to finance projects without being unnecessarily constrained by artificial percentage allocations to different sectors, which may themselves be somewhat subjective. The Bank should be satisfied that an overall balance is being maintained as between the various sectors.

In recent years the Bank has evolved a more sophisticated approach and identified some "Special operational emphases", which are to be pursued aggressively, and will pervade much of the Bank's operational, policy and research work. Some mention of the programmes of special emphasis may be desirable, viz.:

1. *Debt, Financial Intermediation and Adjustment*. The aim is to make the new debt initiatives operational. Considerable research underpinning was provided, e.g. studies on adjustment lending, and the macro-economic effects of public sector deficits, labour market policies and trade policies. Studies were also proposed on the interaction between macro-economic adjustment and private investment. In operations, the Bank's strategy concerning debt was to (a) improve the effectiveness of the adjustment programmes both in the middle income highly indebted countries, and

in the debt-distressed countries of sub-Saharan Africa, and (b) to intensify financial support from commercial and official lenders.

2. *Poverty Reduction and Improvement in Food Security.* Bank documents claim that these objectives pervade the Bank's activities, and efforts to reduce the impact on the poor of necessary adjustments to the economy will continue to be made. Management-oriented research will focus on the effectiveness of alternative approaches and targeting schemes for the delivery of services. The link between agriculture and poverty reduction efforts seems to have attracted attention, and there is full awareness that both these aspects have an important bearing on food security. Broader application of the training and visit system for agricultural extension, means to improve small-holder productivity, and the constraints inhibiting the development and adoption of improved technologies by small farmers are to be examined. Correspondingly, reviews are to be conducted of recent innovations in production technology, particularly bio-technological ones. Food security aspects appear to be concentrated more on the African countries.

3. *Environment.* The Bank responded quickly to the world-wide debate on protecting the environment, and environmental analysis has been integrated into the Bank's operation. The Bank also launched a series of studies on various aspects having a bearing on the environment. A handbook was prepared for mitigating environmental problems related to rail and road infrastructure. Research was undertaken on the agronomic and biological effects of various irrigation and drainage strategies. The FY 1990 programme claimed to include studies on deforestation, and a study on coal utilisation in China to identify options for introducing cleaner technologies.

4. *Human Resources (including Women in Development).* There was universal realisation of the importance of human capital in stimulating economic progress, and improving family welfare, not just for long-run development but also

for short-run adjustment. Education, training, health and nutritional status, as well as adoption of family planning, have all been found to be essential for promoting productive capacity, and improving the quality of life. These emphases have been pursued through lending and sector work in the fields of education, population control, health and nutrition.

5. *Private Sector Development and Public Sector Management.* In keeping with its philosophy and its Articles, the Bank has a commitment to strengthen the private sector. It has a policy and research programme focussed on the business environment, especially the sequencing of policy and regulatory reform, and the *private* provision of public services. The institutional aspects of economic policy reform, and issues of budgeting, civil service reforms, and the management of public sector expenditures generally, are all considered by the Bank. The Energy Strategy, Management and Assessment Programs (ESMAP) seek to improve the management of public power institutions by helping to improve operating efficiency. The finding has been that inspite of massive investments in the power sector, performance has been poor and is deteriorating. The Bank also takes interest in railway reform, and administration of ports, as well as pricing and financing of the transport sector generally.

Certain figures are given in the budget documents to indicate the funds allocated for these Special Emphases, though it has been stated that these should be interpreted with caution, as more than one emphasis may be addressed by a particular operation, and the emphases overlap *inter se.* The sophistication lies in the research work undertaken and the intellectual input provided, e.g. cross-country studies. Of the total funds provided during FY 1990 for the programmes of special emphasis, ($ 160.5 m), some $ 9 million has been allocated for research, and $ 16.9 million on policy issues, though of course, the bulk ($ 118.7 m) goes for operations.

The changes introduced by the FY 1994 budget may be of some interest. There is no mention of the Special Emphases Programmes and the budget document is more focussed and briefer, with a change in format. However, it does lay down some broad goals and priorities which deserve comment. Poverty reduction finds mention in several places, and is being sincerely pursued, if we go by the statement that the work programme centres on enhancing the integration of poverty reduction objectives into country assistance strategies, through country poverty assessments. These seek to effectively address the problems identified. The budget notes the expanding demand for Bank services, and the increase in the membership from 156 a year ago to 174 currently. It adds that a major objective would be to provide effective support to the new members from Eastern Europe and Central Asia during their difficult transition from a command to a market economy. Of interest, is the safeguard that this would be done without impairment of Bank services to existing members. Other objectives are the expansion of the potential of the private sector and safeguarding the environment. An item which is reflected in the budgetary allocations is improvement in the effectiveness of past and future lending, in the light of the findings by the Portfolio Management Task Force. This implies intensified project supervision, and more comprehensive project preparation. The earlier emphasis on policy reform in many countries, including new and re-activating members, would continue. It will be noticed that while the phraseology used may be different, many of the earlier concerns are still prominent, while poverty reduction has moved centre stage, and now professes to permeate the entire country strategy. The debt problem is perhaps being eclipsed somewhat by the programmes in Eastern Europe and Central Asia, which can be expected to gather even greater momentum in future. The bias towards the private sector, as part of the Bank's basic philosophy naturally continues.

An innovation of some significance is the establishment of thematic units under Vice-Presidents. These Central Vice-Presidencies assumed responsibility for best practice dissemination and policy formulation. They will provide increased operational support to the regions. The units are Finance and Private Sector Development, Environmentally Sustainable Development and Human Resource Development and Operations Policy. About 150 higher level staff were transferred from regional Technical Departments to the thematic CVPUs. The move is thus one of centralisation as opposed to the popular trend of decentralisation, and highlights the present policy makers attempts to bring Bank activities more firmly into an overall policy framework.

The allocations reflect the general concerns outlined above. The provisions for 'policy & dissemination' during FY 1994 shows a sharp jump of 26.1% over the provision for FY 1993. Per contra 'Research' shows a drop of 28.2%, indicative of a more hard-nosed approach to such esoteric activities, and a determination to use funds more purposefully for the tasks in hand. While the overall growth in the provisions for the core services has been about 9.3%, higher rates of growth have been provided for 'Lending' (9.9%) and 'Portfolio Management' (11.9%), clearly indicative of the Bank's intention to finance projects only after more comprehensive preparation and examination, and to exercise closer supervision over them during implementation. The changed emphasis is reflected in the completion costs in terms of staff-weeks (SWs). A project on average consumed 106 and 109 SWs in FY 1986 and FY 1987, and peaked in FY 1988 at 121 according to the 1990 document, and was projected at 117 SWs and 114 SWs during FY 1989 and FY 1990, because of staff reductions and greater productivity. The 1994 budget gives higher figures, varying from 125.9 SWs in FY 1992 to 116.3 SWs for FY 1994. The projected figure for FY 1994-96 is higher at 117.9 SWs. The trend is even more noticeable when examining the SWs per project supervised. During the FY 1986 to FY 1990, the SWs per project varied from 12 to 12.9. The actual figure for FY 1992 was 13.3 SWs. The estimates/projections for FY 1993, FY 1994, and FY 1994-96 (average) have been put at 14, 14.9 and 15.5 SWs respectively. Having regard to the tight control exercised on staff by the Bank generally, these figures do presage that the authorities are resolved to tighten up project preparation, and to exercise more stringent supervision over all stages of a project executed with Bank support, and this has lessons for borrowers.

The budget documents go into enormous detail over the staffing provided, the administrative and house-keeping expenses, as well as items such as hospitality and travelling. The Executive Directors, in particular those from the developed countries, keep a close watch on the staffing patterns, and the overall expenditure incurred by the Bank; the reorganisation carried out under the direction of President Conable can be attributed in some measure to the concern expressed by the major shareholders. This resulted in the staff strength going down from 6,466 in FY 1987 to 6,065 in FY 1989. However, the Bank like any other bureaucratic institution, has a tendency to grow. The total staff figures are FY 1991—6,167; FY 1992—6,322; FY 1993—6,716; FY 1994—6,890 (funded). Perhaps justification lies in the increased membership.

Though administrative, supervision and lending costs directly affect the borrowing countries, usually they are not so vociferous in criticising the Management and in calling for a slimming down of the organisation as their confreres from the developed countries. The reasons are complex. Perhaps there is a lurking apprehension that too great a pressure on the Management to cut down staff would damage its effectiveness, and cause further delay in processing loan applications, and also impair the quality of the advice tendered, both of which would act to the detriment of the long term interests of the borrowers themselves. Again, borrowing countries are beholden to the Management in many instances, e.g. for the determination of the size of their country programmes, the allocation of concessionary funds such as IDA credits, the acceptance and vigorous processing of projects posed for Bank financing. Many borrowing countries are somewhat chary of joining issue with the Management on sensitive items, where the Management has a stake.

Reference has been made to the increase in staff numbers despite the reorganisation pushed through by President Conable. While Bank staff are doubtless efficient, giant bureaucracies like those developed by it have a tendency to grow out of control. Perhaps a review of the systems adopted by the Bank, and its methods of work could yield a trimmer and more responsive organisation. To buttress this aspect, information was collected from the FY 1994 budget. It publishes an illuminating chart (Fig. 3.2), which shows that staff costs have been rising faster than the World Bank Budget Price Index. On the contrary, non-staff costs have been keeping well below the index. Over the period 1987 to 1994, the staff costs index has increased from 100 to about 150, while the budget price index has moved from 100 to about 140. Non-staff costs, on the contrary, have moved up to about 120. Another aspect of some significance is that the Bank will employ about 1,260 consultant staff-years in 1994, representing about 22% of higher level staff resources. These figures perhaps suggest an unjustifiable lack of faith in the competence and efficiency of the expert staff employed by the borrowers for preparing the projects and programmes posed to the Bank. The preference for consultants from developed countries adds substance to this criticism.

A final comment on operational travel may be pertinent. The Annual Report mentions that the Committee on Cost Effectiveness and Budget Practices had examined operational travel policy on two occasions and suggested changes in order to reduce costs. Against this background, it is interesting to find that the FY 1994 budget estimates operational travel costs at $ 131.9 million or some $ 10.8 million over the FY 1993 budget. The reason given is mainly to cover an increase of approximately 9% in the number of trips expected in 1994. Perhaps much more reliance for project supervision should be placed on the staff of the Resident Missions, or on local consultants who would have a flavour of the real costs in the borrowing countries, and could also suggest economies that might be missed by foreign experts. Running projects from Washington using repeated missions sent from headquarters may not be a cost-effective method.

Notes and References

1. Figures from Annual Report of World Bank for 1995.
2. P. 147 of the Annual Report for 1995.
3. B.W.C. Report, p. c-200, Financial Operations of the World Bank.
4. Annexure A-1 of FY 1990 Budget , p. 138.
5. Page 82.
6. Page 68.
7. Annual Report, 1993, p. 197, et seq.
8. This and other figures in this portion are taken from the Annual Report, 1989, pp. 192, 200, 61 & Table 4.1.
9. The World Bank Since Bretton Woods, Mason and Asher, pp. 50 and 53.
10. Ch. I—Articles of Agreement (where Article III is considered).

CHAPTER 4

Other Institutions of the World Bank Group

A. INTERNATIONAL DEVELOPMENT ASSOCIATION

The International Development Association (IDA as referred to subsequently) was set up in 1960, as an affiliate of the World Bank to make concessional long term loans to the world's poorest countries. There was a growing realisation that the developing countries had to invest in their infrastructure, e.g. railways, ports, power projects, and telecommunications, and also had to improve their human capital by providing better and more widespread education, by improving skills, and safeguarding health. These activities were time consuming, and tangible benefits could not also be accurately quantified in monetary terms. These were unlikely to attract private investors. Further, such activities though productive in the long run, may not be translatable into foreign exchange earnings, which could be used to service external debt. The problems faced by the developing countries were exemplified by India. Food shortages reflected stagnant agricultural production, and growing population. The growing size of its debt precluded additional borrowings for importing food for consumption, and export earnings were far from buoyant, despite the Second Plan, which emphasised industrialisation. The Articles of the Bank required it to lend prudently, after satisfying itself that the borrower would be able to fulfil its obligations under the loan agreement, i.e. only to credit-worthy Governments. Countries such as India, which had already borrowed heavily, could not be lent more funds on normal terms, as these conditions may not be met. Besides, market perceptions of the IBRD's own financial standing could be undermined if it continued to lend to countries, whose capacity to repay and service its loans was suspect, and this could affect the Bank's ability to raise resources from the global financial markets, essential for discharging its vital intermediation role. It was clear that concessional assistance had to be provided in substantial amounts to ease the situation. The USA was motivated by the following considerations:

(i) It was already shouldering much of the defence burden, and therefore thought that the reviving economies of Germany and Japan should play their part also in providing concessional assistance to the developing countries.

(ii) It was thought that assistance provided through a multilateral agency was likely to be more effective because it would be apolitical, and the criteria adopted for allocations would be more objective, than if the assistance were to be provided bilaterally.

(iii) The USA had built up agricultural surpluses, and legislation such as P L-480 were enacted to sell these surpluses against local currencies.

The U.S. Treasury proposed the establishment of the International Development Association, after modifying the proposals originally put forward by Sen. Mike Monroney. Mr. Eugene Black, the then President of the World Bank, withdrew the earlier objections it had raised to the grant of concessional assistance. The final Articles of Agreement for IDA were completed in January 1960 and became effective in September that year. The role of IDA was to promote development through the provision of finance on terms which are more flexible and bear less heavily on the balance of payments than those of conventional loans.

Though the Articles of IDA were modelled on those of the IBRD, there were crucial differences. IDA was intended to be somewhat more flexible than the IBRD about the projects it financed. IDA was to support anything of high development priority, whether or not the project was revenue-producing or directly productive. Because IDA was both a financial and a cooperative institution, a voting system was devised which could do justice to both these aspects. It combines and tempers a weighted voting structure, dependent on capital contributions, with safeguards that recognise the need for all members to be adequately represented, and hence the high number of membership votes allowed, irrespective of the capital contributions made.

The terms of the 'credits', as they are called, are generous. There is no interest charge, and only a service charge of 0.75%. In addition, there is sometimes a small commitment fee, though this fee has not been levied for the past few years. Further, the repayment period is extremely favourable. Initially the credits were repayable over 50 years, but in recent years, the period has been reduced to 35 years, but even so it is far longer than what the commercial banks adopt, and significantly longer even than what the IBRD offers. Depending upon the prevailing rate of interest, the maturity period and the grace period, the grant element for such credits is therefore substantial. The table below gives some estimates.

Table 4A.1

(Percentage)

Discount rate	Grant element
6	72
10	86
12	89
15	92

Source : IDA in Retrospect.

The World Bank Annual Report 1995 adopts the standard discount rate of 10% used by the Development Assistance Committee of the OECD, and estimates that the typical IDA credit contains a grant element of 75% to 80% of the nominal credit amount at the time the credit was committed (p. 186 of Annual Report).

It is natural, therefore, that all eligible borrowers have been clamouring for IDA funds. Countries which have already borrowed heavily from the IBRD have to meet their debt service obligations, and hence the *net transfer* is relatively small. Because of the relatively long repayment period, and the waiver of interest as such, net transfers for IDA credits are higher and add to its attractiveness for mature borrowers.

The World Bank has been circumspect about the eligibility criteria for IDA credits, and has always ensured that the bulk of IDA funds were made available to the poorest countries by prescribing ceilings for per capita incomes. Another category of 'blend' countries was devised, which were eligible for both IBRD loans, and for IDA credits. Currently there are 63 countries which receive only IDA credits, and 15 'blend' countries, which can be sanctioned IBRD loans as well as IDA credits.[1] Prominent 'blend' countries are China, India and Pakistan in the Indian sub-continent, Egypt, Zimbabwe and Nigeria in Africa, and Armenia, Kyrgyz Republic, Azerbaijan and Georgia of the former Soviet Union. The proportions in which IBRD and IDA funds are loaned out to a country, can be varied depending upon the circumstances, and thus ensure a degree of flexibility. In contrast there are currently some 62 'IBRD only' countries, which are ineligible for IDA credits.

Unlike IBRD funding, which depends upon capital contributions from the shareholders only to some extent, but relies mostly upon the global markets for its intermediation role, IDA has to depend upon grants from various industrialised countries. The Articles called for an initial capitalisation of $ 1 billion, with $ 763 million coming from the industrialised countries. IDA's funds have been periodically 'replenished', normally every three years. Currently, the Association is operating on its tenth replenishment. Each replenishment entails tortuous and complex negotiations with the donor countries, who are represented by their deputies. These negotiations involve several ticklish issues, any one of which can scuttle the negotiations. Illustratively, one can refer to 'burden sharing'. Contributions are supposed to reflect the economic power of the donor, but there is no consensus linking contributions rigidly to the GNP. Since contributions are usually made in the local currency of the donor, and accounts have recently been maintained in SDRs, and earlier were in U.S. dollars, the rate of exchange becomes relevant, as also methods for the maintenance of value of the contributions. Eligibility of borrowers, the policies adopted by them, and the priorities that should be followed in making available IDA credits, all figure in the deliberations of the deputies.

During the writer's tenure as Executive Director, negotiations both on IDA-6 and IDA-7 took place, and are referred to at some length to illustrate the difficulties that confront IDA. The Carter administration had agreed to an IDA replenishment of $ 12 billion, with a U.S. contribution of $ 3.24 billion or 27% over the three year period of 1981-83. Payment was to be made in three equal instalments of $ 1,080 million each. The incoming Reagan administration displayed marked reluctance in meeting the Carter administration's commitment, and the U.S. Congress took the cue. A special feature about the release of public funds in the USA is that Congressional approval has to be obtained before the actual release of any funds, and commitments made by the executive are not binding. In the absence of any U.S. commitment for IDA-6, the agency ran short of commitment authority. An anecdote may provide a welcome digression. The Senior Vice-President, Mr. Qureshi, was presiding at a Board meeting to discuss IDA, as Mr. McNamara, the President, had been summoned to the bedside of his wife, who was ailing. During the discussions, Mr. McNamara returned unheralded, and without resuming his normal seat, announced that IDA was bankrupt, and we should all communicate this position to our respective Governments immediately, and request that diplomatic pressure should be brought to bear on the U.S. Administration to release IDA funds under the sixth replenishment. Regrettably, Mrs. McNamara expired soon thereafter, and the episode provides an insight into the character of Mr. McNamara, and the complete devotion with which he served the World Bank. The U.S. Administration was faced with budgetary constraints, and the Congress was reluctant to provide assistance for the developing countries, when cuts were being imposed on food stamps, and welfare measures generally. The U.S. Administration proposed a revised payment schedule, end-loading the instalments for the relevant years, as shown below:

FY 1981	$ 540 million
FY 1982	$ 850 million
FY 1983	$ 1,850 million
Total	$ 3,240 million

The House of Representatives went even further, stretching out the payments over four years, and reducing the first instalment to $ 500 million, and the total payment for IDA-6 to $ 1,878 million. After several meetings of the deputies, etc. the U.S. Administration eventually agreed to stretch out the IDA-6 payments over four years instead of the normal three years as follows:

FY 1981	$ 500 million
FY 1982	$ 700 million
FY 1983	$ 945 million
FY 1984	$ 1,095 million
Total	$ 3,240 million

This unilateral decision of the USA disturbed the burden-sharing arrangements, and other donors would have been within their rights to have cut their contributions proportionately. However, some donors were not unhappy at the stance of the USA, as they could economise while the opprobrium fell on the USA. Naturally, all diplomatic means were adopted by the developing countries to persuade the USA and other donors to pay their promised contributions. In particular, Prime Minister Indira Gandhi in her talks with the British Prime Minister, Mrs. Thatcher, persuaded Britain to waive its pro-rata rights under the burden-sharing agreement, and to contribute its full share, irrespective of the size of the U.S. contribution in FY 1982. Till FY 1982, the USA paid $ 1.2 billion or about 37% of its total contribution of $ 3.24 billion, when at least 62% should have been contributed in the first two years. There was a resultant erosion in the commitment authority of IDA, and IBRD funds at higher cost were diverted to keep projects going.

There followed various meetings of the deputies at different places, and the diplomatic initiatives by the developing countries may have facilitated the eventual resolution of the impasse by the deputies of the donor Governments. There was an understanding amongst the other donors, except the USA, that for FY 1984 they could contribute an additional one-third of their IDA contributions. However, certain issues were raised by the UK and Germany which necessitated a slight modification. The UK had contributed 10.1% to IDA-6, and it thought that this was too high, and therefore, in order not to prejudice its case during the IDA-7 negotiations, it called for a reduction to 7.6% in its share. The Germans had fixed their contribution in SDRs, and because of exchange rate fluctuations, their payments in domestic currency had risen. Finally, the donors agreed that the contribution to the Special Fund or the FY 1984 account would be so fixed that together with the earlier IDA-6 contributions, the sum was four-thirds of the IDA-6 contributions. Options were given with respect to payment in the national currency, converted at the rate prevailing on a given date (Oct. 5th, 1979). The other donors were, therefore, magnanimous in that they allowed the USA to depart unilaterally from the original burden-sharing arrangement, though they themselves generally abided by it, making an additional contribution for the transitional fiscal year 1984. An interesting stipulation was that for procurement financed out of the Special Fund, the U.S. suppliers would be debarred as the U.S. had not contributed to that fund.

For the IDA-7 replenishment the management prepared an approach paper arguing for a size of about $ 16.5 billion. However, they made suggestions for hardening the terms of the credits, e.g. reducing the maturity period, and suggesting payment of interest, albeit at rates lower than those of the IBRD, for the more creditworthy borrowers. Besides the per capita income, other criteria sought to be introduced was the creditworthiness of the borrower, and its industrial capacity. A series of meetings of the deputies at different centres followed.

Fortunately, the deputies were not persuaded by the industrial capacity criterion, nor were they in favour of charging interest from the more creditworthy borrowers. The size of the replenishment was the most contentious issue. The USA was firm in its resolve that not more than $ 750 million per annum could be provided by their administration, and this was coupled with the stipulation that the USA would not provide more than 25% of the total replenishment, which effectively determined the size at about $ 9 billion for the replenishment.

Despite much canvassing, and President Clausen's efforts, including a meeting with the President of the USA, the outcome was disappointing. The deputies were influenced by the adamant stand of the USA, and though many thought that $ 9 billion was inadequate, this figure was adopted in the interest of equitable burden sharing. Some countries were prepared to adopt a replenishment of $12 billion, without demanding a higher contribution from the USA, as most donors thought that the level of $ 12 billion represented the minimum resources required by IDA for its programme during FY 1985-87. The possibility of raising supplementary resources was left open.

What can one learn from the experience with these two replenishments? Clearly, it will remain a daunting task to persuade sovereign Governments to voluntarily part with sizeable funds for replenishing IDA, especially when there are many competing demands and in difficult times, when there may be inflexible budgetary constraints. The World Bank has to educate public opinion in the donor countries, that in an increasingly inter-dependent world, development of the Third World confers significant benefits on the donor countries themselves. The case for the size of the IDA replenishment requested has to be made out very convincingly. It does not reflect well on all parties involved that the World Bank claim for an IDA-7 replenishment with a minimum size of about $ 16 billion should have been given short shrift, and the eventual size should have been fixed at $ 9 billion. The World Bank also was inept in gauging the opinions of the donor Governments, and put forward suggestions for charging interest from the more credit-worthy beneficiaries, and for the adoption of industrial capacity as one of the allocation criteria. Better liaison might have avoided the putting forward initially of these suggestions, which got rejected. These proposals also, did not improve the image of IDA amongst the borrowers. In the course of the negotiations, the practice is that the Management alone deals with the IDA deputies, and the Board is usually presented with a 'fait accompli', which it is called upon to endorse. Active participation by the Board is thus somewhat limited. During these negotiations, there was a time when seasoned Bank personnel like the Senior Vice-President were replaced by a comparative outsider, Mr. Andre de Lattre, who appeared clearly out of his depth and may have failed to press the IDA case adequately. The Senior Vice-President was soon back in the saddle. A personal view is that it may be desirable to ensure that the initial claim presented to the donor Governments and considered by the deputies bears the imprimatur of the Board. These Governments are represented on the Board, and it should be possible to arrive at a mutually acceptable target figure or range even before the start of formal negotiations. The donor Governments should be aware of how much can be spared out of available resources for IDA and the concerned ED should be kept in the picture. Per contra, the ED should be in a position to brief the decision makers in his constituency on the essential requirements for IDA. This two way traffic and full utilisation of the services of the ED should help to avoid the difficulties which were witnessed with both IDA-6 and IDA-7.

The drastic curtailment in IDA's commitment authority, as a result of the USA reneging on its earlier commitments, caused considerable dislocation to the IDA-6 lending operations, and the substitution of IBRD funds for IDA funds, cast an additional burden on the borrowers. Arrangements should be devised to ensure that similar situations do not arise in future. Because of the long drawn and tortuous negotiations involved, and the many extraneous issues that are thrust into these negotiations for bilateral purposes, it may be actively considered whether the replenishment period should not be extended to five years instead of the present three years, as was once suggested by the Americans.

It is now proposed to consider the present position, and the strategy that IDA has been enjoined to follow by the deputies, and the donor Governments. Currently, IDA is operating under the 10th replenishment (July 1st, 1993 to June 30th, 1996). After five negotiating sessions, the deputies reached agreement in December 1992 on a replenishment of SDR 13 billion ($ 18 billion). When combined with advance commitments against future repayments by IDA borrowers, and the approved transfer of $ 375 million from the IBRD's surplus, IDA's commitment authority during the three year period would total about SDR 16 billion ($ 22 billion). This amount could be augmented by additional amounts transferred from the IBRD's surplus.[2] This overall figure would suggest that annual lending by IDA during the IDA-10 period might be comparable to the levels achieved in the preceding few years.

However, it is disquieting to read in the Annual Report, 1995 (p. 136) that the USA had reneged on its commitments to IDA-10, reminiscent of its role in IDA-6. Part of the second tranche of IDA-10 contributions was not available by June 30th, 1995, as the USA's payment to IDA-10 was about 8% less than the agreed schedule. Unlike the accommodation shown by other donors during IDA-6, this time round, Germany and Canada exercised their right to withhold their contributions proportionately to the shortfall in the USA's contribution. This development is indicative of the hardening of attitudes all round, and does not augur well for the future of IDA.

The Annual Report 1995 gives a gist of the discussions by the IDA deputies during FY 1995 in the context of IDA-11 (FY 1997-99). On the positive side, there was recognition of the needs of IDA borrowers to reduce poverty and the related goals of labour-intensive growth, and environmental sustainability. The problems of debt sustainability also emerged prominently. On the negative side, serious concern was expressed about the prospect of resources for IDA and their adequacy, because of budgetary pressures and overall financial uncertainty. Press reports indicate that the size of IDA-11 has been settled at $ 22 billion, but this is an aggregate figure, including repayments of past IDA credits, the IBRD's own contributions, and significantly, the arrears of the USA's contribution to IDA-10 ($ 935 million), which it earlier withheld. Fresh contributions are said to amount to only one-half, a substantial reduction from IDA-10 even in monetary terms.

However, the need for adoption of sound economic policies by recipients, and their performance in implementing projects, was stressed for determining allocations. Emphasis was placed on Country Assistance Strategies for achieving the desired goals, and for anchoring the lending projections. Encouragement of the private sector and its growth were accepted as goals. Further discussions on the size of IDA-11 and on burden-sharing are scheduled. The outlook for IDA-11 is, therefore, not promising both with respect to its size, and the degree of conditionality that is likely to be imposed on recipients.

The shares of the large donors over the years provides an interesting contrast. USA's share in the initial IDA contribution and IDA-1 was 42%. In IDA-6 it declined to 27%, and further to 25% in IDA-7. The trend has continued in IDA-10, where her share is down to 20.86%. UK's share has dwindled from the initial 17% to 6.15% in the tenth replenishment. France has been relatively constant in the 5% to 8% range since the 1960s. Germany (earlier FRG) contributed 10% to IDA-1, and her share in the tenth replenishment is 11%, though it touched 13% in IDA-6. Japan's share has recorded a spectacular increase from 4% in the initial contribution to its present share of 18.7%, besides a supplementary contribution of $ 169 million which would raise its total share to about 21.2%. However, the Japanese have been using their IDA contributions during negotiations to also improve their ranking in the IBRD, where they have gone to the second position. The USA too has not been above settling unconnected bilateral issues with Japan in the course of the IDA replenishment negotiations (vide IDA-7 negotiations).

The credits approved by IDA over the years have displayed an upward trend till the early 1980s, when these suffered a set-back for the reasons already discussed. During 1961-68, the credits averaged $ 229 million annually. In 1980, credits totalled $ 3,838 million, but these tapered off to $ 2,686 million in 1982. In the 1990s there was a steady increase from $ 5,549 million in 1990 to $ 6,751 million in 1993. In 1994, there was a decline to $ 6,592 million.

The cumulative total of IDA credits stands at $ 97,793 million as on 30th June 1995 or well over one-half of the corresponding IBRD figure.[3]

These figures are significant, and indicative of the effort that the international community has put in, despite formidable odds and at considerable sacrifice, for improving the lot of the poorest countries. As a result, IDA is the most effective and influential agency providing concessional assistance.

Though IDA is a separate entity with its own Articles of Agreement, distinct from the IBRD, nevertheless the Board is common, and the same personnel operate both the institutions. Though the lending by IDA may be on 'soft' terms, there is nothing soft about its functioning. A reference has already been made (vide Chapter 2) to a study undertaken in 1982 comparing the rate of return of 273 IBRD projects, and that of 183 IDA projects. The findings showed that IDA projects on an average achieved a marginally higher rate of return (17.9%) than the IBRD projects (17%). It was significant that in the agriculture sector (which traditionally is a difficult sector, and records lower rates of return in the IBRD than usual infrastructure projects), the 95 IDA projects achieved a return of 19.5% compared with 14.2% return yielded by 74 IBRD projects. The higher proportion of agriculture projects under IDA (about 52%) as compared with IBRD (27%) is in conformity with the objective of helping the poor, as in most populous developing countries, farms are usually small and subsistence or peasant farming is the general rule.[4] These figures were compiled in the early 1980s and relate to projects that were taken up earlier, but are nevertheless still relevant.

When approving IDA-10, the deputies laid down certain principles and practices which might have far-reaching effects, and deserve to be commented upon. They endorsed the objectives outlined at the time of the ninth replenishment, agreeing that they remained an accurate reflection of the *key* development challenges facing the poorest countries. These were:

(i) Poverty reduction,
(ii) Economic reform and adjustment to promote growth, and
(iii) Environmental protection and improvement.

The expectation was that higher shares of poverty-related investment and social sector lending would be attained in IDA-10 than were attained in IDA-9. The deputies enjoined that the Executive Directors should keep track of the expenditure incurred by borrowers, and how closely expenditure patterns reflected development priorities. In particular, they were asked to keep a watch on non-development expenditure, especially military expenditure (about which we have commented elsewhere), and assess the efforts being made to reduce such expenditure to the maximum extent feasible. In conformity with Bank philosophy, IDA was asked to heighten its support for efforts to create the right environment for the private sector to respond to sound economic policies. It was also enjoined to improve the efficiency of the public sector.

The IDA deputies discussed how best to allocate IDA resources to meet these objectives, and they reviewed the three selected criteria viz.

(i) per capita income,
(ii) performance, and
(iii) creditworthiness.

It is noteworthy that previously the emphasis was on the poverty aspect, e.g. number of persons below the poverty line. The present formulation had a different nuance, as per capita income was to be used for determining eligibility for IDA funding only. Further, instead of the passive indicator of the number living in poverty, an active indicator was chosen, viz. the effort put in to reduce poverty. The changes resulting from the application of these criteria are considered in Part B of Chapter 5 which deals with poverty reduction.

For judging performance, the criteria were application of sound economic policies, commitment to poverty reduction, and implementation of environmentally responsible programmes. The need for good governance was highlighted, and four aspects were identified as being critical for effective use of donor resources, and the effectiveness of the development process, viz.

(i) accountability,
(ii) transparency,
(iii) rule of law, and
(iv) participation by the affected people in the design and implementation of the programme.

While much of what the deputies enjoined was already an integral part of standard Bank practice as it has evolved in recent years, its real importance lies in the enforcement provisions, which were also specified, viz.

(i) When allocating resources by country and by sector, IDA should focus on those countries that have *demonstrated* their commitment to IDA's three main objectives (poverty reduction, economic growth, and environment).
(ii) Access to IDA resources should be based on an annual assessment of performance.
(iv) In countries where performance was lax, lending should be limited to the *minimum* necessary for keeping the policy dialogue going.

Borrowers would be well advised, therefore, to be prepared for close scrutiny of their policies, expenditure patterns and implementation procedures by IDA across a wide field, and if there are shortcomings, then their IDA allocations are likely to be cut.

Clearly, there is ample scope for value judgements in assessing performance in the light of the factors mentioned. Also, if there is a difference of opinion, it is not clear what redress would be available to the borrower, should it feel aggrieved, and consider the finding discriminatory. In some ways, the scrutiny exercised by IDA may be closer and more refined than that exercised by the erstwhile colonial powers—but with the crucial difference that while the latter could apply political and military power, IDA's only sanction is to cut allocations. However, this is not to under-estimate the effectiveness of the financial disincentive as IDA funds are not only scarce, but are much sought after. Perhaps these arrangements do provide a "modus vivendi" which the developing countries will have to learn to live with. In some cases, IDA's interventions or even the possibility of such intervention, could provide the needed 'stiffener' to an otherwise 'soft State'. It does mean, however, that the borrowers will have to be ever mindful of achieving the three objectives, which in themselves are unexceptionable. IDA, on its part, will have to ensure objectivity and fairness in its dealings, so as to inspire confidence amongst its clientele.

With regard to the third criterion of 'creditworthiness' there was a distinct shift away from the 'blend' countries, prominent amongst them being China, India and Pakistan. The deputies indicated that greater weight should be given to creditworthiness considerations when allocating funds to 'blend' countries. Specifically, they enjoined that IDA should reduce its allocations by reducing the IBRD/IDA blend to a range of 30% to 35% of total IDA allocations, down from 40% during IDA-9. Further, they recommended that assistance to these countries should be directed primarily to poverty-focussed activities, or to those that promote environmental sustainability. Apparently, concern was expressed by some deputies that these measures would unduly lower the overall share of Asia, home to the largest number of poor people. The upshot was that they agreed to maintain approximate parity between allocations to sub-Saharan Africa and Asia during IDA-10. Sub-Saharan Africa's share was put at 45% to 50%.[5] It needs to be mentioned that since IDA was created to deal with countries such as India, during the first four years, India received about 50% and Pakistan about 23% of commitments. During 1971-76, and 1977-

82, India's share was reduced, but it still was about 39% and 38% respectively of total commitments, while sub-Saharan Africa got about 25%. With the induction of mainland China, and its eligibility for IDA assistance, a rough allocation was to provide about 40% of commitments to both India and China in the aggregate. In 1994, India and China were allocated respectively 12.7% and 14%, or 26.7% in the aggregate. Sub-Saharan Africa's allocation was about 40.65%. The present dispensation by the IDA deputies is thus a continuation of the earlier trend, as sub-Saharan Africa's share is to increase and to lie within the range of 45% to 50%, while the Asian 'blend' countries are to suffer a further curtailment.

By and large, the criteria for allocations have remained basically the same, though there might have been changes in emphasis. It might be interesting to compare how different countries have fared with the adoption of these criteria over the years. Accordingly, cumulative lending till FY 1994 under both IBRD and IDA were tabulated, and the per capita figures worked out (Table 4A. 2) for some selected countries. The figures are startlingly different from country to country. China's case may not be comparable because she joined the Bank in the early 1980s, and credits were approved thereafter. Others have been regular borrowers. India with a per capita cumulative total of $ 24.09 is near the bottom (excluding China, and Indonesia which is a 'Bank only' country). Pakistan, too, is comparatively low in the rankings, with a per capita figure of $ 37.05. On the other hand Ghana is entitled to a per capita cumulative total of $ 158.18, even though its per capita income at $ 450 p.a. is higher than that of India and Pakistan. Senegal with a per capita income of $ 780 p.a. and an IDA cumulative allocation of $ 134.9 has been similarly treated favourably. Several other African countries, e.g. Cote d'Ivoire, and Zimbabwe with higher per capita incomes, have done better than India and Pakistan in IDA allocations. Almost all African countries with comparable per capita incomes have also fared better than their Asian counterparts. At one stage, India's share of about 40% of IDA allocations was the cynosure of other developing countries, even though this represented a restriction on her borrowings, as on a population basis her entitlement was higher. The wide gap apparent from the per capita allocations figures between India and the other African

Table 4A.2

Cumulative IDA and IBRD lending to selected countries

Country	Population (millions)	Per capita GNP (US $)	Cumulative IDA credit		Cumulative World Bank loans	
			Credits (US $ millions)	Per capita credit (US $)	Loans (US $ millions)	Per capita loans (US $)
Bangladesh	114.4	220	6,729.9	58.83	46.1	0.40
China	1162.2	470	7,795.7	6.71	11,759.4	10.12
Cote d'Ivoire	12.9	670	522.2	40.48	2,887.9	223.86
Egypt	54.7	640	1,376.5	25.16	3,955.8	72.32
Ethiopia	54.8	110	1,860.6	33.95	108.6	1.98
Ghana	15.8	450	2,499.2	158.18	207.0	13.10
India	883.6	310	21,284.1	24.09	21,838.2	24.71
Indonesia	184.3	670	931.8	5.05	20,411.7	110.75
Kenya	25.7	310	2,202.2	85.68	1,200.0	46.69
Madagascar	12.4	230	1,191.5	96.09	32.9	2.65
Malawi	9.1	210	1,269.8	139.54	124.1	13.63
Mozambique	16.5	60	1,401.3	84.93	-	-
Nepal	19.9	170	1,394.1	70.05	-	-
Pakistan	119.3	420	4,420.6	37.05	5,163.2	43.28
Senegal	7.8	780	1,052.2	134.9	164.9	21.14
Sri Lanka	17.4	540	1,862.0	107.0	210.7	12.11
Tanzania	25.9	110	2,691.5	103.92	318.2	12.28
Uganda	17.5	170	2,116.9	120.96	8.4	0.48
Yemen	13.0	-	1,088.4	83.72	-	-
Zaire	39.8	-	1,151.5	28.93	330.0	8.29
Zambia	8.3	-	1,234.5	148.73	679.1	81.82
Zimbabwe	10.4	570	443.4	42.63	893.2	85.88

Source: Annual Report, 1994, Appendix 6 and W.D.R.

countries suggests that India is entitled to a better deal. It will be noticed that the extent of IBRD lending to India at $ 24.71 per capita is moderate and has not redressed the position; Cote d'Ivoire, Egypt, Indonesia and Kenya have received respectively $ 223.86, $ 72.32, $ 110.75 and $ 46.69, i.e. many times higher than what India received. IBRD cumulative lending per capita to other countries in Latin America and South-East Asia is also very much higher (e.g. Argentina—$ 264.10, Brazil—$ 140.93, Mexico—$ 275.51 and Thailand—$ 81.62).

If one were to consider some smaller Asian countries, e.g. Nepal, the differences are suggestive again of a tilt against Asian countries. Nepal by all accounts is a small and poor country with a per capita income of a mere $ 170 p.a. Uganda has the same per capita income, and a slightly lower population, but has a cumulative IDA allocation of $ 120.96 against the corresponding Nepalese figure of $ 70.05. Madagascar and Malawi are also relatively small countries, but with a per capita income appreciably higher than that of Nepal and yet their cumulative per capita IDA allocations at $ 96.09 and $ 139.54 are far higher than that of Nepal.

Regional figures of cumulative lending by IDA reinforce the country-wise figures cited above, as shown below:

Table 4A.3

Region	Cumulative IDA credits to borrowers	Population (millions)	Per capita cumulative IDA credits
Africa	$ 35,982.9 million	487.8	$ 73.76
South Asia	$ 31,304.9 million	1036.8	$ 30.19

Source : Annual Report 1994, p. 229.

These trends are difficult to justify and it would appear that a reconsideration is required. The enormous and unwarranted disparities in the per capita cumulative allocations of IDA funds to different countries as detailed above, would suggest that the application of the selected criteria, or the criteria themselves used so long, have been defective. Clearly, IDA funds will not be allocated if projects or programmes are not prepared and posed to the Association. Country assessments should ensure that suitable projects or programmes are duly posed before IDA in time and in an orderly manner. The need of a particular country for concessional assistance should also be assessed having regard to its indebtedness position, debt service burden, B.O.P. problems, and essential development objectives. What is necessary is a coordinating mechanism that ensures equitable distribution of scarce IDA resources by rationing it out on the basis of need, size of the country, extent of poverty and performance, as available concessional resources will invariably fall short of requirements.

These drastic reductions in the allocations of IDA credit have taken place for India and Pakistan without a corresponding improvement in the B.O.P. situation. In fact, India was on the verge of defaulting in her debt servicing obligations in 1991. The present buoyancy in her foreign exchange reserves, though welcome, cannot be a cause for complacency, as some of the funds, e.g. portfolio investments are volatile, and could well be repatriated. The fundamental feature that needs emphasising is that India, like many other developing countries, is in chronic and sizeable trade deficit with the rest of the world. The considerations which led to the creation of IDA in the first instance, still remain valid, and necessitate the influx of large sums by way of concessional finance for development purposes.

It is not being suggested by any means that the African countries should be deprived of concessional assistance, as their needs are also genuine. All that is being suggested is a still greater effort by the international community to mobilise additional concessional resources, and a more equitable basis of distribution of the available funds. If a long term view is taken, the problems of the Asian countries will be found to be intractable because of the population pressure on the land, and the relatively few natural endowments. This is not the case in most African countries, which possess immense physical and natural resources, and have a more favourable land to population ratio. Their potential for development is immense, given good administration and guidance. Concentration on these aspects under the aegis of the World Bank may yield rich dividends.

B. INTERNATIONAL FINANCE CORPORATION

The International Finance Corporation (or IFC) is a relatively small but important member of the World Bank group. Like other members of the group, it shares the common objective of improving living standards in developing countries, and assisting in their overall development and growth. However, IFC's focus is *private sector* development. As laid down in its Articles of Agreement, its purpose is to "further economic development by encouraging the growth of productive private enterprise in member countries" financing such enterprise in partnership with private investors and helping Governments create conditions that stimulate both domestic and foreign investment. Though set up in the 1960s, i.e. several years after the IBRD came into being, the IFC has now established itself as the largest multilateral institution assisting the private sector.

Though a member of the World Bank group, the IFC is an entirely distinct entity, both juridically and in day-to-day operation. It has its own Articles of Agreement, and unlike IDA, has its own staff. However, being a part of the World Bank group, its policies reflect the basic tenets of the IBRD, and its activities are closely coordinated with those of the other members of the group. There is continuous exchange of information and data at various levels. The organisation of the IFC ensures coordination within the group, and adherence to its overall policies. The supreme authority, viz., the Board of Governors, is more or less the same as that of the IBRD. However, as in the case of the IBRD, most of the powers have been delegated by the Board of Governors to the Executive Board, based in Washington, D.C. This latter Board is identical to the Executive Board of the IBRD, with the modification that the IFC has an Executive Vice-President, who attends Board meetings and is responsible for the day-to-day operations of the Corporation. The IBRD President is also the President of the IFC. Like the IBRD, the IFC has Regional Departments for each of the geographical regions, together with a number of specialised departments that are allotted certain well-defined functions and operate centrally. The IFC raises its own capital from the members, and has a system of weighted voting. As with the IBRD, the USA is the biggest shareholder with a current voting power of 22.67% (compared with 17.14% in the

IBRD). The second largest shareholder in the IFC is Japan (voting power 7.12%, as against 6.47% in the IBRD). Germany is third in both institutions (IFC—5.63%; IBRD—5.00%). The UK and France are tied jointly for the fourth place in both bodies (IFC—5.28%; IBRD—4.79%). Currently the authorised capital is $ 2.45 billion, while the paid in capital is $ 1.7 billion.

The basic activity of the IFC is to finance viable projects put forward by private companies and entrepreneurs in the developing countries, *without* any Government guarantees. The finance is extended both in the form of loans, and as equity. The scope of its activities can be gauged from the relevant figures for FY 1994 given below[6]:

Loans by IFC on its own account	$ 1.7 billion
Equity & quasi-equity by IFC	$ 0.719 billion
Guarantees, Swaps & Stand-by arrangements	$ 0.035 billion
Total	$ 2.454 billion

However, the IFC also arranged for syndications and underwriting, amounting to about $ 1.8 billion, with the result that the total financing extended was of the order of $ 4.3 billion. Some 231 projects were financed, and covered a wide array of activities. The three largest sectors were infrastructure ($ 1.346 billion), capital markets, development finance and financial services ($ 688 million), and chemicals, petrochemicals and fertilisers ($ 417 million), which together constitute 57.16% of the total. Mining, Food and Agribusiness, Cement etc., Energy and General Manufacture, each received over 6% of the total. The approved projects were distributed over 65 countries scattered around the globe. Although assistance raised through IFC, and syndicates, etc. was about $ 4.3 billion, the total cost of these projects was placed at $ 15.8 billion, the balance being raised by the promoters, etc. The leveraging achieved by the IFC was thus substantial. The figures for a single year may not be indicative of the IFC's impact overall. The total committed portfolio on IFC's account as on June 30th, 1994 is put at $ 7.893 billion, with the following break-up:

Loans	$ 6.398 billion
Equity	$ 1.495 billion
Total	$ 7.893 billion

The cumulative commitments both on IFC's account and through syndications are as follows, with respect to the same date:

IFC	$ 14.316 billion
Syndications	$ 7.417 billion
Total	$ 21.733 billion

The commitments relate to 1290 enterprises.

It would be tempting to gauge the relative sizes of the IFC and the IBRD by comparing these figures with the total loans current made by the latter till June 30th, 1994, i.e. $ 164.3 billion. However, in many respects, the comparison may not be fair, as the IFC not only approves loans, but also participates in the equity of the enterprise, and its clientele are all from the private sector. The IBRD, on the other hand, insists on the member-Government's involvement, either directly or by way of a guarantee. The scope for lending is also vastly dissimilar, as the IBRD is dealing with sovereign Governments, having sizeable resources at their disposal, while the IFC is dealing with private entities, some of which may be just starting up.

The IFC's activities have been growing steadily, without displaying the ups and downs witnessed by the IBRD's loan commitments. Some figures relating to the IFC may be of interest. In 1985, the IFC financed 75 projects, and on its own account, provided $ 611 million. The corresponding figures for 1994, as shown above were 231 projects, and $ 2454 million—about a fourfold increase. A commendable feature has been that over the last decade the IFC has operated profitably. In 1985, its net income was $ 28.3 million, while the corresponding figure for 1994 is $ 258.2 million. The IFC derives a sizeable part of its income from interest and financial fees paid by its various clients ($ 355 million). It also earns interest on its deposits and securities ($ 141 million). Dividends and profit participation amounted to only $ 28 million in 1994. However, the IFC made sizeable capital gains on its equity sales ($ 241 million), and has to be commended for the success achieved, as it reflects the good performance of the enterprises it has assisted in setting up and has financed. To finance its operations, the IFC like the IBRD, borrows from the global financial markets, and has also earned a triple 'A' rating. During 1994 its borrowings amounted to $ 1.7 billion, and as on June 30th, 1994, the total amount of borrowings in all currencies stood at $ 5.669 billion. A major item of expenditure is 'charges on borrowings', and it stood at $ 243 million in 1994. Administrative expenses were much less, amounting to $ 175 million. The other major item of expenditure was 'provision for losses' ($ 127 million). The net result was, as stated above, a net income of $ 258 million.

While due care is taken in selecting the projects to be financed, and the parties responsible for these projects, not all projects are successful, and the IFC too has its share of problem-projects. For giving special attention to loss-making projects, a Special Operations Unit has been set up. Often problems are caused by external factors, which are beyond the control of the promoters or of the IFC. Sometimes, however, these projects run into difficulties because of poor design or poor execution, and remedial action may be possible. The total reserve against losses stands at $ 636 million, and is in excess of 10% of total investments by way of loans and equity. During the writer's tenure as Executive Director, several such problem-projects came up for discussion and remedial action by the Board. It was noteworthy that the attitude of both the management and the Board was pragmatic, as it was realised that business has inherent risks, and these are more pronounced in developing countries, especially those facing macro-economic problems. There was full recognition of IFC's role as a developmental institution, and far from being inquisitorial, the Board encouraged the taking of legitimate and calculated risks in order to further the development of the host country. To the writer, coming from a developing country, the Board's attitude provided a refreshing contrast to the attitude adopted generally by Parliamentary Committees, and Central Audit authorities in developing countries, to similar issues.

It would, perhaps, be wrong to judge the IFC on the basis of its financial contributions in the form of equity and loans alone, though as noted above, these are quite substantial. More valuable to the developing countries in some ways, has been the catalytic effect of its activities over the years. It has clearly demonstrated that business enterprises can be run successfully and profitably in developing countries even in new and uncharted sectors. That IFC itself has been operating profitably over long periods, despite considerable turbulence in the financial sector, is a factor weighed by other investors when deciding whether or not to invest in developing countries. Besides investing on its own account, IFC has been contacting other financiers to form syndicates or to underwrite the loans or equity. The contribution from such other parties has been only slightly smaller than the IFC's own contribution. The fact that over the years, the sponsored enterprises have, by and large, prospered, has helped to break the ice, and persuade other parties also to invest in developing countries. It could be claimed that IFC's activities over the years, to some extent, have helped to generate the present favourable climate which has led to a surge in foreign direct investment to some selected developing countries.

A major contribution by IFC, which is likely to have far-reaching consequences for the developing countries, is its pioneering role in the development of capital markets in these countries. The Annual Report for 1994 of the IFC states:

> "Today the evidence is clear that the critical contribution of a country's private sector to investment and growth is directly related to the health and development of its financial sector . . . While IFC's capital market activities have included significant efforts to help supplement domestic resources by mobilising external savings flow to emerging markets, much of IFC's work has focussed on developing domestic financial institutions and capital markets."

This dual approach was predicated upon the basic feature that in most cases, the supply of domestic savings and capital exceeded foreign savings flows. Hence, the emphasis on the domestic capital market, though simultaneously measures were taken to stimulate the flow of foreign investment as a supplement. The IFC's efforts have been assisted to a great extent by the favourable environment, and global developments, such as the dissolution of the USSR, and the world-wide trends towards liberalisation, globalisation and privatisation.

To its credit, IFC has been collecting and disseminating data on stock exchanges and companies in the developing countries for several years. Its Emerging Markets Data Base (EMDB) has increased appreciation of the potential of emerging markets. The EMDB tracks price and share data for the stock of more than 1,400 companies in 25 emerging markets, and IFC publishes more than 100 indices. The data serve as benchmarks, and are used by many foreign investors to guide their investment decisions.

To develop the domestic capital market, IFC claims to have helped establish or improve nearly 200 financial institutions over the past 23 years, in the process making equity investments and loans exceeding $ 1.1 billion. The gamut of the institutions covered is wide, ranging from basic institutions such as commercial and housing banks, to mutual funds, leasing and venture companies, credit rating institutions and even stock exchanges. It has made efforts to broaden the emerging markets. While equity markets exist, bond markets are practically non-existent, and IFC has attempted to include a wider range of financial instruments in these markets, e.g. long term debt instruments. Innovative techniques such as revenue bonds and receivable-backed securities have also been explored. IFC claims to have studied and recommended changes in the relevant laws and regulations of various countries to create a more conducive legal and regulatory environment. It is also said to have engaged itself in drafting security market laws and regulations. Because it was in a position to commit funds for the purpose, reforms and improvements could be implemented in some countries.

In tandem, IFC took steps to generate greater interest in emerging markets amongst foreign investors. It is said that till the late 1980s, few international investors were interested in the markets of the developing countries. The few that were, had been attracted by the ready availability of raw materials for their business purposes, and the cheap labour. IFC has been repeatedly pointing out the advantages of diversification between the markets of the developed countries and those of the developing countries, e.g. emerging markets are less prone to cyclical fluctuations, and diversification with some investments in those markets can reduce overall volatility in the earnings and also result in lower risks. This message seems to have gone home and gained general acceptance now, as the *Economist* writes:

> "Yet although the ups and downs of Asian markets can be nerve-wracking, it remains true that most American investors could reduce risk and boost returns by putting some of their portfolio into the region. That is because the movements of Asian markets have not correlated with New York's ups and downs. Paul Schultz, a strategist with CS First Boston, claims that in recent years putting 40% of a wholly American portfolio of stock into a mixture of non-Japanese Asian shares would have increased expected returns from 15% to 17%, while reducing risk from 15% to 11%."[7]

The wide dissemination of data by the EMDB to influential clients did demonstrate that yields in emerging markets could be considerably higher than those available in the industrial countries, provided investments were made intelligently and with discrimination.

The widespread dismantling of trade and financial barriers coming in the wake of moves to liberalise and globalise, as well as the revolution in information technology resulting in almost instant communication world-wide, created an awareness amongst companies in the industrial countries that they should achieve a global presence. Large companies and institutional investors became conscious of the growing business opportunities in the emerging markets of the world, and thought that activity in these markets should constitute an important component of their global strategy. The IFC's prompting fell on receptive ears, and therefore, the preparatory work done by the IFC could be said to have been seminal. The IFC claims that it has stimulated portfolio investment in emerging markets by promoting over 35 pooled investment vehicles—"country funds"—which have mobilised more than $ 3 billion for these markets. The IFC estimates that there has been an increase in foreign portfolio investment flows (including debt issues) to emerging markets from less than $ 7 billion in 1989 to over $ 60 billion in 1993, exceeding foreign direct investment and O.D.A. for the first time. While portfolio investments are welcome, developing countries should be on their guard. Such investments are fair weather friends, and should the host country investments prove less attractive than opportunities available elsewhere, portfolio investments can prove to be highly volatile. As some countries have found, there can also be an embarrassment of riches, in that too large an inflow of foreign funds can lead to inflationary pressures. The overall result of these trends and developments has been that IFC's capital market activities have increased greatly not only in scale, but also in scope and complexity. Its capital markets programme now spans more than 100 countries.

Conversely, the IFC has played a major role in assisting companies and institutions in developing countries to access global markets. The tally is put at 18 companies (till 30th June, 1994). It is claimed that these international security issues have helped encourage local practices in connection with securities issuance, disclosure, and trading to be more in line with international standards and practices. Besides "country funds" mentioned earlier, IFC is also engaged in mobilising external resources through specialised investment funds that focus on key sectors or regions, and through direct security issues. Another area where IFC's expertise has been utilised is in privatisation of public sector enterprises and in ways of enlarging the scope of private sector participation in providing much needed infrastructure to developing countries.

It may be appropriate to refer to the Foreign Investment Advisory Service (FIAS) in this connection. It was set up in 1986 with the objective of helping Governments to fill long term development needs by getting the greatest possible benefit from foreign investment—not only capital, but also technology and managerial expertise. FIAS has also helped Governments to build an effective institutional framework for interacting with investors, and to develop investment promotion strategies. It is also said to have worked on laws, policies, and procedures needed to create an attractive investment climate. The FIAS is funded to the extent of 50% by the World Bank group, the balance 50% coming partly from a Trust fund set up by several developed countries and from contributions by several multilateral and bilateral agencies, as also from the clients themselves.

In Chapter 7 (Concluding Observations) the recommendations of the Bretton Woods Commission (BWC) have been referred to, and the heavy emphasis given to development of the private sector noted. The instrument of choice seems to be the IFC, and the World Bank has been exhorted to lend through the IFC rather than directly to private entities. The BWC represents a section of influential opinion, and most industrial country Governments are likely to share similar views. It is, therefore, quite likely that in the foreseeable future the IFC will be called upon to play an even more decisive role concerning developing countries, and the resources at its command will be substantially augmented.

It might be desirable to try and anticipate what the enhanced role of the IFC presages for the development of Third World countries, and how these countries should react. Despite all that has been said about development of the capital markets, and the surge in portfolio investments by "country funds", pension funds, etc. in the emerging markets, Third World countries should not de-emphasise investments made by the IFC whether as equity or as loan. The volatile nature of portfolio investments has already been commented upon. Industrialisation in the developing countries has a long way to go, particularly in the more sophisticated and high wage sectors. Third World countries, perhaps, would find it worthwhile to enlist the support of the IFC, and to persuade it to invest the maximum possible, whether as equity or loan, in furthering industrialisation of their countries. The sectors covered could be both the traditional industries as well as the 'hi-tech' new industries. From this point of view, a larger and well endowed IFC with the requisite financial muscle should be welcomed.

The services of both the IFC, and its associate, the FIAS, should be enlisted to augment the flow of foreign direct investment. Not only are such flows much more stable, but usually these bring with them new technology, and managerial expertise. Often foreign companies can assist in export promotion because of their contacts in their own home countries, and their intimate knowledge of the precise requirements of the home consumer. With the heavy external indebtedness of most developing countries, and the pre-emption of foreign exchange for servicing their debts, the paramount importance of export promotion cannot be gainsaid. Foreign direct investment would be needed for the setting up of the new generation of industries in the Third World countries, as MNCs alone seem to have mastered the technology, and would be reluctant to part with it except to their own subsidiaries.

The services of the IFC should be welcomed for improving the domestic capital market, and for carrying out institutional changes which would lead to greater transparency, and reduce paperwork, making it safer and more profitable for the investor, particularly the small man. With improving living standards, it is the numbers in the populous developing countries, that have to be sought after, so that even if their individual mite is severely limited, in the aggregate, a significant accretion of capital takes place.

It might be of interest to consider the implications of IFC's efforts to promote both direct foreign investment and external portfolio investment. Partly because of IFC's past activities, it appears that industrial countries will be participating to a growing extent in the business activities of the developing countries, though on a selective basis. Barriers to trade, especially after the successful completion of the Uruguay round, and also financial barriers, are being rapidly dismantled. It is probable, therefore, that most countries with relatively open economies will have to fall in line with international trends. This would presumably mean that the wide differences in interest rates currently prevalent, especially between the industrial countries and the developing countries, would narrow considerably, with all the attendant consequences across the entire field of economic activity. Not only trading practices, but also accounting, banking and disclosure practices, would have to be gradually attuned to international norms. Developing countries would have to be particularly circumspect about inflation, as failure to control prices may affect exports and the exchange rate. Possibilities of capital flight would also have to be countered. Competition, both internal and external, will make it more difficult to run business enterprises.

The dangers inherent in globalisation, and the necessity for continuous vigil over economic developments is exemplified by the Mexican crisis of late 1994 and early 1995. The Mexican crisis has some lessons for other developing countries also, and is elaborated upon to help formulate policies in those countries, should they be required to face similar problems. Mexico was the first country to head for a debt crisis in the early 1980s. There followed a series of adjustments, and help under the Brady initiative. The World Bank opines that Mexico's stabilisation and structural reforms were highly successful in restoring macroeconomic stability, and controlling inflation, which by 1993 had fallen to single digits from an average of 65% during 1987-90. During 1990-93, Mexico had benefited from some $ 91 billion of capital inflows. Nevertheless, Mexico faced a full blown financial crisis towards the end of 1994. In retrospect, it is thought that the crisis was caused by real appreciation of the Mexican peso, owing to large external inflows, which were not matched by an increase in productivity. This, in turn, was caused by low investment. The current account deficit was sought to be met by borrowings, some of which were short-term.[8] There were also non-economic factors which helped to trigger the crisis, e.g. the Chiapas insurrection, and political assassinations. There was a flight of capital in the absence of any exchange control, even on capital transfers. The situation was compounded by faulty and tardy policy responses, e.g.

(i) Non-adjustment of the exchange rate despite loss of investor confidence;
(ii) Rise in interest rates was moderated, and the contractionary effect of loss of reserves was sought to be sterilised;
(iii) Reliance was placed on short term borrowings in the form of dollar-indexed 'tesobonos';
(iv) The fiscal stance was expansionary.

The lessons drawn from the Mexican crisis, can be summed up as:

(a) Large persistent deficits on current account result in an unsustainable situation if the foreign savings are not used to increase productive investments.
(b) Reliance on monetary policy alone to restrict aggregate demand may be self-defeating, as higher interest rates may attract more capital inflows.
(c) Continued real exchange rate appreciation in excess of productivity gains increases vulnerability. Two ways of offsetting exchange rate appreciation are: (i) to restrain aggregate demand by use of fiscal measures, and (ii) to improve productivity. This method, however, yields results only over a period, and it would be risky to deal with a crisis in the expectation of productivity gains.

(d) The composition and maturity structure of public debt matters. Thus, credits such as those given by IDA are less pernicious than short term commercial borrowing.
(e) Financial liberalisation necessitates a higher level of foreign exchange reserves than what may be required for only meeting trade-flow needs.
(f) The health and resilience of the financial system is crucial to ensure sound use of capital inflows and to reduce vulnerability. It follows that an effective system of bank supervision has to be installed, and remedial measures adopted as required. It has been argued that because of the weak banking system in Mexico, necessary measures such as raising the interest rates were not taken.
(g) Constant vigilance is required, and the authorities should monitor warning signals, and take prompt action. The full range of macroeconomic measures available to the Government may have to be resorted to, including monetary policy, reduction in the fiscal deficit, promotion of savings, and exchange-rate changes.

The repercussions of the Mexican crisis were considerable, and besides affecting the neighbouring countries, these were felt in other emerging markets also. Thus, the IFC's global emerging market index declined by 13% in the first quarter of 1995, with virtually all emerging markets recording significant declines. However, some markets fared better than others, the Latin American markets declining most (by about 30%), while the East Asian markets declined by less than 10%. Later, all these markets recovered strongly in the second quarter of 1995, when the rescue package proved effective and contained the crisis. However, investors became more discerning, and evaluated the economic fundamentals of each market more closely, differentiating between markets accordingly.

The rescue package that was put together initially comprised a loan of $ 20 billion from the USA, $ 18 billion from the IMF, $ 10 billion from the Bank of International Settlements and about $ 3 billion from commercial banks, or over $ 50 billion in the aggregate. In the event, only the funds assured by the USA and the IMF became available. Some comments arising from the Mexican crisis may be of relevance to policy makers in other Third World countries:

(i) The role of the Government has perhaps acquired even greater importance in the context of globalisation and liberalisation. The crisis, perhaps, could have been moderated, if not averted, by prompt and effective macro-economic measures at the outset. The steps actually taken seem to have exacerbated the crisis.

(ii) Constant vigilance and monitoring of the economy are essential, prompt and forceful measures are required at the very onset of the crisis. Because of the speed of communication, and the marvels of the electronic age, a higher degree of instability has been injected into the international financial system.

(iii) Modern conditions have made the age-old verities more meaningful, and thus, call for more stringent financial control. Besides monetary policy, reliance has to be placed on fiscal measures also, and the Government cannot live beyond its means for long. Similarly, a Third World country cannot incur current account deficits indefinitely, and has to increase exports to close the gap. The exchange rate has to be adjusted flexibly in keeping with the ground realities. It has to be assured that loans are well-used and productivity improves.

(iv) Capital account convertibility is only warranted in a country, when its current account deficit is negligible and inflation has been brought down to the levels prevailing in countries which are its trading partners.

(v) For a country wishing to pursue an independent line, it has to be doubly careful about the sound management of its economy. Mexico was fortunate in being a member of NAFTA, and having large amounts of U.S. capital invested there, which resulted in the release of massive funds by the USA. The only other large contributor to the rescue package was the IMF. For other Third World countries, perhaps, the only succour they can hope for in a similar situation would be from the Bretton Woods 'twins'. The Mexican crisis emphasises the continuing need for these two organisations to play a helpful role in the future, which is likely to be equally turbulent, and to ensure that they have adequate resources at their disposal.

In the changed context, the task of administration will call for a higher degree of sophistication, based upon incentives and disincentives, and a different style of functioning, relying far less upon administrative fiats than before. The trends started up by the World Bank, and competently nurtured by the IFC can thus have far-reaching effects, and their implications for various categories, especially the poor and the underprivileged, are far from clear, and will only emerge in the fullness of time.

C. MULTILATERAL INVESTMENT GUARANTEE AGENCY

The Multilateral Investment Guarantee Agency (MIGA) is a relatively recent organisation which is still growing. Its scale of operations, as compared with those of other members of the World Bank group, is therefore small. Its purpose is to increase the flow of productive investments to developing countries by providing cost efficient services to its clients. These services include (a) guaranteeing (or insuring) investments in developing countries made by private investors against specific *non-commercial* risks; and (b) advising and assisting these countries' efforts to attract and retain these investments.

MIGA was first mooted in the early 1980s. However, it did not straightaway take root because many of the prospective members were not convinced that such an organisation sponsored by the World Bank had an important role to play in promoting foreign investment flows, especially since many industrial (and other) countries had their own national organisations providing insurance cover to prospective investors in developing countries. Further, at that time, the surge in either foreign direct investments, or in portfolio investments, to the emerging markets had not occurred. However, the bank authorities persisted with their endeavours, and eventually, MIGA came into being in 1988. Nevertheless, even by 1992, 115 countries had signed up as members, with 14 new members that year. After completion of membership requirements the number of full members was only 85 in 1992. Important countries such as India, Brazil, Colombia and Mexico became signatories only later. Even an industrial country like Belgium took time to join MIGA. For 1994, the Annual Report states that the number of countries paying their capital subscription in full and becoming members of the agency increased from 107 to 121, substantially less than the number of member-countries of the IBRD (178).

The organisation of MIGA is modelled somewhat on the lines of the IFC. It has its Board of Governors, and its Executive Board, to which most of the powers have been delegated. Like the IFC, it has its own Executive Vice-President. Similarly, the representatives on these Boards are mostly common with those of the corresponding IBRD Board, though of course, representation on the MIGA Board is restricted only to its members.

During FY 1994, MIGA entered into 38 contracts under its guarantee programme, and earned an income from the premia and commitment fees of $ 9.9 million. The commitments entered into, because of the potential coverage, were put at $ 140 million. These 38 contracts involved an associated total direct investment of some $ 1.3 billion and created 7,800 jobs directly in 14 host countries. Cumulatively, over the last five years MIGA has signed some 100 contracts of guarantee, and its total contingent liabilities exceeded the one billion dollars mark. The categories of risks covered are (a) currency transfer, (b) expropriation, (c) war and civil disturbance, and (d) breach of contract. Clients seem inclined to cover expropriation and currency transfer risks more frequently than the other two categories.

Another task undertaken by MIGA is the promotion of foreign investment in the developing countries. Till the end of FY 1994, it has been doing so either directly or through the Foreign Investment Advisory Service (FIAS). It is reported that technical assistance to stimulate foreign investment is now focussed primarily on investment promotion and information dissemination on investment opportunities in Category Two countries, i.e. the transitional economies of the former Soviet Union and of Eastern Europe. MIGA has conducted major multi-country promotional events, e.g. for the tourism sector in South America, and for the mining sector in sub-

Saharan Africa. MIGA has also conducted strategy workshops designed to help member-countries in capacity building for marketing, and workshops to strengthen investor services and linkages. MIGA has launched schemes for the dissemination of information on investment opportunities through the electronic network. Like the IFC, MIGA provides advice to member-countries on their investment legislation so as to stimulate foreign investment. There is thus, some overlap in the functions of these two bodies.

It is interesting to note that as from July 1st, 1994, MIGA has severed its links with FIAS, which it was jointly funding partially with other members of the World Bank group. The reason given is to conserve MIGA's resources and to build up its reserves.

When MIGA was first mooted, foreign investors were not particularly interested in the developing countries, except as sources of essential raw materials. In recent years, however, as already observed, there has been a major change, and foreign investors are keen on diversifying and some MNCs desire to acquire a global presence. The preliminary work done in establishing MIGA has, therefore, been opportune, and it has succeeded in catching the tide of external flows to the developing countries. The foreign investors find some comfort in the coverage provided by MIGA because of its international character, and the high financial standing of the World Bank. Besides, other insurers also sometimes find it worthwhile to re-insure with MIGA. It is reported that since MIGA provides long term, non-cancellable insurance against political risks and is a member of the World Bank group, bank regulators in some countries have exempted commercial banks from special provisioning requirements for country risk on their loans on investments insured by MIGA.[9] This is perceived as an advantage. MIGA has re-insurance and co-insurance agreements with national insurers in some countries (e.g. USA, Canada, Denmark, Japan and the UK). It has also agreed to re-insure a private insurer of political risks (Nordia). The facts of this case are illustrative of the utility of MIGA in dealing with some special cases and are, therefore, given below. AVX Corporation, a U.S.-owned company, was engaged in making capacitors in E1 Salvador. It was insured with the U.S. Government agency, Overseas Private Investment Corporation (OPIC). Thereafter, AVX merged with Kyocers of Japan, and consequently became ineligible for OPIC coverage. On the other hand, it was not eligible for Japanese Government political risk insurance, as it was based in the USA. The private insurer, Nordia, and MIGA jointly came to their rescue, MIGA directly insuring the expansion project, and reinsuring the existing project, covered by Nordia.

From this brief outline, it would thus appear that it was fortunate that the World Bank had the foresight to create MIGA at a time when foreign investments were still relatively unimportant. With the surge in external flows and the dramatic changes in the former Soviet Union, and in Eastern Europe, coupled with world-wide trends such as liberalisation, globalisation, and privatisation, there is significant interest both in promoting foreign investment, and per contra, in insuring investments made in countries, where considerable uncertainty and turbulence still prevail. Summing up, it would appear that MIGA is fulfilling a genuine need, and helping to promote external flows to developing countries in a vastly changed milieu to the one that prevailed when it was first contemplated.

D. DEVELOPMENT COMMITTEE

The Development Committee had its origins in a recommendation of a Committee of the Board of Governors of the IMF on reform of the international monetary system (The Committee of Twenty) established in July 1972. This Committee presented its report in June 1974, together with an Outline on Reform. Various technical groups were set up to assist the Committee, and its deputies. One such was dealing with the Transfer of Real Resources to developing countries, in the context of the 'Outline' and its Annex 10 which dealt with the special interests of the developing countries. The 'Outline' listed as one of the main features of a reformed international monetary system the promotion of the net flow of real resources to developing countries. The 'Outline' recognised that the promotion of economic development was an important objective of reform. To study the various aspects of aid and development, and in particular, the broad question of the transfer of real resources to developing countries, the Committee recommended that a joint ministerial committee of the Fund and the Bank be established, (subsequently known as the Development Committee).[10]

The then prevailing economic climate provided the relevant background to the setting up of the Development Committee, and was a contributory factor towards this welcome innovation. Compounding the uncertain economic outlook, was the sharp increase in the price of oil that occurred in 1974-75 (first oil shock). The oil-importing developing countries had to cope with the situation by borrowing or drawing down on their foreign exchange reserves, while they adjusted to increased oil prices. Similarly, some of the industrial countries also incurred large current account deficits, but the Technical Group of the Committee of Twenty advised against any reduction in aid flows to the developing countries. The group thought that a mechanism had to be devised for transferring some of the surpluses generated by the oil exporters to developing countries, particularly those finding it difficult to borrow in the international market. Pursuant to these recommendations, the Boards of Governors of the IMF and the World Bank adopted parallel resolutions for the establishment of a joint ministerial committee of the Boards of Governors of the Fund and the Bank to carry forward the study of the broad question of the transfer of real resources to the developing countries, and to recommend measures for the implementation of their conclusions. The Development Committee thereby came into being in October 1974.

The Development Committee comprises Governors of the Fund and the Bank, and thus Finance Ministers, or dignitaries of comparable rank are its members. They have two year tenures, and the Chairman is selected from amongst the members of the Committee. By convention, the Chairman normally hails from one or other of the developing countries. The Executive Secretary, who services the Committee, normally comes from a developed country, and thus some balance is sought to be achieved between these two groups of countries. The Executive Secretary is authorised to draw upon the staff of the World Bank and the Fund for servicing the Committee, preparing studies, etc., and thus costs are minimised. The arrangement is suited to the requirements of the Committee, which meets only periodically (usually twice a year, in Spring and in the Fall), and the work-load drops after a meeting is held, picking up again before the next meeting.

The Terms of Reference of the Development Committee were

laid down by para 4 of the parallel resolution creating it.[11] Inter-alia, the salient points covered by these terms of reference were:

(i) To maintain an overview of the development process, and to advise and report to the Boards of Governors of the Bank and the Fund on *all* aspects of the transfer of real resources to the developing countries.
(ii) To make suggestions to those concerned, regarding the implementation of its conclusions, and to review, on a continuing basis, the progress made.
(iii) To establish a detailed programme of work, taking account of the topics listed in Annex 10 of the Outline of Reform (i.e. the special interests of developing countries). The promotion of economic development was recognised as an important objective of reform. The Development Committee was also enjoined to bear in mind the need for coordination with other international bodies.
(iv) To give urgent attention to the problems of the least developed countries, and of those developing countries most seriously affected by balance of payment difficulties in the then current situation (1974).

Built into the parallel resolutions of the Fund and the Bank, was a review of the performance of the Development Committee by the Boards of Governors at the end of two years. There have been three reviews since the Development Committee came into existence, the last one in 1981. Suggestions were made for improving its effectiveness, an important one being the greater involvement of the Executive Directors in the preparatory work of the Committee, including drawing up the agenda for the meetings, its work programme, and review of the meeting papers.

The activities of the Development Committee can be conveniently categorised into three phases, viz. first phase, responding to the first oil shock of 1974, and to the emergence of generalised floating; the second phase, which reacted to the recycling of the OPEC surpluses generated by the increase in oil price, and increased commercial bank lending to the developing countries; the third phase, in the 1980s. This phase reflected the work of the Development Committee in responding to the external debt crisis, and to the process of adjustment that the developing countries were required to undertake.

It might be worthwhile discussing the main initiatives taken by the Development Committee, and its achievements, since its inception, before commenting on its future role. For brevity it is not proposed to catalogue a comprehensive list of its activities, and achievements, but to refer to only those main activities which have had a more than transient influence on the World Bank. Though it is a joint Fund/Bank committee, since the discussion here is centered on the World Bank, only the Development Committee's work relating to the Bank will be considered, and not that relating to the Fund. The Development Committee can claim credit for the opening of the 'Third Window' for the benefit of those developing countries that were seriously affected by the first oil crisis. This facility was established by the Bank for one year beginning July 1st, 1975, and provided assistance up to $ 1 billion in the forthcoming fiscal year, as a supplement to the Bank's regular operations. The Development Committee was also instrumental in creating an interest subsidy fund that permitted lending on terms which were intermediate to the terms normally adopted by the World Bank, and the concessional terms offered by IDA.

In the Spring of 1980, the Development Committee provided political support for the World Bank's proposals to increase programme lending for countries facing severe balance of payment problems, so as to enable them to undertake structural adjustment measures.

The theme during this period was the need for structural adjustment to promote economic growth. During 1985-86 there was strong endorsement by the Development Committee for expansion of lending to the heavily indebted countries so as to further structural and sectoral reforms. Simultaneously, the Development Committee kept in mind the interests of the poor, and advised that the adjustment programmes should be designed and implemented so as to minimise their adverse impact on the poor. It recommended targetted compensatory measures for those likely to be affected, and adoption of steps to generate employment, and to augment the income of the poor. Significantly, the Development Committee emphasised the importance of the industrial countries adopting policies that were supportive of the adjustment measures undertaken by the developing countries.

In mid-1982, the external debt crisis initially involving Mexico, thrust itself upon the financial world's attention, and the crisis soon deepened and engulfed other countries as well. This issue was to become pervasive in all the discussions of the Development Committee for several years thereafter, and to demand action. In the Spring and Fall meetings of the Development Committee held in 1985, the issue was comprehensively examined, and the Committee advised adjustment efforts as appropriate in each case for the heavily indebted countries, to be supported by adequate financial flows. The Development Committee was particularly concerned about the situation in the Latin American countries. The next significant measure was the initiative proposed by the then Secretary of the U.S. Treasury (the Baker initiative). The initiative involved, first, the continuance of the adjustment measures by the debtor countries; second, a continued central role for the IMF, in conjunction with increased lending by other multilateral institutions in support of market-oriented policies for growth; thirdly, increased lending by private commercial banks. The World Bank was assigned an increased role for assisting adjustment efforts within a consistent framework, which would strengthen growth prospects. While the debt crisis continued to cause concern, it was realised that besides the severely indebted middle income countries, other countries (e.g. low income countries) were also in difficulty. The next major development was the initiative proposed by the then U.S. Secretary of the Treasury, Mr. Nicholas Brady, in April 1989. For the first time, debt reduction was accepted (as had been urged by the Group of 24) which was to be supported by the World Bank and the IMF with resources set aside by these institutions for the purpose. The Bank and the Fund moved quickly to develop operational guidelines for support of voluntary debt reduction by commercial banks, rescheduling, and debt-service-charge reduction. The external debt crisis currently seems to be on the way to resolution, though it has entailed high costs on the part of the lending institutions, considerable sacrifices on the part of the debtor countries, and the diversion of substantial resources by the multilateral institutions, which could have been utilised to better purpose by assisting traditional bank-financed activities in the remaining developing countries.

While the debt problems of the severely indebted middle income countries hogged the limelight, other countries were also facing severe difficulties. Mr. Nigel Lawson, the U.K. Chancellor of the Exchequer took the initiative in September 1987 to lighten the debt burden of the low income countries in sub-Saharan Africa. The steps proposed were, first, the conversion of some loans into outright grants; second, rescheduling of other loans; and third, reducing the rate of interest generally. While the first two suggestions were accepted, consensus on the third, involving reduction of interest rates on non-concessional official loans, proved elusive. The Development Committee noted progress internationally on conversion of loans into grants, and the extension of grace and maturity periods by the Paris Club. The Committee agreed to encourage creditors and debtors to consider measures, where possible, for interest rate reduction in official rescheduling or alternative measures having a similar impact. A year later at the Berlin meeting (Fall 1988) against the background of the debt relief measures agreed to earlier that year by the Toronto Economic Summit, and with the political support of the Development Committee, the meeting was able to note with satisfaction that the Paris Club had worked out a framework of options involving cancellation of a portion of debt, extension of maturities and concessional terms on market interest rates applicable to non-concessional debt.

In 1983, the Development Committee asked the Bank to put forward proposals which would allow an expansion of the Bank's lending programme, subject to financial prudence. The Bank had meanwhile intended to expand its lending by about 5% annually. The Eighth General Review of quotas for the IMF had taken place. In the Fall of 1983 discussions took place on the size of the appropriate Selective Capital Increase for IBRD consequent upon the revised IMF quotas. Within the suggested range of $ 3 billion to $ 20 billion, a consensus amongst the members was reached on an increase of about $ 8 billion. Negotiations for a selective capital increase of $ 8.4 billion were completed in 1984.

As already outlined elsewhere (vide Chapter 6), an intensive discussion took place in the Executive Board seeking to define the future role of the Bank. The issue was discussed by the Development Committee and it endorsed the broad consensus emerging from those discussions, calling for an expansion in the Bank's lending programme in order to respond more effectively to the needs of the borrowing members. The Committee called for a projection of the IBRD's lending during the ensuing five years, and its future financial requirements, including the possibility of a general capital increase (GCI). The issue was considered at the Seoul meeting (Fall 1985), and an important political consensus was reached, paving the way for a GCI. A year later the Development Committee concluded that a substantial GCI would be required, and at successive meetings, it exerted considerable pressure for an expeditious conclusion of the deliberations for a GCI. By the Spring of 1988, the Development Committee was able to welcome the agreement on a $ 74.8 billion increase in the capital of the IBRD.

In the Spring of 1990, further discussions on the role of the Bank group took place. In keeping with the general philosophy of the Bank, the Development Committee encouraged the Bank to accord very high priority to private sector development, and also to achieve full coordination within the Bank group so as to ensure that private sector considerations were more closely integrated with the Bank's operations. A capital increase for the IFC, which was under discussion, was encouraged, so that the IFC would have the resources to adequately fulfil its role of assisting private sector development.

The subject of IDA replenishments has been considered at some length in the relevant section. Suffice it to state here that the Development Committee was helpful in resolving the problem arising out of the lack of commitment authority under IDA-6 because of the U.S. stand. It was also helpful in getting the negotiations finalised for the subsequent replenishments.

The Development Committee has played a major and decisive role during the 1980s and subsequently in raising the level of international awareness about the plight of the sub-Sahara African countries. In 1981, a major study by the World Bank on sub-Saharan Africa, and an agenda for action to promote accelerated development, was considered by the Development Committee. The World Bank was asked to take the lead in promoting dialogue for joint action by African Governments, donors and international agencies with a view to promote accelerated growth. In response to the request made at Helsinki in the Spring of 1982, the World Bank formulated a specific programme of action. In the Fall of 1984, a joint programme of action prepared by the Bank was endorsed by the Development Committee. By January 1985, because of its efforts, a Special Facility for sub-Saharan Africa amounting to $ 1.2 billion was established. The Development Committee has been reviewing subsequent progress and maintaining a close watch.

As outlined elsewhere, the World Bank has geared itself fully to deal with environmental issues, and has ensured that its lending activities are fully integrated with measures to minimise environmental degradation. The Development Committee was fully attuned to these issues. Following the Brundtland Report, the topic 'Environment and Development' was discussed by the Development Committee in the Spring of 1988. A consensus emerged there that close linkages existed between development and the environment on the one hand, and between environmental degradation and poverty on the other. The Development Committee recognised that integrating environmental considerations into development projects would entail heavy costs for the developing countries. In the Fall 1989 meeting, the German Minister, Warnke, and the French Minister, Pierre Beregovoy, proposed studies of the mechanisms and the finances required to meet the environmental challenges confronting the developing world, and the establishment of a new facility within the Bank to assist developing countries with global environmental problems. The Committee encouraged the Bank's proposal of creating a Global Environmental Facility, and this body subsequently came into being.

It will be recalled that the key mandate given to the Development Committee when it was set up was to deliberate upon *all aspects* of the transfer of real resources to the developing countries in order to promote their economic development. It is proposed to consider how successful the Development Committee has been in fulfilling this crucial mandate. During the 1970s and 1980s, the Committee focussed on the slow growth of ODA, and its decline as a percentage of GNP in many donor countries. The Committee directed attention to the problems faced by the developing countries in gaining access to the capital markets of the industrial countries, and in promoting foreign direct investment in these countries. It also emphasised the need for an increase in the flows by multilateral financial institutions.

Probably influenced by the tougher stand on aid adopted by the Reagan administration, the budgetary constraints flowing from the incipient recession, and aid fatigue manifesting itself in the developed countries, the Development Committee set up a Special Task Force on Concessional Flows with Prof. John Lewis, of Princeton University as its Chairman; it had representatives from industrial countries, OPEC and other developing countries as its members. The Task Force was required to carry forward and widen the continuing study of the problems affecting the volume and quality of concessional flows and its effective use in the shorter and longer terms. The Task Force, which reported in July 1985, reached three broad conclusions, viz.,

1. that most aid has been productive and helpful to development,
2. that there is need for political leadership to play a role in strengthening support for aid, and
3. that donor Governments should redouble their efforts to increase aid flows to low income countries, particularly as ODA was forecast to grow by only about 2% annually for the rest of the decade, compared to 6% in the 1970s.

The Development Committee endorsed the report and urged all the Governments concerned to take account of these findings. It further called upon the World Bank to play a leadership role in following up the Task Force's recommendations, and to report progress to the Committee periodically. By Spring 1988, the Development Committee decided to address specifically as a major item on the agenda the "adequacy of all forms of resource transfers to all developing countries to enhance the momentum of their development." The focus was on the adequacy of Resource Flows to meet the needs of the highly indebted countries, of sub-Saharan Africa, and of low income Asia. It was accepted that low income Asia needed capital inflows which could be targeted to poverty reduction objectives.

It might be useful to pause here, and to revert to the labours of the above-mentioned Task Force, and to refer to some studies it commissioned to assist it in coming to the findings outlined above. One such was the Independent Consultant's Study on Aid Effectiveness, prepared by Prof. R.H. Cassen of the University of Sussex. This study provides some illuminating insights about the way aid functions, and the many factors that influence its effectiveness. It needs emphasising that the basic finding of the detailed and meticulous study carried out was that most aid *works* in terms of its own objectives. It adds that it can be said with confidence that most aid does obtain a reasonable rate of return. When considering the effectiveness of aid, it is not realised often enough that a good deal of aid takes on very difficult and innovative investments in the poorest regions of the world, often lacking the facilities taken for granted in advanced countries. As the report says, such investments are quite liable to go wrong. In fact, one is pleasantly surprised that the success rate for aid projects is nevertheless quite high, and failures are relatively infrequent, enabling the author of the report to state "one might conclude that the record compared well with the average for complex human endeavours."

The fact, however, remains that a significant proportion of aided projects does fail. The natural tendency would be to point an accusing finger at the recipient of aid for the failures. It can be conceded that in many cases the policies adopted by the recipient country, poor management and design shortcomings have contributed to these failures. However, these lapses, regrettable as they are, do *not* fully explain the failures, and as pointed out below, there are many other shortcomings, for which the recipient country cannot be held responsible, that militate against the full effectiveness of aid, and have a greater impact than the actions of the recipient. They are discussed below.

It has been found that the effectiveness of development assistance depends importantly on the breadth and depth of knowledge of conditions in recipient countries on the part of the donor. To build and maintain that capacity necessitates expenditure well beyond the feasibility of most bilateral donors.[12] It is in this respect that the World Bank scores a decisive advantage. Consequently, most bilateral aid is *ab initio* lacking in effectiveness, because the project is incompatible with the prevalent conditions in the recipient country.

The report finds that the principal measure to improve effectiveness, that arose out of their discussions, was simply that the funding of the multilaterals had to be at a level which permits them to fulfil their role, which is essential to the effectiveness of aid as a whole. It adds that the World Bank, in particular, has a critical role to play in aid coordination, in policy dialogue, in economic reporting, and in the analysis and evaluation of aid and its performance and policies. In short, this means that if aid is to be effective, it must be adequate for discharging the tasks in hand. We have elsewhere dealt at some length with the challenges faced by the World Bank, and the need for additional funds to meet the requirements of Eastern Europe, the countries of the former Soviet Union, and for the development of infrastructure, and the social sector, so essential for the amelioration of poverty in other developing countries. If the international community wants to ensure effective utilisation of aid, it must simultaneously ensure that funds are not provided in penny packets over an unconscionably long period, but promptly and in adequate measure. Elaborating on this aspect, the Cassen report argues that reduction of aid below some critical level means reduction in effectiveness. Experience confirms that the volume and the nature of development assistance strongly influences the kind and level of policy dialogue. *Continuity* of operation and exposure, has an important influence on the capacity for dialogue. Unless lending is regular, contact with the concerned agencies of the recipient is lost, and with it the multilateral "loses its seat at the policy level."[13]

Effectiveness of aid depends largely on practices and procedures adopted by the donors, either singly or collectively. Thus, donors should coordinate their efforts, and their procedural requirements so that recipients are not confronted with conflicting demands, and avoidable administrative labour is reduced. The Bretton Woods Commission had suggested that prime coordination should be carried out by the World Bank. The international community should empower the World Bank to effectively perform this role.

It is found that much bilateral assistance is directed to further the political and commercial interests of the donor. Frequently, aid is seen as yet another instrument of foreign policy, and large sums are spent by way of military assistance to particular favoured countries. With the end of the cold war, and the possibility of reduced tensions in the Middle East, the time would appear opportune, to improve the effectiveness of the available aid by directing it much more purposefully to economic growth, reduction of poverty, and improvement of living standards in the recipient countries. It is with some sadness that one has to highlight the findings in the Cassen Report that aid activities in a number of countries do *not* correspond to development priorities (para S. 47). The World Bank writes:

> "As aid budgets decline aid effectiveness becomes a paramount concern. D.A.C. donors are increasingly directing their aid to poverty reduction and to countries pursuing sound policies" (W. Debt Tables 1996, p. 26).

The onus for achieving greater efficiency is, therefore, neatly passed on to the recipients. On the other hand, the factual position is that aid is highly concentrated, and its allocation country-wise somewhat sub-optimal, if the objective is to benefit the largest number to the maximum extent feasible. Thus, during 1990-94, only some donors (viz. the Nordics, Portugal and the U.K.) allocated 70% of their cumulative net ODA flows to the low income countries. The four largest donors (France, Germany, Japan and the USA) directed on an average 44% of their aid to those countries. It would appear that a dollar of aid would go further and have greater utility in a low income country, rather than in a middle or high income country. Poverty is more pervasive in the former than in the latter groups. It is an interesting finding that the combined share of aggregate net ODA and official aid *going to low-income countries has been declining* from 52% of the total in 1990 to 45% in 1994. The shares of the middle income and high income groups have remained more or less stable at around 35% and 7% respectively. The share absorbed by the transition economies has risen from 4% in 1990 to 13% in 1994. These figures suggest that there has been diversion of aid from the poor to the not so badly off. The emphasis in this study that aid to the transitional economies should be *in addition* to the resources already allocated to the poor countries is justified by these figures.

A final word on tied aid may not be inappropriate at this stage. Such tying increases the cost to the recipient, as the equipment, works contract, etc. could have been purchased or executed on more favourable terms in most cases, if competitive global bidding had been permitted. Besides the initial expenditure, recipients have to bear the recurring expenditure of maintenance. Over the life of major items of plant and equipment, these maintenance costs add up to substantial amounts, perhaps exceeding the initial cost. There is little or no support from aid agencies to meet these recurring costs, and frequently the recipient country has to fend for itself. Many items are proprietary items, and the recipient country is left with no option but to purchase spares, etc. from the original suppliers at the price demanded, and irrespective of intrinsic worth. These remarks may be treated as an elaboration of the point made earlier that bilateral assistance furthers the commercial interests of the donor.

The issue about aid-effectiveness has been considered in some detail because of the Development Committee's pre-occupation with it. The Committee's communique of September 1993 states that the Development Committee believes it is more than ever important to enhance the effectiveness of development assistance, and proposes to address the matter again next year. In the communique of October 1994, several paragraphs are devoted to aid-effectiveness, and much of what is said is valid. There is the important admission that for aid to be most effective, it has to be adequate. Recipients are advised that appropriate domestic policies are essential if aid is to be effective. They are also told that strong administrative and institutional capacity is required for effective use of aid. Donors are called upon to collaborate with recipients, and told that best conditions and policies for aid cannot substitute for strong 'ownership' by recipient Governments and good governance. Significantly, the Development Committee clearly recognises that aid programmes should be consistent with the sound framework for macro-economic and structural policies put in place by the recipient country. These programmes should also be consistent with the country's own development priorities. The Committee correctly enjoins donors to coordinate and simplify aid procedures and practices, improve accountability, and make them more transparent. The Committee lent its support to the efforts of the DAC to reduce the use of tied credits. Overall, there is unequivocal support for the development of the private sector.

The counsel given by the Development Committee is unexceptionable so far as it goes. The criticism is that it does not go far enough, and leaves much unsaid that is even more significant. Further, what is not clear is the emphasis being given to aid-effectiveness, and its timing. The points mentioned are not new, as the Task Force under Prof. Lewis, and the study by Prof. Cassen made a decade ago, are comprehensive, covering these points besides some others. The emphasis on sound policies, good governance, and strong administration demanded from the recipients, may be mis-interpreted in the public mind, and suggest that aid funds are going down the drain. While there is welcome recognition that for effectiveness, aid must be adequate, there is no specific suggestion as to how such adequacy has to be ensured. Meanwhile, the target of 0.7% of GNP for aid adopted by the U.N. and re-affirmed at the Rio conference, seems to be receding ever further into the background. There is also no mention of the need for aid to achieve a minimum critical volume in order to be effective, and for a certain degree of regularity and orderliness in its disbursement. On the contrary, the tendency is to make the quantum of aid dependent on the response of the recipient to the suggestions put forward during the policy dialogue. There is no attempt to rectify the declining share of ODA going to the low income countries, and the gross mis-allocation of aid, referred to above.

One could also expect the Development Committee to take the lead in the context of the vastly altered global conditions, and to suggest diversion of military aid to economic development and growth. The advantage of multilateral assistance is that it strives to be apolitical. Also, multilateral institutions have the capacity, the resources, and the strengths to assess the economic conditions in the recipient country, assess its financial and administrative capacity, and suggest schemes and projects which are best suited to the prevailing conditions, and are designed to meet the urgently-felt needs. Bilateral assistance often does not have the essential underpinning provided by prior economic and sector work. Overall effectiveness would improve if more bilateral assistance were to be channelled through multilateral institutions.

In recent years, the Development Committee has launched two important initiatives. The first concerns the heavily indebted poor countries. It was becoming increasingly apparent that even with the relief admissible under the Toronto terms and the Naples terms, some poor countries were finding the debt burden crushing and additional concessions were required. In October 1995, the Committee asked the Boards of the IMF and the World Bank to come up with a 'framework of action'. This document was duly considered at the April 1996 meeting of the Committee, and the Boards were requested to prepare a 'programme of action' based upon their preliminary proposals, after further study of the issues. The aim was to have this second document ready for consideration at the ensuing Annual Meeting of the Fund and the Bank. The suggestions made in the 'framework' have been outlined and commented upon where necessary in Chapter 6, and the reader is referred to that chapter.

The second initiative concerned the role of the multilateral development banks (MDBs) in the light of the recent vast economic changes, and the task of efficiently coordinating their work. The Committee set up a Task Force for examining the issues in October 1994. Their report was considered by the Committee in April 1996, and the recommendations were generally approved, the MDBs being enjoined to act upon the recommendations of the Task Force as a matter of priority. The findings of the Task Force have been outlined and where necessary commented upon in Chapter 6, as important issues have been raised. The reader is referred to that chapter for further particulars.

The Development Committee comprises the Finance Ministers, or comparable dignitaries, of both the developed and the developing countries. It is difficult to think of a more influential and powerful group dealing with financial matters. If it so desires, it can give sound advice to the Bank and the IMF, and provide the appropriate guidance in formulating new policies for development. Various types of financial crises like the external debt crisis of the 1980s are likely to erupt from time to time, and the Development Committee should be able to provide expert guidance about the countervailing measures that the IMF and the World Bank should adopt, to limit damage and to restore normalcy.

There is a curious dichotomy in that while the Development Committee in its collective capacity suggests more ODA, its members from the industrial countries pay scant heed to these suggestions. While the Development Committee has considerable achievements to its credit, much more should be expected from such a powerful group, particularly with regard to achieving the U.N. target of 0.7% of GNP for ODA, and in respect of future IDA replenishments.

That humankind lives in an inter-dependent world is now universally recognised. The interactions between the developed countries and the developing countries can either be of immense mutual benefit, or can lead to deleterious consequences, depending upon how these countries conduct their affairs. Trends towards increasing globalisation have accentuated this inter-dependence. The policies followed by the developed countries, in particular, have a marked impact on the developing countries. Budgetary constraints, and large fiscal deficits in the advanced countries influence interest rates. In turn, developing countries find their debt servicing burden rising, and foreign direct investment also gets affected. Exchange rate fluctuations profoundly affect the debt servicing burden, besides disrupting trade. Business cycles, and recessions in industrial countries likewise impact on growth and development in the Third World. The creation of trading blocs such as the European Union, and NAFTA, have the tendency to shut out trade with the non-members, and deny them a fair share of trade. With the completion of the Uruguay Round of trade discussions, many issues relating to intellectual property rights, patents and services are likely to demand attention, and mutual goodwill in ample measure will be required for a satisfactory resolution of these issues. The setting up of the World Trade Organisation will also throw up problems, especially because its mandate requires it to strive for global comparability and to coordinate global economic policies. Its functions may, therefore, impinge on those of the IMF and the World Bank. The Development Committee may provide a useful forum for discussion of these ticklish issues, with Finance Ministers of both the developing and the developed countries being able to interact, and explore the possibility of harmonising policies to the mutual benefit of both groups. The Finance Ministers of both the groups can exchange notes and become sensitised to the problems and difficulties confronting their counterparts, in a relatively friendly and congenial atmosphere. Once a fair degree of goodwill and rapport is established, it should not be beyond the wit of the civil servants to identify the problem areas, and suggest pragmatic solutions of mutual benefit. Given the vast scope that the Development Committee has in focussing attention on crucial issues and problems, it is a pity that so much time should be spent on discussing aid-effectiveness, and that too, without coming to grips with the core issues determining such effectiveness.

For the Development Committee to function at or near its full potential, it will require some rethinking of the manner in which it is being serviced. Too limited a view is taken of the agenda to be placed before the Development Committee, and the writer's experience is that interested parties strive to restrict the items for consideration. Uncomfortable or controversial items get short shrift. The review of the Development Committee's work suggested a greater role for EDs, as the representatives of their respective Governments. Elsewhere, this study has also suggested a greater role for the EDs when negotiating IDA replenishments. The review's recommendation needs to be implemented and more intensive preparation well before the scheduled Development Committee meeting should help to focus attention on crucial issues, and make the subsequent discussions at ministerial level more vibrant and purposeful. There also seems to be scope for closer liaison between the Bank management and the officials of the member-Governments, particularly the G-7, which plays a powerful role. The practice of set speeches during the meeting is not conducive to fruitful dialogue and negotiations. Perhaps more time should be allotted to personal level discussions between the Finance Ministers on items that are of mutual interest.

In summary, it can be said that the Development Committee is a unique forum with enormous potentialities. It has considerable achievements to its credit as mentioned earlier, but these do not even come near to what it can and should achieve. It should be a much more effective group for guiding the Bank (and the IMF), and mobilising additional resources, at a time of bewildering change, if the world is to take full advantage of the emerging opportunities.

Notes and References

1. Annual Report, 1995, p. 204.
2. Annual Report, 1993, p. 56.
3. Annual Report, 1994.
4. IDA in Retrospect, p. 62/T.5.1.
5. Annual Report, 1993, p. 59.
6. Most of the figures, etc. quoted in the Chapter have been taken from the IFC's Annual Report, 1994.
7. 'Economist' of November 12th, 1994, Survey of Asian Finance, p. 10.
8. World Debt Tables, 1996, Vol. I, p. 9 et. seq.
9. MIGA Annual Report, 1992.
10. Much of the factual information in this section has been obtained from the World Bank publication 'The Development Committee—Its Origins and Achievements, 1974-1990'.
11. IBRD Governor's Resolution 294 of October 2nd, 1974; IMF Governors Resolution 29-9 of October 2nd, 1974.
12. Para 9.31 of Cassen Report, January 1985.
13. Para 9.39 and 9.40, ibid.

CHAPTER 5

THE WORLD BANK, ENVIRONMENT AND POVERTY

A. THE WORLD BANK AND ENVIRONMENTAL ISSUES

Chapter 2 on World Bank Lending has not touched upon environmental issues. The following pages attempt to rectify this omission. The activities of environmentalists in recent years have succeeded in arousing the consciousness of the public, and they have pointedly agitated against the World Bank, and the financial help it has extended to certain projects, which were deemed by the former to be detrimental to the environment.

It will perhaps be conceded that during the 1970s and the early 1980s, environmental issues did not command the attention of the World Bank and the project authorities to the extent that these do now. During the beginning of the writer's tenure as Executive Director, certain Indonesian and Brazilian resettlement and similar projects were approved by the Board, though these involved large scale felling of tropical virgin forests. It is noteworthy that these projects evoked little criticism either from individual Board members, or even from environmentalists. Soon afterwards, however, there were rumblings of disapproval. In particular, the then Canadian Executive Director was trenchant in his criticism of some earlier South American transportation projects, which he alleged, had a deleterious effect on the environment, and had been approved by the Bank without paying due heed to the environmental costs involved. The Bank's current attitude to environmental issues contrasts markedly with its earlier indifference.

To provide a sound underpinning for the Bank's strategy and

its approach to environmental issues, the World Development Report 1992 focussed on these issues, and analysed the wealth of factual material that was collected. The conclusions from this informative study are both relevant and significant for the design and adoption of a suitable strategy for development. There is the heartening finding that no conflict exists between sound development on the one hand, and the environment on the other. It states that continued, and even accelerated, economic and human development is sustainable and can be consistent with improving environmental conditions, *if* major policy, programme, and institutional shifts take place. The report cautions that without adequate environmental protection, development will be undermined, but without development, environmental protection will fail. Two types of policies are advocated, viz. those that build on the positive links between development and the environment, and those that break the negative links. The report stresses the need to reform industrial and agricultural practices so as to reduce pollution, waste and damage to the environment. The instruments to be relied upon for the purpose are price, tax and other economic incentives, and the creation of strong public institutions, which will ensure public participation, considered essential for sound policy-making, project design, monitoring and enforcement. The report stresses the need for early action to *prevent* environmental degradation in the first instance, pointing out that this would be much cheaper, and more effective, than attempting to reverse the damage at a later stage. The report also estimated the costs of enabling countries to develop in an environmentally sound manner. The figure mentioned was $ 75 billion annually, or about 1.4% of the developing country gross domestic product over the current decade. It was further pointed out that these environmental investments would require an expansion of private and official capital flows to developing countries. Even more significant was the recommendation that this expanded funding should be *additional* to the development aid that would otherwise be available.

Besides preparing the W.D.R 92 as an important input for the U.N. Conference on Environment and Development (UNCED) held at Rio de Janeiro in June 1992, the World Bank carried out much preparatory work on all the important issues at the conference, and sent a large delegation headed by the President himself, Mr. Preston. It is, therefore, not surprising to read in the Annual Report that the World Bank is fully seized of the importance of environmental issues, it has reorganised itself, and suitably strengthened the concerned departments, so that the requisite capability has been built into the system, and the lending activities can now address environmental issues when appraising and approving various projects. The Annual Report for 1992 mentions that of the 222 projects approved during the year, nineteen had *primarily* environmental objectives, and these represented lending of about $ 1.2 billion. In addition, the approved projects for that year included 43 other projects which addressed one or more environmental issues, though these were not the primary objectives, as was the case in the earlier 19 projects.[1] The report goes on to state that for the Africa region a National Environmental Action Plan (NEAP) is prepared for each country in consultation with the donors, and this plan provides the framework for integrating the country's economic and social development with the environmental issue. The report mentions that ever since 1989, an operational directive has been in force which mandates an environmental assessment for *all* projects that may have a negative impact on the environment. This directive appears to have been revised recently, streamlining the provisions, and also requiring that the people affected by Bank-supported projects have access to the information in the assessment. The report significantly highlights the over-arching importance given to environmental issues, and the prospect of yet closer scrutiny in future in the following words:[2] "As elsewhere in the Bank, the environmental strategy of the East Asia and Pacific and South Asia regions consists of combining more stringent environmental assessments of projects with a range of non-project activities designed to improve the ability of Governments to manage their resources". The implication, therefore, is that more stringent assessments will spill over from the concerned project or sector, to other activities of the Government as well. This should also be read with the statement that in *all* regions progress was made with the national environmental plans. These are not to be one time exercises, but are to provide a strategic framework for investment planning. The Bank also states that it has learnt that in future it should follow a more transparent and pro-active process of handling environmental issues.[3]

These statements provide an interesting background to what transpired with the Sardar Sarovar (Narmada) project in India. The project was approved and loans were sanctioned for it some years ago, even though it was known that the project involved the resettlement of large numbers from the areas that would be submerged by the impounded waters. The affected persons' cause was taken up by some influential and dedicated environmentalists, and agitations were organised not only in India, but also in the World Bank. This resulted in the setting up of an international Committee and its findings were not favourable. Eventually, the Government of India decided to withdraw the project from the World Bank, but to continue with the project on its own, foregoing any further loans from the World Bank. What transpired behind the scenes is not known, but can be surmised. The Government of India probably thought that enough was enough and the conditions stipulated by the Bank on environmental considerations were too onerous and costly to be acceptable. Doubtless, the World Bank must have heaved a sigh of relief that it was saved from any further controversy and embarrassment.

However, these developments raise some concerns. Large sums had already been spent with the full knowledge and consent of the Bank. The project is likely to go through in any case because of the backing and the resources of the Government of India, but perhaps with some delay, and considerable sacrifice, as the Bank support will be missed, leading to considerable escalation in costs. Meanwhile, the large number of beneficiaries, who far out-number the displaced persons, will have to forego the benefits from the project in the shape of irrigation, higher yields of foodgrains, and greater availability of power in an energy-starved region of the country.

The Bank was quick to respond to the developments concerning the Sardar Sarovar Project, and set up a task force[4] in 1993 to analyse 146 projects approved between 1986 and 1993, and having resettlement components. Nearly 2 million persons were in various stages of resettlement in these projects. The review appears to have re-affirmed the basic elements of the Bank's resettlement policy as it evolved since the 1980s, though it identified certain shortcomings, and specified some exacting norms, besides tightening supervision.

The basic elements of the Bank's resettlement policy are said to be:

(a) to avoid or minimise involuntary displacement wherever feasible,
(b) to assist displaced persons to improve upon their former living standards, or to at least restore them, upon resettlement,
(c) to pay compensation at replacement costs,
(d) to involve both the displaced persons, and the host organisations in the resettlement process,
(e) to provide adequate land, infrastructure, and other compensation for groups that may have *informal customary rights* to the land, etc. acquired for the project.

The task force seems to have delivered the important message that good resettlement is justified on both economic and ethical grounds. Poor resettlement has repercussions not only on the displaced persons but also on the host population and the regional economy. It can result in local resistance and deferring benefits from the project, while the resultant escalation in costs could well outweigh the marginal costs of a good resettlement package. Other relevant findings and follow up action are outlined below:

(a) The Bank should avoid or reduce displacement as much as possible through technical and social studies for project design and execution.
(b) All projects should internalise the full cost of resettlement and of the investments required for income restoration within the total project costs.
(c) The Bank could adopt the twin-project approach for large scale civil works. While the project proper could be assisted with IBRD funds, the resettlement and rehabilitation costs for the displaced persons could be funded with low cost IDA funds. The Xiaolongdi project in China is cited as an example, as it received a $ 110 million IDA credit for resettlement, besides a $ 460 million IBRD loan for the main project.
(d) While full implementation responsibility rests with the borrowing Governments, the Bank has assumed responsi-

bility to follow up carefully on performance, impacts and outcomes.

(e) The content and frequency of resettlement supervision will be further improved, and supervision missions will take place at least every 12 months. These missions will visit and inspect the sites where displacement and relocation occur. Regional units are also enjoined to prepare annual reports on projects with resettlement components.

There is much in the Bank's resettlement policy and the task force's recommendations that is unexceptionable, particularly the emphasis on good resettlement schemes, and the need to safeguard the interests of the displaced persons. Further, the twin-project approach to such projects deserves to be heartily welcomed, as the rehabilitation costs will be funded by soft IDA credits, and borrowers will be encouraged to take up sound rehabilitation packages, and thus ensure a square deal to the displaced persons, who suffer not only materially, but sometimes also psychologically, and therefore deserve sympathy. However, taken as a whole, there are some misgivings, which too should be placed on record.

Firstly, the informal and customary rights of the displaced persons are to be protected. Having regard to widespread encroachments, illegal acquisition of lands in forest areas, and unlawful activities such as grazing of cattle, poaching, and illicit removal of timber, it would be unjustified to burden the project with compensation for these unauthorised and surreptitious activities. Also, in the absence of formal documentation, the recognition or rejection of such informal and customary rights can be contentious.

Secondly, while restoration of living standards for the displaced is a laudable objective, it may not always be feasible to restore the same precise benefits in the rehabilitated mode. Land in populous countries is a scarce commodity and parity area-wise for the displaced persons may be impossible to achieve upon resettlement. Also, irrigated fertile land may be given for infertile dry land. In extreme cases, an agriculturist may have to be resettled in industry or in trade. The objective should be to at least restore original income levels.

Thirdly, the Bank seems to be assuming too great a responsibility by committing itself to follow up carefully on performance, impact and outcome of the project. Many extraneous factors can intervene, as Bank experience would corroborate, and mid-course changes may become necessary. The more the Bank intervenes actively, the more it will expose itself to criticism, constructive and destructive, from environmental groups and vested interests. It would be well advised to conduct its supervisory exercise at one remove, so that the borrowing Government is held squarely responsible, and has to face the critics. This aspect of the Bank's direct involvement in project execution has been further examined in Chapter 6.

The exacting resettlement requirements, and the tight supervision, coupled with the likelihood of intervention by the Bank during execution appear to present daunting challenges to posing multi-purpose projects, etc. with resettlement components for financing by the World Bank. The question of balancing such considerations thus needs to be addressed. Recent press reports[5] cause even greater disquiet. The retiring Managing Director of the World Bank (Mr. Ernest Stern) is reported to have hinted at the possibility of the World Bank pulling out of the business of financing multi-purpose development projects. The campaign waged by environmentalist groups against the Narmada and the Arun projects (the latter in Nepal) had a "chilling effect" on the World Bank. This retreat by the Bank is contemplated despite the realisation that it is the poor masses in the developing countries who will suffer the most because of the Bank's withdrawal from these multi-purpose projects, though those threatened with displacement will be able to continue with their life-style, however inadequate this might be.

Should not the World Bank take into account these other factors as well, and not succumb so readily to pressure from environmentalists? Should not the Bank steel itself to adopt the right course as determined by the experts, even if this means warding off criticism, and some controversy? It may be appropriate at this stage to pause, and ask what should be the answers to these questions, and in general what should be the rational and cost effective approach that the World Bank should evolve for dealing with environmental issues. The Bank is the premier developmental institution, and has the well-being of the developing countries at heart. Its thinking often influences the thinking of other financial institutions, such as the Regional International Banks, and the donor community generally. It is, therefore, vital that the World Bank should hit upon the correct approach. For the discussion to proceed on an informed basis, it may be in order to digress a little, and to consider the views of some authoritative and well-reputed bodies.

The World Commission on Environment and Development in its report "Our Common Future" (Brundtland Report) has made some suggestions of considerable relevance. Recognising that economic growth and development must obviously involve changes in the physical ecosystem, it has given content to the concept of sustainable development by stressing that such development should meet the needs of the present without compromising the ability of future generations to meet their own needs. This concept subsumes two further concepts, viz. first, there should be social equity not only between generations, but also within each generation. Sustainable development requires meeting the basic needs of all, and in particular the essential needs of the world's poor, to which over-riding priority should be given. Secondly, it recognises the limitations imposed by the state of technology and social organisation on the environment's ability to meet present and future needs.[6] The report goes on to recommend that the strategy of sustainable development requires the integration of economic and ecological considerations in decision making, and by way of elaboration calls for the ecological dimensions of policy to be considered at the same time as the economic, trade and other dimensions on the *same agendas by the same institutions,* whether national or international. The budgets of the concerned agencies should be so formulated that environmental considerations are built into the planning and implementation of all programmes and projects.[7] It accords priority to the diffusion of sustainability considerations throughout the work of all financial institutions, and considers the roles of the World Bank and the IMF to be crucial, because their lending conditions are being used as benchmarks by other institutions, e.g. commercial banks and export credit agencies. The World Bank is also enjoined to take account of these considerations in its own lending. Various international bodies, particularly the World Bank, are called upon to help the developing countries make the transition to sustainable development. The World Bank is singled out for playing an especially important role because it is the largest source of development finance, and it exerts significant influence on both developing countries and on donors owing to the pre-eminent position it has established over the years in formulating and handling policy issues. While acknowledging that the Bank has now developed a greater sensitivity to environmental issues in its lending programmes than before, the report terms it only a promising beginning, and calls for a fundamental commitment on the Bank's part to sustainable development. The demand is for the transformation of its internal structure and processes so as to ensure its capacity to carry it out.[8]

One of the inter-Governmental documents to emerge from the Rio conference of June 1992 was the 'Rio Declaration', a statement of environmental principles, which was originally conceived as an 'Earth Charter'. Some of these principles have a bearing on development and should be taken into account by policy makers in both the developed and developing countries. Principle (2) recognises a State's sovereign right to exploit its own resources pursuant to its own environmental and developmental policies, but it has a responsibility to ensure that its activities do not cause damage to the environment of other States. Principle (3) requires that the right of development must be fulfilled so as to equitably meet the development and environmental needs of present and future generations. Principle (4) states that environmental protection should constitute an integral part of the development process. Principle (6) states that the special situation and needs of the developing countries shall be given priority. Principle (12) enjoins that States should co-operate to promote a supportive and open international cooperative system. Trade policy measures for environmental purposes should not constitute a means of arbitrary and unjustifiable discrimination. Environmental measures addressing trans-boundary issues should be based on international consensus. Principle (16) states that national authorities should endeavour to promote the *internalisation* of environment costs taking into account the principle that the polluter bears the costs of pollution.

An important document to emerge from UNCED, which may have far-reaching consequences if handled cooperatively was Agenda 21. It is a comprehensive document which attempts to cover the entire development and environment agenda. Though signed by the participants, it is not a legally binding document, but rather a 'work plan' and an 'agenda for action'. With the backing of the U.N. General Assembly it may become 'soft law', and secure the political commitment to pursue a set of identified goals. The cost of implementing Agenda 21 has been estimated by the Secretariat of the Conference at $ 600 billion per annum, which includes $ 125 billion as grant of concessional assistance from the international community. As the document itself points out, these figures are indicative only and order of magnitude estimates, and have not been reviewed by the concerned Governments (Chap. 33, item 20). It will be recalled that the W.D.R. 92 estimate for measures which would enable countries to develop in an environmentally sound manner was only $ 75 billion p.a., and it had presumably set its sights more realistically. The negotiations regarding resources appear to have been the most difficult, and what emerged was merely a reaffirmation by the developed countries of their previous commitment to reach the accepted U.N. target of 0.7% of G.N.P. for ODA, and to the extent they have not achieved the target, they agreed to augment their aid programmes in order to reach the target *as soon as possible.*[9] An interesting side issue is that neither the USA nor Switzerland were touched by the reaffirmation, since they had not accepted the target of 0.7% of GNP initially. In any case, the wording is such that even the other countries were merely recording their intent to move towards the target when circumstances so warranted. The problem of resources is thus likely to prove perennially difficult. As in the Rio declaration, the key issue of integrating development with the protection of the environment was also considered in Section I (Chapter 8) of Agenda 21. The need to integrate environmental factors into policy making, law, economic instruments, and national accounting appears to have been stressed. The document candidly mentions that environmental standards may pose severe economic and social costs if these are uniformly applied in developing countries. The primary need is identified as the integration of environmental and developmental decision-making processes. It advocates a national review, and improvement in the decision-making processes so as to achieve progressive integration of economic, social and environmental issues in pursuit of development. However, the emphasis on a *domestically* formulated policy framework, the establishment of *domestically* determined ways and means to ensure coherence of sectoral, economic and environmental policies, etc. is unmistakable, and seems to be motivated by a desire to eliminate outside interference. The document mentions the need to reverse the tendency to treat the environment as a 'free good', and favours the increasing use of economic approaches, and a market orientation, e.g. the polluter-pays principle and the natural-resource-user-pays principle. As a corollary, introduction of systems of integrated environmental and economic accounting (IEEA) are suggested.

While the suggestions, etc. are unexceptionable, the layman may be left wondering what the practical implications are likely to be. A high level of technical competence is an essential pre-requisite and the skilled manpower may be difficult to find and deploy in developing countries. Also, Governments must be in a position to find the resources in both finances and material to make these suggestions workable. More often than not Governments are distracted by a series of emergencies, e.g. plague epidemics, natural calamities, subversive militancy from across the international border posing threats to territorial integrity, and by acute budgetary constraints. All the proposals call for large funds, and enlightened political leadership, before these can yield tangible results, which are likely only in the long term.

Disputes regarding terms for the transfer of environmentally sound technology were resolved with a statement in Section 4, Chapter 34, that enhanced access to technology should be promoted, facilitated and financed as appropriate. However, simultaneously the industrialised nations ensured that a provision should be added requiring States to take measures to prevent the abuse of intellectual property rights. Because of the technological lead established by the industrial countries, the developing countries will perforce have to depend upon the former for environmentally sound and efficient processes, and for treatment of pollutants, etc. One can only hope that up-to-date technologies will be transferred, and industrial countries will refrain from charging unfair and prohibitively costly fees.

Section 4, Chapter 39 dealt with some controversial issues concerning large scale environmental destruction that cannot be justified under international law. The issue was eventually restricted only to war-time activities, and a lukewarm suggestion to refer it to the General Assembly and its sixth Committee followed. The other issue of some importance for development purposes was the possibility of framing environmental standards so as to operate as trade barriers. The document recognises that environmental policies should deal with the root causes of environmental degradation and unnecessary restrictions on trade should be avoided. [Chap. 39.2, sub-para (d)]. There follows the caveat: "Trade policy measures for environmental purposes should not constitute a means of arbitrary or unjustifiable discrimination or a disguised restriction on international trade". Should trade policy measures, nevertheless, be found necessary for enforcement of environmental policies, these should be non-discriminatory and transparent. The need to give consideration to the special conditions and development requirements of the developing countries was stressed. Undoubtedly, the framework set out by Agenda 21 appears equitable, but the moot question is how far these well-meaning principles will be followed in practice, especially in difficult times. The tendency would naturally be to protect domestic industry and employment at the cost of international understandings, and to devise clever measures for circumventing the uncomfortable provisions. In such a situation, trade restrictions on ostensibly environmental grounds could come in handy, and the international community should be prepared to combat such moves. Naturally, developing countries will have to be ever vigilant. The discussions here are reminiscent of the provisions of Principle (12) of the Rio declaration, and are symptomatic of the apprehensions of developing countries that on some pretext or other, their access to the markets of the industrialised countries will be denied to them.

To round off the discussion, it might be appropriate to refer to the Global Environment Facility (GEF). It started as a three-year pilot project that provides grants for investment projects, technical assistance, etc. The four programmatic areas that it dealt with initially were climate-change, ozone layer depletion, pollution of international waters, and biodiversity. Responsibility for implementing the GEF is shared amongst the UNDP, UNEP, and the World Bank, the last named being the administrator, and the repository of the $ 1 billion Trust Fund. This facility has been a bone of contention between the developing and the developed countries, with the former demanding more transparency, and universal membership, while the latter have been suspicious and apprehensive that the resources would be wasted by inefficient policies, and have been demanding more reliable oversight mechanisms, and stricter screening of proposals. In April 1992, the participating Governments agreed to a restructuring of the facility. The UNCED appears to have endorsed the proposals. Universal membership was seen as a key to the Facility's success. Matters would normally be decided by consensus. However, where this did not prove possible, a voting system would be developed that guaranteed a balanced and equitable representation of the interests of developing countries, while giving due weight to the financing efforts of donors. The scope of the Facility was enhanced by adding to the initial four programmatic areas, a new item, viz. reversing land degradation, primarily desertification and deforestation. An important development was the designation of the Facility as the financial mechanism for the climatic change and biodiversity conventions. There was also agreement that the Facility was the appropriate financial mechanism to cover the agreed incremental costs of measures designed to achieve global environmental benefits. The Annual Report of the Bank mentions that fiscal year 1992 was the first full year of activity of the GEF, and that six investment projects had been approved. Besides, as of June 30th, 1992, the GEF was considering over 70 projects worth $ 580 million.

The Annual Report of the Bank for 1995 also comments on the GEF. The World Bank continues to play a crucial role,

(a) being the trustee, and as such responsible for raising resources,
(b) being the agency for implementing GEF projects, and
(c) providing administrative support for the GEF secretariat.

The Bank appears to have decided to treat regular Bank projects and GEF projects implemented by the Bank alike; thus, the latter projects have to adhere to the project cycle, are approved by the Board, and are subject to portfolio-performance reviews. The scale of operations of the GEF may be of interest. Through the end of fiscal year 1995, 148 projects worth $ 869 million had been endorsed by the GEF participants and the new Council. Of these, 63 projects worth $ 558 million were allocated for World Bank/GEF investment projects. On an average, therefore, these projects were costing less than $ 9 million each, and thus must be adjudged to be minor projects compared to projects regularly financed by the Bank. The allocation by focal areas is as follows:

Areas	(Percentages)
Biodiversity	50
Climate change	30
International waters	12
Reduction of Ozone depleting substances	7
Multiple thematic areas	1
Total	100

It is noteworthy that since 1992, there has not been a spectacular surge in projects taken up by the GEF. It is also disappointing that land degradation, which is of great significance to the Third World countries, has not been given prominence.

Having regard to the expanded mandate and the designation of the Facility as the appropriate financial mechanism for these activities, the Trust Fund of $ 1 billion (subsequently raised to $ 2 billion) appears minuscule especially in the light of its expanded role. For the body to be effective, there has to be a major spurt in its activities, and it should be provided all the necessary resources by way of finances, manpower and infrastructure. The international community will, therefore, have to mount a major effort to make the Facility truly beneficial, and statesmanship and vision of the highest order will be demanded for a genuine cooperative endeavour to emerge.

With the passage of time, public awareness of ecological damage caused by poorly designed projects has become pervasive, both in developed and developing countries. Issues such as global warming and depletion of the protective ozone layer raise widespread concern. Environmental groups are often able to raise controversial issues concerning most major projects. Some groups are well organised and articulate, and can touch responsive chords in the highest echelons of various Governments and international financial institutions. Where serious damage to the environment is a genuine issue, the activities of such groups are to be warmly welcomed, but cases also arise where there is opposition to a project merely for the sake of opposition, and the benefits from a sorely needed project are denied indefinitely to a deserving section of society. A mechanism should be devised and put in place for distinguishing between these two categories, and maintaining a proper balance, so that the greatest good occurs to the largest number.

The emphasis given by the World Bank to sustainable development is to be warmly welcomed, and in principle, the holistic approach linking both development and ecological aspects is commendable. This approach is fully backed by principle 4 of the Rio Declaration. The Bank has followed up its statements by positive action, and it is significant that in fiscal year 1994 lending in support of environmentally sustainable development totalled $ 10.203 billion or 49% of total Bank lending. Developing countries are always short of resources and it would be prudent for them to build in, even at the initial stage, costs required for environmental protection and sound resource management, so as to prevent damage, rather than be obliged to undertake costlier restorative measures at a later stage. While commending the assumption of added responsibilities by the Bank for safeguarding the environment, it may be only proper to draw attention also to certain implications which may cause concern amongst the developing countries.

Much of the present pollution, and degradation of the environment including the greenhouse effect, and the depletion of the ozone layer, can be attributed to the activities of the developed countries, both in the past and during present times. This is so both because of the much larger scale of their industrial and energy operations as also of the longer time horizon within which their industries have been operating, as compared with those of the developing countries. On the contrary, the developing countries have only recently embarked on large scale industrialisation. The per capita energy consumption for low income countries is 330 kg. of oil equivalent (kg.o.e.) compared with 5,182 kg.o.e. for OECD member countries (W.D.R. 1991, Table 5). The middle income developing countries have an intermediate level of 1,242 kg.o.e. Growth and development will necessarily entail an increased level of energy consumption by the developing countries over their current low levels, even if account is taken of possible energy conservation measures, and improvements in efficiency. It will be recalled that the Rio Declaration recognised a State's sovereign right to exploit its own resources pursuant to its developmental and environmental policies, provided it did not damage the environment of other States. Thus no checks can, or should, be imposed thwarting the process of development, subject of course, to essential safeguards. It will be generally accepted that as the system approaches its ecological limits, inequalities will sharpen. The poor will be harder hit, and late-comers in the industrial field will suffer more from the effects of depletion of mineral resources, while the rich with their greater resilience will be able to cope better with emerging difficulties. The strategy of the international institutions and of the enlightened Governments in the industrialised countries should be to devise and implement measures to ameliorate the lot of the poorer countries, even if this entails a modicum of sacrifice by the richer countries, so that all can benefit from a cooperative endeavour.

Poverty, and particularly abject poverty, causes major ecological damage, and is a phenomenon confined almost solely to the developing countries. The poor are compelled to cultivate marginal lands, or lands encroaching on the spill area of rivers, causing damage to the soil, and interfering with drainage. They may also encroach on depleted forests just to eke out a living, and tribals may over-exploit forests, which are already being progressively depleted because of diversion of land to agriculture, industry and multi-purpose projects. Poverty militates against the use of resources in a sustainable manner. The Brundtland report states categorically that a necessary, but not a sufficient, condition for the elimination of absolute poverty is a relatively rapid rise in per capita income in the Third World. It estimates that overall national income growth of around 5% a year in the developing economies of Asia and 6% per year in Africa would be required to significantly reduce poverty, having regard to current population growth.[10] Estimates of the time required may also be of interest. With a static population, and a per capita income growth of 3% per annum, coupled with the re-distribution of 25% of the incremental income of the richest one-fifth of the population, 18 years would be required to reduce the poverty ratio from 50% to 10%, which is an unconscionably long period in a fast-changing world.

Rapid growth will only result from a major developmental thrust. It is almost axiomatic that any significant developmental endeavour has an impact on the environment. This is the basic problem that has to be resolved equitably by the world community. Large dams constructed to generate hydro-electricity, or to provide irrigation, result in submergence of inhabited areas, or of forest lands. Coal-fired power stations call for large investments in new mines, which can scar the countryside, and burning coal can exacerbate the greenhouse effect, besides polluting the atmosphere not only with noxious gases, but also with particulate matter. Clearly, the attempt should be to minimise these environmental costs, and to design the project specifically with this objective in view, using the most modern and effective 'clean' technologies. Afforestation of the upper catchment areas of dams can more than offset the loss of forest cover caused by submergence besides checking soil erosion. Resettlement of displaced persons can be carried out humanely, and their quality of life improved. Experience with some of the dams constructed by the Damodar Valley Corporation in eastern India would show that these aspects were given due attention even decades ago. Electrostatic precipitators can reduce the discharge of particulate matter from power stations, etc. and sufficiently high smoke stacks can spread the gaseous emissions over a wider area, and so reduce concentration levels and damage.

Efforts of environmental groups could profitably be channelised into ensuring that environmental aspects are given proper attention by the project authorities, and adequate provisions are made during the planning stage itself for measures deemed necessary to minimise the environmental damage. It would, of course, be incumbent on the decision-makers to ensure that the overall benefits flowing from a major project far outweigh the environmental costs. Perhaps, constructive criticism along these lines by environmental groups would serve the community better than destructive criticism focussed on scuttling the project as a whole, which might cause irreparable harm to a far larger section of the community than those directly affected by submergence, etc.

There can be no gainsaying that the ameliorative measures designed to minimise ecological damage will entail heavy expenditure as the earlier illustrations will show. Other instances come to mind where the additional burden resulting from environmental considerations will be even heavier, e.g. industrial projects calling for treatment of effluents to comply with internationally accepted safety standards, and chemical plants handling noxious and dangerous chemicals. It will be recalled that these costs have been estimated at $ 600 billion per annum in Agenda 21. Developing countries face a chronic shortage of capital, and these additional demands, generated by environmental considerations place crippling burdens on them. As earlier mentioned, newcomers and the poor are already handicapped, as compared with the rich industrialised countries. The environment, however, is a common heritage, for rich and poor alike, and minimising damage benefits all. A powerful case can, therefore, be made out not only for the transfer of much larger resources to the developing countries for tackling ecological issues, but also for softer terms, as the benefits would not be restricted only to the developing countries, but would also spread to the developed countries. The World Bank can lend its powerful support to make such transfers not only possible but also significant, though the current climate for aid is not propitious.

The Brundtland report has drawn attention to the crucial role that the World Bank can play in dealing with environmental issues. Some elaboration of this theme, in the context of its lending activities may be in order. The Bank has enormous experience world-wide covering a vast array of projects in many sectors, and spanning decades, and therefore can be expected to give invaluable advice on environmental issues that has crystallised out of this experience. The Bank is also unique in that this experience is recorded, and is readily retrievable. It has the further advantage of being able to hire the best consultants to provide expert advice when required. Environmental safeguards, which are deemed necessary in densely populated industrialised and urban communities of the rich nations could be safely relaxed for plants, etc. installed in the rural or semi-urban areas of the developing countries. The degree of sophistication and instrumentation demanded in rich countries may also call for modification if used in a country with ample manpower, and relatively low wages. The Bank should be in a position to guide and counsel on the type of environmental safeguards best suited to the specific conditions prevailing in the borrowing country, and thus reducing costs. Agenda 21, Chapter 34 does discuss the promotion, facilitation, and financing of enhanced access to technology for environmental purposes. The Bank has a useful role to play in this context because of the strengths it has developed. The Bank has for long scrutinised rates and tariffs for electricity, water, fertilisers, etc. The experience it has acquired, and the capability it has developed in laying down conditions, etc. could be utilised for environmental purposes also. The Rio Declaration referred to the internalisation of the environmental costs (Principle 16) taking into account the principle that the polluter should bear the cost of pollution. When approving loans for projects, etc., and scrutinising the rates and the tariffs, the Bank could, with advantage, combine the financial and economic viability aspects with the environmental aspects and the principles of making the polluter and the natural resource user pay.

Environmental groups are likely to be more active in the years to come and to take their pleadings to the World Bank, demanding that no funds be provided for particular projects, citing likely environmental damage. It is to be hoped that the Bank will take a balanced and sensible view on these pleadings, and projects will not be discarded on emotive grounds. Recent press reports that the World Bank is contemplating withdrawal from all multi-purpose development projects, therefore, cause serious disquiet. It is to be further hoped that a rational and scientific view would be taken by the Bank both of the likely benefits from the project, and the costs to the environment, after all feasible measures have been built into the estimates for minimising the ecological damage. After verifying their credentials, the Bank will doubtless give these groups a sympathetic hearing, and for its own image as well as for the benefit of the community take note of the useful suggestions made in the course of the discussions. Clearly a balanced and objective view will be required so that corrective measures are not thrust forward irrespective of the costs in time and money. In any case final decisions will have to be taken by the project authorities and the borrowing country, though the Bank would have a major role to play in giving expert technical advice, augmenting resources and smoothening the discussions, which may sometimes prove stormy.

The environmental dimension for most projects has now become highly significant, and is a cause of some concern. Developing countries whose resources are exiguous, feel that besides securing financial sanction, and obtaining the approval of other affected departments, and of the planning authorities, they now have yet another hurdle to clear from the environmental angle. Moreover, the additional costs required to protect the environment have to be arranged for, and in the process may adversely affect the economics and financial viability of the project. The ecological dimension will also be scrutinised closely by the Bank, and may further lengthen the Bank's already protracted project cycle.

The need to integrate development with the protection of the environment is generally accepted, as is the incorporation of environmental factors into policy making and economic instruments (vide Rio Declaration and Agenda 21, Ch. 8), but what requires clarification is the manner of doing so, and its timing. The Bank's annual report, as mentioned earlier, promises the combination of a more stringent environmental assessment of projects with a range of non-project activities designed to improve the ability of Governments to manage their resources. Some caution may be indicated here, as the Bank should be pragmatic, and should not start chasing environmental will-o'-the-wisps to the detriment of much needed development. The old adage of the greatest good to the largest number is still valid, and perhaps we all have something to learn following the withdrawal of the Narmada project from the World Bank. The pendulum may have swung a trifle too far and could move back to centre in the overall interest.

B. THE WORLD BANK AND POVERTY REDUCTION

We have earlier made the point that poverty, particularly abject poverty, causes major ecological damage. The World Development Report 1992 reinforces the same point and has identified a number of links across a wide range of issues (including agriculture, forestry, water-supply, sanitation, energy, industry and biodiversity) between poverty, environmental protection, and demographic factors. No sophistication is required to appreciate the reasons for some of these links. Poor people, living at or near the subsistence level are prone to eke out a living by over-utilisation of the land, water and forestry resources, to the long term detriment of these resources, and therefore, contribute to environmental degradation. Alleviation of poverty consequently subserves the objective of environmental protection. It was felt that because of these links, the section on poverty reduction could be juxtaposed with that on the environment.

Since Mr. Robert McNamara's address to the Board of Governors at Nairobi,[11] poverty alleviation and related issues have been continuously addressed by the World Bank, and many studies have been undertaken to understand the problem, assess its extent, and to suggest practical measures for the benefit of the poor. Under Mr. Clausen, though poverty reduction remained an important issue, some slackening in the momentum to devise positive measures for dealing with the issue could be discerned. Mr. Clausen himself was well-intentioned, and there could be no mistaking his sense of shock when first exposed to the depth of rural poverty in India. He was appalled when he visited a rural homestead in Lakshimpur Kheri (Uttar Pradesh) while inspecting some large irrigation projects in India. However, there were many pressing problems which demanded much of his time and energy, e.g. the attitude of the Reagan administration, IDA replenishment and the prospective General Capital Increase, and these good intentions were not translated into positive measures.

In recent years, the World Development Report of 1990, suggested a strategy for tackling poverty. Based on a review of experience gained in various countries, a key element for reducing poverty was the promotion of broad-based growth, making efficient use of the only resource that the poor have in abundance, viz. human labour. This was complemented by easier access to basic social services, including primary education and health services. The suggestions made in the WDR 1990 were seminal, and according to a recent World Bank publication[12] it has been increasingly placing poverty reduction at the centre of the policy dialogue and its country assistance strategies. This publication points out (p. 13) that the concern with poverty reduction is particularly evident in the ways in which the composition of the Bank's lending has changed. However, some of the figures cited substantiate this statement only partially. Poverty-focussed sectors are identified as human resource development, agriculture and rural development, and finally water supply and sanitation. While total lending in dollar terms in these sectors has increased from $ 4.77 billion per annum in 1981-83 to $ 7.8 billion per annum in 1990-92, as a share of total Bank lending, in percentage terms there has been a marginal fall, i.e. from 37% in 1981-83 to 36% in 1990-92. Nevertheless, the emphasis on human resource development, which impacts most on the poor, is unmistakable, as its share of total Bank lending has risen from 5% in 1981-83 to 14% in 1990-92. The monetary figures for this item are impressive—from $ 659 million per year in 1981-83 to $ 3.028 billion per year in 1990-92 or well over a four-fold increase. This share further rose to 16% in fiscal year 1993 (Governance—1994 World Bank). However, lending for agriculture and rural development has been somewhat stagnant at a little over $ 3.5 billion per year, even though it has a vast potential for generating employment in the rural areas. (p. 17, ibid)

The World Bank being an international financial institution, and subject to tight control by its Executive. Board, is particular that funds are spent efficiently, and poverty reduction projects do not have relaxed standards. It is laid down:

> "Bank financed poverty reduction projects must pass the same economic tests that apply to other projects. They must have a satisfactory economic rate of return . . . . Rather than relaxing the standard investment criteria for Bank financing of projects, greater operational attention should be paid to identifying projects and project designs that *both benefit the poor and have high returns* . . . ."
>
> —O.D. 4.15 quoted in Wapenhans Report, Ann. C, p. 17

The World Bank's approach to poverty reduction is comprehensive and systematic, as is only to be expected from an organisation with a high calibre professional staff providing the intellectual inputs. Poverty assessments have been carried out or are proposed to be completed in 88 countries by end of 1995. These assessments are meant to provide the basis of collaboration between the borrowing country officials and the Bank and to identify the economy-wide policies, the institutional factors and the public expenditure patterns which are inhibiting poverty reduction. Further, the objective of these exercises is also to assess how far the Government's long term management of the economy is helping to generate the kind of growth that will create efficient demand for labour, and develop human capital. The World Bank's view, that *all* public policies affect the poor either for better or for worse, has been sought to be buttressed by the findings of selected studies on the impact of reform upon poverty, outlined in the 1993 publication referred to earlier (Box 11, p. 29). In India's case, it was claimed that reducing macro-economic imbalances, implementing policies to promote growth, and encouraging efficient labour demand were the most important ways of bringing about a sustained improvement in the incomes of the poor. Reduction in tariffs, especially on capital goods, and reforming the licencing system were said to encourage demand for labour. The experience so far in India is not very clear cut. For these reforms to take hold and to produce tangible results takes time; initially after the reforms, industrial production slackened, and it is only some three years later, that it is again picking up. It is not surprising, therefore, that simultaneously the Bank calls for safety nets for the vulnerable, and emphasises targeted programmes. In the longer term, the Bank's advocacy of improving access of the poor to better basic education, and improved health care, is sound and calls for universal support. This emphasis on policy issues entails very close scrutiny of public expenditure, and it is significant that under the rubric of deepening implementation strategy, public expenditure finds mention thrice in a couple of pages, the last being as follows:

> "At the top of the agenda is the need to give greater attention to the incidence, composition, and management of public expenditures" (ibid, p. 37)

While the World Bank's efforts at poverty reduction are commendable, and the suggested remedy of providing employment for the poor is sound, it is to be hoped that its decision-makers will not put the policy dialogue into a straitjacket. Within developing countries, circumstances and conditions differ markedly, and the development process is still not fully understood. Remedies and approaches to development will necessarily have to be country-specific, and tailored to the particular needs and strengths of the concerned country. While labour intensive activities, and the generation of employment opportunities for the poor have their proper place, some caution has to exercised in scrutinising public expenditure and in thrusting policy options upon the borrower. Technology is developing rapidly, and the developing countries have a lot of leeway to make up. Over-emphasising employment generation should be tempered by the need for the introduction of new and sophisticated technologies in the developing countries also, to ensure that the technology gap does not widen further, and these countries are not condemned in perpetuity to be suppliers of raw materials and primary commodities to the industrialised countries, with a leavening of some low value exports of simple and unsophisticated manufactures. The concerned Governments in the developing countries, and the peoples' representatives should be credited with the necessary insights to decide what is best for the economic growth of these countries in the specific prevalent conditions. Adoption of sophisticated technologies calls for a high level of trained manpower, and a well-developed educational and industrial base, which is closely associated with research institutions keeping abreast of current advances. Such endowments and facilities take time to develop, and a danger to be guarded against is that initial efforts in this direction for modernising a country, should not be thwarted because of a misplaced zeal to create more employment at relatively low wages, and to curtail public expenditure. Similar cautions are relevant for defence expenditure and defence research, which have been commented upon elsewhere. While one may have differences over some of the nuances in the policies suggested by the World Bank for the reduction of poverty, there can be no doubting its earnestness in dealing with this scourge. It has adopted a highly focussed approach on its own part, and simultaneously given incentives to the borrowers to take effective steps for the reduction of poverty as the following illustration demonstrates. IDA credits are much sought after by borrowers because of the generous terms. Even in the 1970s, the extent of poverty, the performance of the borrower in implementing World Bank programmes, and the creditworthiness of the borrower (with a negative correlation) were factors in allocating IDA credits, which were perpetually in short supply. The Bank publication of 1993 on poverty, referred to earlier, indicates that IDA allocations have been used as powerful incentives for borrowers to pay greater heed to poverty reduction. Instead of the earlier passive criterion of the extent of poverty, currently the determinant used is the Government's commitment for reducing poverty. The quality of the Government's short and long term economic management is taken into account. It is ascertained whether the policies adopted have succeeded in generating the kind of growth that makes productive use of labour, in expanding the delivery of social services to the poor, and improving the effectiveness of the safety nets. The publication points out that as a result, per capita allocations have been more sharply differentiated in recent years. During the ninth IDA replenishment, it is claimed that amongst IDA-only countries, those in the top twenty-fifth percentile in terms of poverty effort have received per capita allocations that are about four times higher on average than the allocations to countries in the lowest twenty-fifth percentile. During the eighth IDA replenishment, the corresponding factor was about three in favour of the top twenty-fifth percentile in terms of poverty effort (*source*: ibid, p. 16, Box 6). It is perhaps not a mere coincidence that in India's case concessional aid in 1994-95 will be 43%[13] as compared with the corresponding figure of 28% in 1993-94. Of this concessional aid of $ 6 billion, as much as $ 3.5 billion came from IDA, and the rest mostly from bilateral donors.

Without being termed parochial, attention is proposed to be invited to certain figures and comments in the above-mentioned publication of the World Bank. The number of poor in Eastern Europe in 1990 was estimated at 5 million. The corresponding figure for South Asia is 562 million. The head count index for the same year is shown as 7.1% for Eastern Europe and 49% for South Asia. The Annual Report, 1994, estimates that South Asia is home to half the world's poor. It is claimed that poverty exists in Eastern Europe, and during the economic transition, it is increasing in some of these countries. Poverty reduction efforts are to be concentrated on investments for social protection and human resource development. There can be no doubt that the international community should assist the poor of Eastern Europe, particularly during the period of economic transition that they are currently undergoing. However, it is incumbent on the international community and the international financial institutions to provide the necessary wherewithal for the purpose as an *additional* amount, so that the poor of the Third World, and of South Asia in particular, are not called upon to sacrifice for their brethren in Eastern Europe, who may be relatively better off, especially in the long term. The depth of poverty in South Asia, and the lack of endowments is far more severe than what prevails in Eastern Europe. The situation is further aggravated by the prevailing high population density in South Asia, which puts enormous pressure on the land etc., and by the unremitting growth in numbers despite population control measures. The figures already cited show how much more pervasive the poverty problem is in the Third World. The plea is for a balanced and rational approach that is equitable for all.

Notes and References

1. Annual Report, 1992.
2. Ibid., p. 56.
3. Ibid., pp. 58-59.
4. Annual Report, 1994, p. 44, Box 3.2.
5. *Economic Times*, 28th January, 1995.
6. P. 43, et seq, Brundtland Report.
7. Pp. 62, 313, 323, ibid.
8. Pp. 78 and 337, ibid.
9. Section 4, Chapter 33.
10. P. 50, Brundtland Report.
11. Speech to Board of Governors, 1973.
12. Implementing the World Bank's Strategy to Reduce Poverty, 1993.
13. *Statesman*, July 7th, 1994.

CHAPTER 6

The Changing Role of the World Bank and Its Place in the Emerging World Order

As mentioned earlier, initially the World Bank was primarily concerned with project lending dealing with traditional power, irrigation, railway and transportation projects. During Mr. Robert McNamara's long and dynamic stewardship, not only did the Bank increase the quantum of its annual lending manifold, but also a new thrust was imparted to its activities. In his Nairobi annual meeting speech, Mr. McNamara emphasised the poverty aspect,[1] and this was in keeping with the extension of Bank lending to cover the social sector as well. Projects in the on-farm sector, and the education, health, water supply and sanitation sectors were now also financed, besides the traditional infrastructure projects.

When President Reagan succeeded President Carter, there was reconsideration about the role of the multilateral institutions in the light of economic thinking permeating the Republican Party, and the policy makers in the U.S. Administration. The Treasury prepared a paper analysing the role played by the multilateral financial institutions, and this document attracted much attention amongst World Bank officials, as the USA was the largest shareholder, and exercised veto powers on certain issues. Although this paper did not arrive at an unfavorable conclusion regarding the continuance of U.S. support to these institutions, it did question some of the policies, and resulted in considerable rethinking, especially on the role of the World Bank, and generated a ferment for change. At about the same time, it was found necessary to press for a General Capital increase, as the 'headroom' available for fresh lending was beginning to act as a constraint.

An elaborate exercise was launched to review the role played by the World Bank, and to re-define it having regard to the current thinking amongst the shareholders. For this purpose 12 working groups were set up with some 100 staff members to prepare various papers for discussion. A number of seminars with the EDs were held, and luncheon discussions were organised. In the words of the then British Executive Director, it was necessary to prepare a 'prospectus' for the purpose of raising the fresh capital required by the IBRD. The thrust of the papers and the salient points made, which were generally endorsed by the industrialised countries, were:

(a) Policies followed by the borrowing country were relevant for the success of *all* developmental schemes that it undertook. However sound a project might be in its conception, it was unlikely to succeed, unless the policies followed by the borrower were sound, e.g. macro-economic policies, tariff and pricing policies.
(b) In future, there would be no predetermined levels of lending for a country or for a particular sector. The management reserved the right to alter levels of lending to a particular country depending upon its response to the policy changes proposed, i.e. rewarding those countries which accepted the policy advice proffered by the Bank in the course of the negotiations during the processing of the loan or credit, and withholding loans or credits, where the response was deemed inadequate.
(c) There would be closer coordination between the World Bank and the IMF, and at one remove, with the commercial banks.

There was divergence of views, especially between the borrowing countries on the one hand, and the major industrialised countries on the other. The former generally thought that policy dialogue of the nature envisaged was an unacceptable intrusion into the sovereignty of the borrowing country. They also thought that there was a divorce of authority from responsibility, as the World Bank officials were not accountable, while the elected Ministers, etc. in the borrowing Government (if it was a popular one) had to answer to the electorate for policies which were being thrust upon them. Further, it was argued that World Bank officials could not claim to possess the quintessence of wisdom and may not be fully aware of local conditions. In fact, they may be at a considerable disadvantage, not being able to accurately assess which policies would work, and which were unlikely to succeed in the prevailing conditions. There were misgivings that if the level of lending in future years by the World Bank were left indeterminate, as was envisaged, a further element of uncertainty would be introduced, compounding the difficulties already faced by borrowers in successfully implementing a medium term plan or programme. On the procedural aspect, it was pointed out that too elaborate an exercise, with a fragmented approach, conducted at a leisurely pace, could delay the General Capital increase, when it was required to urgently expand Bank lending.

The discussions seem to have been effective, because President Clausen clarified that the Bank's policy role was meant to be supportive and not confrontational. The policy advice was meant to stimulate the borrowing Government and to elicit a response. The approach was evolutionary, and the Bank would be building on its known strengths. There was unanimity that the Bank's financial standing built up over the years had to remain inviolate, and that its effectiveness would depend mainly upon the resources that it was able to raise and lend out to the borrowing countries. Coordination with the IMF was recognised as desirable, but it was also pointed out that the Bank and the IMF were two distinct institutions with their own charters. Apprehension was expressed about the possibility of the two institutions acting in concert, and perhaps in connivance with the commercial banks, pressurising borrowing Governments to adopt policies which they would have otherwise eschewed. It was emphasised that there should be no cross-conditionality, and agreement with the IMF should not be made a pre-requisite for the sanction of loans or credits by the World Bank.

Some Executive Directors desired that Bank lending should be confined to projects, as non-project lending was not backed by tangible assets, and could thereby undermine the Bank's financial standing. This view did not prevail, however, as it was thought that its acceptance would unduly circumscribe the scope for Bank lending, especially to the heavily indebted countries. In turn, such an approach would weaken the case for a General Capital increase.

The discussions did portend, however, that the Bank would attach much more importance to the macro-economic policies, etc. adopted by the borrowing Government, that policy dialogue would be both broadened and deepened when considering loans to borrowers, and tougher conditions would be attached. However, there were some inklings that the conditions imposed would be moderated from one country to another depending upon the borrowing strength of the borrower, its staying power, and the weight of the arguments that it could marshal in support of its stand.

During the writer's tenure several Structural Adjustment Loans (SALs) were approved by the Board. There was no mistaking the extent of the policy dialogue, and the usual practice was to obtain a communication from the Finance Minister or comparable functionary of the borrowing Government indicating the policy measures (macro-economic *et al*) that would be adopted within a particular time-frame. During 1980-82, and 1983-85, SALs to the extent[2] of $ 741 million and $ 910 million per annum were approved. There has been an increase in SALs since 1989, and the quantum committed under this item in 1991 was $ 3,050 million. SALs are usually repeated, as the reforms take time to implement. Thus, in the case of Turkey five SALs besides a supplementary loan were approved during 1980-84. The Board discussions during approval were somewhat ambivalent, and the Board desired information about the effectiveness of the SALs and the lessons that could be learnt from the experience with this form of lending. There have been three reports on adjustment lending, the last one in April 1992. Adjustment lending includes not only SALs but also Sector Adjustment Loans (SECALs) covering a particular sector. The third report, which draws on the findings of the earlier reports, and also benefits from the experience gained over a few more years makes some valuable points which shed light on the role of the World Bank and the tasks likely to devolve on it in the future. It also has implications for traditional Third World countries, and for devising the strategy that they should adopt to protect their interests, and further their own development, making the fullest use of their membership of the Bank, and the facilities it offered.

The Bank had committed $ 41 billion in adjustment loans by the end of calendar year 1991, and such loans accounted for about 25% of total Bank lending. Seventy-five countries had received adjustment loans, and 22 countries had got five or more SALs or SECALs. The wide coverage of these loans and experience covering more than a decade inspire confidence in the findings of the report. The report states emphatically that adjustment lending has worked, especially for middle-income countries. It points out that both low and middle-income countries, which had borrowed intensively from this source, had achieved growth rates in the late 1980s comparable to those in the 1970s, and had significantly recovered from the set-backs of the early 1980s. It further points out that if initial conditions, external shocks, official inflows, etc. are controlled for, the middle-income countries enjoyed growth four percentage points higher than would otherwise have occurred, and the low-income group had growth two percentage points higher.[3] The report mentions that substantial improvements in policies have taken place, as indicated by reduction in the fiscal deficit, lower inflation, trade liberalisation, and reduction in the black-market premia for foreign exchange. It adds that this is consistent with the fact that 70% of adjustment loan conditions were fully implemented by final tranche release, and 80% were substantially implemented. These achievements are certainly impressive, and the Bank and its staff deserve commendation. The report draws attention to a significant feature, viz. that the outcome of the adjustment measures was different in the middle-income countries, as compared with that for the low-income countries, despite the latter having adjusted more than the former. The relatively unfavorable outcome for the low-income countries is attributed to the difference in the level of development.[4] It mentions that to lift the growth rates of the low-income countries to desirable levels would require tackling longer term development problems. While there have been some star performers, others have not persisted with the adjustment measures, and outcomes have been mixed, varying from country to country. Having regard to the enormous diversity that prevails within the borrowing countries, this finding is not surprising. By and large, the World Bank's prescription for adjustment conforms to a pattern, involving achievement of macro-economic stability, reduction in the fiscal deficit, liberalisation of trade, devaluation, improvement in the business environment by ensuring freer exit and entry, and reform of public enterprises. It may be a promising field of enquiry as to why the shortcomings noticed are so widely prevalent, and why the recommended measures seem to work. Developing countries have had different histories, some having come under foreign rule, while others have avoided foreign domination. Even for the former category, the colonial legacy has differed widely. What is surprising is that authorities under widely different circumstances have found it expedient to embark on courses of development which have many common features, and during implementation, have suffered from similar infirmities.

The report mentions that the evidence to date for low-income countries suggests that adjustment lending is a necessary—but not sufficient—condition for transition to a sustainable growth path. Further, it is pointed out that adjustment lending will pay off in high growth *only if* long run development problems are tackled. For this purpose, simultaneous action has to be taken on several fronts, e.g. development of infrastructure, which is usually inadequate, provision of suitable education and health facilities, without which a skilled and competent labour force would not be available, widening and deepening of the financial sector, reforming the legal and judicial process and the functioning of the courts. Each of these call for massive investments in the form of power stations, telecommunications, roads, ports and railways for meeting transportation needs, schools, colleges, technical institutions, health centres and hospitals. Moreover, improvements can only be carried out in a relatively long time-frame, and call for sophisticated leadership of a high order in the borrowing country. The report states that according to their experience, a decade is not uncommon for the adjustments to be carried out. This means that the Bank should be prepared not only to lend for adjustment purposes but also should complement this lending by investment lending for dealing with the longer term developmental issues, and the infrastructure. The latter may call for the injection of larger funds than the former, and the Bank should be prepared for a long haul. A significant finding is that the recovery of private investment has taken longer than originally anticipated. Private investment will occur, whether from domestic sources, or in the form of foreign direct investment, only if the conditions are deemed suitable, viz. the infrastructure, the financial markets, and the legal and regulatory framework are conducive to stable growth. Credibility will be achieved only over a long period of sustained and effective action by the concerned Government.

As outlined in its Articles, the philosophy of the World Bank favors private trade and industry, and would like to see the role of the Government confined to those sectors, where it alone can function, or where experience has proved that the Government can discharge its responsibilities efficiently and economically. This implies that the private sector would be forthcoming and co-operative, and explains the emphasis on the creation of a congenial business environment. The pattern usually advocated by the World Bank involves trade liberalisation, removal of quantitative restrictions, reduction in tariffs, adoption of a realistic exchange rate, de-regulating industry, so that both entry and exit are less restrictive, and maintaining macro-economic balance by reducing the fiscal deficit, etc. Some of the measures are conflicting, e.g. tariff reductions impose additional budgetary strains, and make the task of fiscal deficit reduction all the more arduous. As a concomitant, the role of the Government is predicated to shrink, the traditional functions of law and order, and the social sector, involving health and education, and rural development inclusive of agriculture and irrigation, being recognised as legitimate functions. It is also accepted, in part, for certain countries that the Government has to play a direct and active role in the energy, power and transportation sectors. Industry, manufacturing, and service sectors run by the Government are frowned upon—and the role of public enterprises comes under close scrutiny, especially where these enterprises have not performed satisfactorily, as is the case only too frequently. Inevitably, because of budgetary and other constraints, the size of the Government, the wage-bill and the numbers employed by it and by the enterprises, etc. that it controls, all are subjected to close scrutiny. To get the Government to accept these suggestions, which usually have strong political overtones, requires intense policy dialogue between the Bank and the Government. As indicated later, the Bank wields disproportionate bargaining power during the negotiations, and considerable skill and dexterity, combined with skilful marshalling of data, are required to make a stand, and preserve the national interest, seen according to the lights of the concerned Governmental authorities.

Policy dialogue is of the essence in an adjustment operation. The Bank's "country economic and sector work" usually lays the foundation for the reform programme and contributes to the design of the adjustment operations. Part of the 'artistry' consists of identifying quantifiable and monitorable indicators which can be used to objectively assess the progress made and to ascertain whether the targets have been met. Because of the many uncertainties, supervision and policy dialogue are essential during the implementation stage as well. Modifications may be called for in the programme because of unforeseen developments, or to rectify shortcomings in the design stage itself, which come to light subsequently. Even after completion, the policy dialogue continues. As the report points out, because of the complexity of the policy changes, and the general uncertainty, strategies to improve the business environment must build on the complementarities between adjustment loans, and appropriately designed *investment* loans.[5] It will be noticed that this is a re-affirmation of the point made in the papers prepared by the Working Groups, etc. when the role of the Bank was being discussed, viz. the policies followed by the borrower are relevant when considering loans for *all* projects posed for financing by the Bank.

As is to be expected, structural lending and the connected policy dialogue, have been controversial. Criticisms often heard are that the Bank adopted more extreme measures than were really necessary, and thus brought about a sharper recession in the borrowing country than what was unavoidable. The impact on the poor and the under-privileged has been disproportionately heavy. Another line of attack is that the World Bank has paid too little attention to the role of the State, the interventions that it carried out and the developmental policies that were followed, which nurtured industries in countries such as South Korea, Taiwan and Singapore, or going back further in time, in Japan. There was no need to denigrate the role of the State as the success achieved by these countries is the result of the efforts put in and the policies followed by their respective Governments. The Bank's rejoinder[6] is that, wherever the State has intervened in the present developing world, it has abused and over-used protection, and subsidised credit.

It would, perhaps, be a fair comment that intervention by the State cannot *ipso facto* be characterised as bad. The real issue is whether the policies followed were the right ones in the prevailing circumstances, and whether the administration was efficient, responsive and knowledgeable. The sorry pass in which so many developing countries find themselves may be because of the inefficient and corrupt administration that they have been saddled with. Vested interests also have thrived, and pressed for maintenance of the *status quo* which benefits them, with the result that policies, which may have had a rationale when first introduced, have continued despite the sea change in the prevailing circumstances, making persistence with policies, which are now out of tune, harmful for the country. Even according to the World Bank's dispensation, the State would continue to have a crucially important role to play. Besides raising resources, and reducing fiscal deficits, the State is called upon to play a vital role in providing education, health care, and adequate maintenance of assets including roads, irrigation works and ports. Moreover, the World Bank also envisages a role for the State in providing an adequate infrastructure without which business cannot thrive, e.g. power, energy, railways, highways and telecommunications.

One of the measures generally advocated by the Bank as a part of structural adjustment is liberalisation of trade, abolition of quantitative controls, adoption of a realistic exchange rate, reduction in import tariffs, and free imports. The argument is that these measures are essential to make domestic industry competitive, and to promote exports as exporters are handicapped because of high duties on imported machinery and components. There is also a general recommendation to increase exports so as to improve the balance of payments position. Undoubtedly, there is much force in the arguments advanced by the Bank, and the advice given. However, some worry arises, because it is not free from doubt whether the Bank has fully thought through the repercussions of their advice. *First*, although, there may be no problems if a few countries abide by the advice given, questions may arise when a multitude of countries, including large ones, follow the same advice. Easing import restrictions implies that the concerned countries will be satisfying their pent up demand for imports, and at least in the short term, demands for foreign exchange will increase sharply. For exports to grow at the same pace, realistically requires a considerable time lag, allowing exporters time to reorganise, produce the exportable goods at competitive prices, and sell these abroad in a fiercely competitive market. The World Bank, the IMF and other financial institutions must, therefore, be prepared to provide the necessary free foreign exchange straightaway in order to cushion the shock. It would be obligatory on the part of these bodies to provide the resources required by *all* adjusting countries in order to enable the policies advocated by themselves to work in practice. *Secondly*, universal acceptance of the Bank's advice to promote exports can collectively put pressure on the prices of the exportable items, to the benefit of the consumers in the importing countries. The World Bank's 'Global Economic Prospects—1993' states that non-fuel primary commodity prices have fallen sharply in real terms since the early 1980s, the relevant price index having almost halved over this period, declining from 168.2 in 1980 to 86.1 in 1992 (1990 = 100).[7] Prices in 1992 were by far at their lowest level since the starting point for the index in 1948. While developing countries have been diversifying exports, and manufactures constitute an increasing proportion of their exports, the same trend may apply to the diversified exports also for similar reasons. This apprehension is fortified by the findings of a World Bank publication, which flatly states "But an increase in the export volume from one country is almost certain to have an adverse effect on the welfare of competitor countries. This would be true whether the export is a manufactured good or a primary commodity, whether global demand is elastic or inelastic."[8] The same publication refers to the 'adding up problem', which arises because global demand tends to be inelastic for primary commodities, i.e. an increase or decrease in supply of a commodity, leads to a large percentage change in its price. It may thus even be possible that the export revenues of major exporters of a particular commodity may decline, though the volume of their exports of this commodity has grown. *Thirdly,* the advice of the Bank would make sense if the developing countries gain access to the markets of the developed countries, and can export freely. The present trends, however, are not encouraging. The 1993 publication mentioned above records that the exports of Hungary, Pakistan, Poland, Thailand and Sri Lanka, out of 14 countries studied, encountered non-tariff barriers covering over 50% of their exports. India, which has a relatively diversified export trade, faces non-tariff barriers which cover 49.2% of her exports. The 1994 issue of 'Global Economic Prospects' states that "non-tariff barriers have become the principal means of protection, especially since the start of the last Uruguay round." It also draws attention to other distortions in trade which have an adverse effect on export revenues of developing countries, e.g. subsidies for agricultural products produced domestically and undue concentration of international trade in some commodities with a few trans-national corporations, e.g. diamonds and beverages, resulting in inadequate price realisation by the producing countries. The total transfer to protect domestic agriculture in the OECD countries by adopting various measures has been estimated in this publication at $ 350 billion in 1992 or about six times the ODA provided to the developing countries (p. 42, ibid). The one bright feature in an otherwise gloomy scenario, is the successful conclusion of the Uruguay Round after long and tortuous negotiations. Meanwhile, the USA has been threatening action under its 301 and super-301 provisions, which could run counter to GATT. Each nation seems to be interested in protecting its own domestic industry, irrespective of efficiency and cost-competitiveness, and little heed is paid to the economic well-being of the entire international community. *Fourthly*, regional trading blocs make it even more difficult for non-members to compete on equal terms. The European Community is a prime example. The relatively under-developed members, e.g. Portugal and Greece, have a decided advantage over Third World exporters when tapping this growing and enormous market. Similarly, with the implementation of the North American Free Trade Agreement, other developing countries will have to compete with exports from Mexico to this affluent and gigantic market. Being a member, Mexico enjoys many facilities in the form of capital investment, and transfer of technology, which augment its advantages from proximity to the USA and duty-free access. It is perhaps time that decision-makers and international financial institutions should take effective action to tackle these vexing questions so that developing countries as a group can compete on equal terms and have a reasonable chance of improving their lot.

Another frequent advice given by the Bank is to de-regulate industry, and eliminate licensing, etc. The objective is to make both entry and exit easier. As a corollary, retrenchment and lay-offs of workers should be made less difficult. There can be little doubt that over-regulation of industry can be stifling, and there are instances where such over-regulation has been carried to absurd levels. On the other hand, as in most cases, some balance has to be achieved. Developing countries usually suffer from a chronic shortage of capital, and it would appear sensible to optimise the use of whatever is available. This would suggest that the public interest required that capital should not be diverted to industries which have only a limited social utility, or may even be harmful. The tobacco industry, and the manufacture of intoxicating liquors and beverages readily come to mind. Similarly, developing countries should be wary of mimicking the practices of affluent countries without full consideration. Competitive forces call for frequent introduction of new models of motor cars, air-conditioners, refrigerators, etc. in industrial countries. Where there are substantial technological improvements which outweigh the costs of re-tooling and refurbishing the manufacturing units, such changes may be justified, but changing models just for the sake of change, may be a luxury that developing countries can ill afford. For these various reasons, complete *laissez faire* may not be in order, and the concerned Government may still find it advisable to retain a measure of control and regulation, and they should not be castigated for doing so. Clearly it would be incumbent on the Government to exercise these powers sensibly keeping in mind the broad objectives of development.

The World Bank admits that in an adjustment programme, stabilisation measures have a temporary negative effect on investment. The reasons are fairly clear; thus, import substituting industries suffer a shock and prefer to bide their time, reduction of fiscal deficits and monetary contraction both have an adverse effect on investment, especially if the measures tip the economy into a recession. Trade liberalisation and reduction in import tariffs present challenges to some units, and may result in an increased proportion of non-performing assets in the loan portfolios of banks, which in turn, are reluctant to make fresh loans, or raise their interest rates to off-set the higher risk.

The report in Box 3.4[9] makes an interesting comparison between two low-income countries, both of which have been leaders in the intensity and consistency of the adjustment effort that they have put in, and yet the outcome has been significantly different. Thus, Bolivia adjusted in 1985 but even by 1990, private investment had not responded, and remained at the low level of 1985, which was significantly lower than the investment level of about 6% of GNP achieved in 1980. Ghana adopted structural reforms in 1983, and private investment fell sharply from a little over 6% of GNP to about 2% in 1986. However, thereafter private investment has recovered smartly and stood at a little over 8% of GNP in 1990. The implication is that economic recovery and development depend upon many imponderables, and the process is still imperfectly understood. The risks of adjustment measures misfiring are thus not negligible. Besides private investment, the conditionality imposed by the adjustment loans also influences Government expenditure. To reduce the fiscal deficit, the tendency for the Government is to curb capital expenditure. The report[10] notes that when Governments are faced with tough choices, they find it more expedient to cut capital expenditure, and to try and preserve *present* welfare and security interests. The tendency is understandable, because welfare cuts affect many, and security, whether internal or external, is a highly sensitive issue with the risk that expenditure cuts in either case, can become politically explosive. It needs emphasising, however, that cuts in capital expenditure, especially those relating to infrastructure, irrigation works, and agricultural development would inevitably have adverse consequences for future growth and development. Decision-makers and the World Bank should therefore be circumspect in introducing adjustment measures that result in a fall in investment, which can slow down development, and cause critical shortages in future. It is also necessary to ensure that the fall in investment is reversed speedily after the reforms are underway.

The report makes the interesting point that measures to adjust the level and composition of public sector spending have become more prevalent in recent years.[11] It is especially striking, says that report, that 100% of SALs and almost three-quarters of all SECALs have conditions for rationalising Government finance and expenditure. The Bank stresses the importance of allocating Government expenditure to the social sectors, particularly to education and health, correctly pointing out that such expenditure is of particular benefit to the poor and the under-privileged. The Bank is critical of expenditure on higher education, which may occur at the expense of primary education. While the importance of primary education, especially in countries with a high level of illiteracy and the resultant enormous gains in productivity cannot be gainsaid, some caution has to be exercised regarding cuts in technical and higher education. The rate of technological change is enormous, and there are no signs of its abating. To be attuned to the highly complex and sophisticated manufacturing and servicing industries of the modern world, and to develop the capacity to earn a living in this milieu, necessitates the building of quality institutions imparting higher education and training. Scientists and research workers also have to be provided adequate facilities if they are to keep abreast of modern developments, and be able to probe the frontiers of knowledge. Any failure on this front would condemn the developing countries to perpetual scientific and technological inferiority, at a time when every developing country should aspire to close the technology gap between it and advanced industrialised countries. Similarly, while primary health care is of paramount importance, neglecting hospitals, and the adoption of modern medical and surgical techniques, would deprive citizens living in developing countries of essential life-saving facilities. Another common criticism by the Bank is directed against subsidies. Here again, the Bank is justified in calling for the elimination of many subsidies, e.g. those given for fuel, power and foodstuffs, especially if consumed also by the affluent sections of society. The case for elimination, however, is not so clear cut when the subsidy is given for agricultural inputs. In many developing countries there is a race between the growth rate of population, and growth rate of food production.

Any measure which tilts the balance by slowing down the growth rate of food production can have deleterious effects on the economy of the concerned developing country. Subsidies on fertilizers and other agricultural inputs were given initially to popularise their use, and have resulted in substantially increasing food production. To remove or reduce these subsidies, without taking all factors into account, can cause food production to fall, and in most densely populated developing countries, such an outcome would not be countenanced by the authorities. To argue that *pari passu* with the elimination or reduction of these subsidies, the support price and the market price of the foodgrains or other product would be raised proportionately, so that there is no disincentive to increased production, is flawed. The factual position is that in most populous developing countries, there is a high proportion of subsistence farmers, who do not have a marketable surplus to sell in the open market, taking the year as a whole. Any increase in the price of fertiliser, or other input, owing to the reduction or elimination of a subsidy, results in pressure on the subsistence farmers' meagre budget, and the outcome frequently is that less of the input is purchased, and this is inevitably reflected in lower agricultural production.

It is apparent, therefore, that any measure designed to reduce subsidies which have a bearing on agricultural production, e.g. fertilizer subsidy, should bear in mind these possible consequences, and should introduce the correctives at the very outset. For the reduction of fertilizer subsidies, a pre-requisite would be to simultaneously devise and introduce a method of targeting the subsidy to the small and marginal farmers only. Such correctives should be effective, and simple to administer, so as to ensure that abuse is minimised. While such a prescription is easy to lay down, implementation can present formidable difficulties especially in densely populated countries with a high proportion of small peasant farmers.

A repeated refrain in World Bank papers is the need to downsize the Government, and to reduce the wage-bill of the employees. Few will deny that overstaffing exists in most Governments and their enterprises and that Government employees are often a pampered lot with indexed pay-scales, which place them in a privileged position as compared to the public at large, whom they are expected to serve. However, it has to be realised that in many developing countries, there is no social security system, and with chronic unemployment and underemployment, it is difficult for a retrenched person to find alternative employment. The consequences of retrenchment in these countries can, therefore, be grim. Trade unions and associations are strong, and where there are popular elected Governments, they wield much political power. It is, therefore, not surprising to read that overall progress in civil service reform has been modest. Most adjusting countries are said to have kept employment roughly constant, squeezing down wages as necessary to stay within constraints of the wage-bill, as often stipulated in IMF and World Bank adjustment loans. It is further mentioned that declines in the public sector wage-bill, either in absolute or relative terms, have been difficult to achieve. Nevertheless, the conclusion seems to be that this 'stickiness' in wage shares suggested that the down-sizing of bloated public bureaucracies remains an important requirement for sustainable fiscal adjustment, which would demand more attention in future. In important countries, efforts in this direction will have to be made with care and circumspection, lest these prove to be counter-productive, and generate strong resistance to the entire reform process. One suggestion is that instances of gross duplication or overlap of functions, and of activities which have become redundant, either with the lapse of time, or with de-regulation and reform generally, should be prominently brought to public notice. To soften opposition, the surplus personnel can be paid existing remuneration until they are absorbed against vacancies in continuing posts. It is necessary that, in general, there should be *no* new recruitment to vacancies caused by normal attrition, e.g. superannuation or by taking up new activities, or expanding existing ones, so as to allow the surplus to be absorbed within a reasonable period. However, exceptions may have to be made to accommodate especial needs and skills, and also to meet the requirement of regular career services, where recruitment is made annually bearing in mind a time-frame of 25 to 30 years. Measures should not be advocated which cause an already weakened service to run down further. There can be little disagreement with the World Bank view that there should be major civil service reform in most adjusting countries, as the public are not being served by the bureaucracy as well as they deserve to be. However, it may be prudent not to under-estimate the difficulties involved. The Gore proposals under the Clinton administration and the earlier attempts to reform the Government machinery in the USA will bear testimony. In Japan too the Government of Morihiro Mosokawa tried to curb the power of the bureaucracy, but the resilience and resistance offered by the officials gave rise to speculation and comments.[12] What is proving difficult in advanced countries with a good social security system, is likely to prove even more difficult in developing countries, lacking a reasonable social security system.

Alleged excessive military expenditure by developing countries has attracted the attention not only of the World Bank, but also of the donor countries. One of the concerns expressed is that development assistance is used directly or indirectly by developing countries to augment their military expenditure. Mr. Robert McNamara, a distinguished former President of the World Bank, who dealt with problems of development for 13 years in that capacity, and served earlier as Secretary of Defence to the U.S. Government, is reported to have endorsed a proposal made by the Independent Group on Financial Flows that "when decisions concerning allocations of foreign aid are made, special consideration be given to countries spending less than 2% of their GNP in the Security Sector". Again, Denis Healey, the former British Defence Secretary, was quoted as advocating that G-7 nations link aid to developing countries to cuts in defence expenditure.[13] The report is frank enough to admit that given the Bank's charter, loan conditions cannot focus on the level of military spending.[14] Newspaper reports suggest that the Bank officially endorses this stand. This stipulation is circumvented, and military expenditure levels *are* dealt with indirectly, by pointing to the inadequacy of the allocations made for the social sectors, and to the need to reduce the budget deficit. The Bank claims that it addresses the level of military expenditure in the context of the resources needed for economic development. The issue of military expenditure is highly sensitive, involving as it does the security of the country and its territorial integrity, and financial institutions and donors should be discouraged from dabbling in issues about which they have no expert knowledge and cannot claim to possess a comparative advantage. It is surprising that high powered groups and influential persons should lay down arbitrary guidelines such as 2% of GNP for determining defence expenditure. Obviously, the threats faced by various countries are not uniform, and some are far more exposed than others. The position is compounded by some donors who in the furtherance of their foreign policy interests, inject sophisticated weapons into highly sensitive regions, which can and have been used against neighbours by the assisted country. Some countries are also exposed to virulent terrorist and subversive activities, which are actively aided and abetted by neighbouring countries. Such activities in reality amount to an undeclared war. To place such countries in a 'Procrustean bed' and require them to conform to such arbitrary dictates seems not only inequitable but also dangerous. It is, therefore, interesting that the World Bank in its 1994 publication, 'Governance' reporting on the results of 45 consultative Group meetings it chaired, states that "clear consensus did not emerge from any side on reducing military expenditure". While most Governments agreed that military expenditure diverted resources away from development, some Governments very cogently argued that military expenditure ought to be looked at in the geo-political context of the country. The same publication acknowledges the sensitivity of the topic, and with commendable fairness refers to an econometric study of data from 71 non-communist countries (London 1993), which states that no clear relationship could be found between military spending and economic growth, except at very high levels of the former. Further, it adds that a strong correlation, however, was found between military expenditure in one country and the level of military spending in neighbouring countries (p. 43). These excerpts suggest that responsible and sensible elements within the Bank appreciate that they are treading on slippery ground when dealing with military expenditure. Borrowers should unitedly encourage these elements to resist pressures from industrialised countries to curtail military expenditure as a pre-condition for new Bank lending.

A further point that needs emphasising is that the negotiations with the Bank officials can often be unequal because of the disproportionate power that the Bank exercises in some cases. The reason is that prospective borrowers are often hard pressed, especially for foreign exchange, and turn to the Bank and IDA for easing their difficulties, as these institutions command large resources. This position is further accentuated by the fact that borrowers who have been obtaining loans over a long period have heavy repayment and debt service obligations. The figures of net transfers, i.e. gross disbursements less the repayment of the principal amounts already received, the interest due and other debt-service obligations, show a diminishing trend. During 1992, against gross disbursements of $ 16,432 m, net transfers were *minus* $ 1937 m. These figures compare with the corresponding figures for the period 1988-92, which show gross disbursement of $ 80,700 m (average per year $ 16,140 m), and net transfers of *minus* $ 2599 m (average per year *minus* $ 520 m)—vide Table below. Thus, though the gross disbursements during 1992 show no great difference, there has been a substantial deterioration in the net transfers. This deterioration is particularly marked for Latin America and the Caribbean. An interesting point made in the Third Adjustment Lending Report is that because of relatively fast disbursements,

Table of gross disbursements and net transfers by regions

(Million $)

	1992		1988-92	
	Gross dis.	Net trn.	Gross dis.	Net trn.
Africa	2,550	783	12,912	5,017
East Asia and Pacific	3,612	- 264	17,606	- 2,452
South Asia	3,321	1,429	15,847	8,406
Europe & Central Asia	1,646	- 430	6,446	- 6,469
Latin America & Caribbean	3,927	- 3,317	22,131	- 6,003
Middle East & N. Africa	1,376	- 138	5,758	- 1,098
Total	16,432	- 1,937	80,700	- 2,599
	Average per year		16,140	- 520

Source: Annual Report, 1992.

adjustment lending has a much higher share of IBRD *net disbursements* (i.e. gross disbursements less principal repayments)—82% in 1990 and 98% in 1991—than of commitments or gross disbursements.[15] This feature greatly enhances the attraction of fast disbursing loans/credits admissible for adjustment lending, and most borrowers are in no position to resist the policy advice proffered by the Bank. A consequence is that World Bank officials (and those of other multi-lateral financial institutions) exercise great power, while remaining anonymous, and are not accountable to the people of the borrowing country, even though the latter's lives can be greatly influenced by this advice. Often the measures recommended can cause hardship to sections of the community, e.g. removal or reduction of subsidies, down-sizing the Government, reforming the civil service, restructuring public sector enterprises and reducing import duties. The political consequences of these decisions, however, fall squarely upon the elected representatives, if it is a popular Government. As already mentioned, the adjustment process initially results in a hiatus in investment, and thus conflicts with long term development. Visitors from developing countries are greatly impressed by the circumspection and extreme caution with which the Governments in the advanced industrial countries handle issues such as additional taxation, health care, reduction in subsidies, even in mild doses or trade issues such as NAFTA (compare USA, France and Canada). It seems only appropriate that World Bank officials should approach the daunting problems confronting Third World countries with a sense of humility, and develop the necessary acumen to anticipate with reasonable accuracy the political consequences of the advice that they tender. This will ensure that the advice falls on receptive ears, and full involvement of the borrowing country heightens the chances of success for the adjustment process. It is noteworthy that the Wapenhans Report (referred to later in this chapter) set great store on the involvement of the borrower, and the concept of ownership.

The increase in adjustment lending had resulted not only in more intensive policy dialogue but also in the laying down of more conditions and in greater detail. These conditions cover a wide gamut of policies, as mentioned above. However, there has been a reaction, and with a consensus developing on a market-friendly approach to development, the need for SALs is perhaps diminishing. It is interesting to read in the Annual Report for 1994 that there has been a shift in lending to human resources and away from adjustment loans.[16] The Bank has always stressed the need for supervision, and even for investment projects, supervision was tight, as missions used to go out from Washington regularly to inspect the Bank-financed projects. Annually, regional portfolios are reviewed in the Annual Report on Implementation and Supervision, which is presented to the Board. For years the Bank has advised on the overall policy directions to be adopted by borrowers, but with the advent of adjustment lending, the Bank had at its disposal a powerful new instrument with which it could directly support policy reform, and play a larger role in shaping policy. What is more, supervision of the adjustment operations melds with the policy dialogue. Even after the intensive adjustment period is over, lending activity tends to shift to more specific investment operations, and the actual monitoring of the *adjustment* process may occur through subsequent *projects*, policy discussions, etc. The relatively greater use of SECALs in recent years has not only added more specificity to the conditionality but has also placed an added burden on the staff to assure appropriate linkage between sector and macroeconomic conditions. It is, therefore, not surprising to read in the Report that on an annual per loan basis, recorded time spent on supervision of adjustment operations is much higher than for investment lending —15.6 staff-weeks (SW) per adjustment operation in FY 1991, compared to 11.8 S.W. for an investment loan. While these are Bank-wide figures there are considerable regional differences. For Africa and Asia the figures are as follows:

	Staff-weeks/operation	
	Africa	Asia
Adjustment Operations	18.0	12.2
Investment Lending	13.7	12.9

The report points out that since these are recorded times, the figures substantially underestimate the staff effort in overall monitoring of adjustment operations, which is carried out with other activities as well. Unforeseen developments in internal and external circumstances often necessitate changes in the adjustment operations, and call for adaptation. This in turn, calls for the exercise of a great deal of judgement, and makes demands on the time and effort of the senior management. At the time of tranche releases, the progress with the adjustment operations is reviewed, and there is further scrutiny.

The report makes an interesting comparison between two countries, Ghana and Kenya, which have been receiving adjustment loans. In the former, substantial progress was achieved by the reforms which included re-allocation of Government expenditure. Not only was there an increase in both capital and current expenditure, but also *non-wage* O&M expenditure in health, education and agriculture increased, showing that more benefits in kind were flowing to the public. Real per capita education spending increased 150% between 1984 and 1989, while real per capita health expenditure tripled. The Government of Ghana retrenched 50,000 surplus staff, but increased average pay levels and carried out other civil service reforms. On the other hand, the position in Kenya provides some contrasts. Little progress has been made in improving the composition of public expenditure. Government employment has grown. *Non-wage* operations and maintenance expenditure had declined in real terms. It is said that the Government does not have a public investment programme that constitutes a basis for determining priorities for public investment. In primary education, teacher salaries account for 85% of total expenditure and milk distribution, a further 13% (i.e. both items constitute 98%). The *non-wage* expenditures have dropped sharply, now amounting to less than half the price of a textbook on a per student basis. It will be recalled that earlier attention had been drawn to another comparison between the performance of Ghana (which is common), and Bolivia. There too, Ghana's performance was found more commendable than that of Bolivia.

The question then arises that if such contrasts persist between countries, what is the utility of the formidable supervision provisions and the large staff employed for the purpose? In sovereign countries, it is the political leadership which is responsible and which runs the country. The Bank can only achieve the desired objectives through the borrowing Government, and with its active participation.

The World Bank as an institution has to be commended for conducting a regular, systematic and vigorous evaluation of assisted projects after their completion. It also carries out impact evaluation of selected projects, ascertains whether the benefits and objectives envisaged at the inception of the project have been fulfilled, and if so, to what extent. This post facto evaluation is entrusted to the Operations Evaluation Department (OED) which functions independently of the Management and reports to the Board. Experience shows that the OED is impartial, objective and perceptive, pulling no punches when shortcomings come to light. The previous President, Mr. Preston, constituted a task-force under Mr. Wapenhans in early 1992 to look into portfolio management and the evaluation process, and to assess the development impact, so that timely lessons would be drawn from the lending operations, and disseminated. The report of the task force provides valuable insights into the functioning of the Bank group, as it objectively analyses a wealth of data, and does not hesitate to be critical, where necessary. It also should help to clarify the proper role of the World Bank, and the improvements that could be made in its functioning. President Preston is on record that the report validates his initial concerns that all was not well with the results of Bank-financed projects and with the processes and procedures which affect lending for assisted projects, and their supervision and implementation.

The Wapenhans report's finding that there has been a deterioration in portfolio performance is a matter of grave concern, not so much for the Bank, as for the borrowers, as they have to repay the loans or credits, and even more worrisome is the indication that the benefits flowing from these assisted projects may not be coming up to expectations. The report adds that the deterioration has accelerated in the last three years (i.e. from 1989). The figures cited are alarming. Problem projects under execution have increased from 10% in FY 1979-81 to 17% in FY 1989-91. Data on completed projects confirm the trend, and 'Unsatisfactory' projects constitute 35%. Significantly, this figure is higher than the number so graded on data based on current active portfolios, hinting at probable optimistic assessments during implementation. The overall success rate is said to have declined from an average of 87% in FY 1979-81 to 65.7% in FY 1989-91. As can be surmised, the pattern changes across sectors. Agriculture over several years has been rated to be relatively weak. However, the finding that traditionally strong sectors such as power, telecommunications and industry also appear to have been affected by the malaise does not augur well. The new areas of lending such as poverty reduction, and the environment are said to be encountering major problems though perhaps, these will improve as more experience is gained. Analysing the causes for the deterioration in the portfolio over the years, the report suggests that the commitment of the borrower, and related powerful sense of ownership are essential pre-requisites for success. The significant finding is that inadequate attention is paid by the Bank to local commitment and ownership necessary to sustain the project through the implementation process. While recognising that Bank leadership may often be indispensable, especially in areas of special emphasis, it enters a caveat. If leadership is exercised through coercion rather than persuasion, then it may weaken the borrowers' commitment resulting in poor implementation. The indication is that Bank authorities assume too great a direct responsibility during the implementation stage, and thus alienate the borrower. There is the further finding that projects are designed with too many objectives, resulting in built-in complications which are not realistically calibrated to the borrowers' implementation capacity. An interesting finding, which should have major policy implications, is that the use of more Bank resources (e.g. staff time) on preparation, appraisal and negotiations is *not* correlated with project success. The most satisfactory projects tend to be those in which there has been most borrower participation during preparation, and as a result, the greatest likelihood of high borrower commitment.

A reason advanced by the task-force for inadequate supervision, and portfolio performance is the Bank's pervasive pre-occupation with new lending, involving an active role by the Bank in the preparation stage which is characterised as being "promotional" rather than "objective". While supervision and implementation of projects are crucial, issue can be joined with criticism of new lending. Even as it is, the Bank takes an unconscionably long time in approving projects, and if a well-defined and planned programme of development over a reasonable period has to be undertaken, sufficient projects should be in the pipeline, and approvals should be received as scheduled. Any downgrading of the importance of new lending is fraught with risk, especially when the Bank is known to have been unable to fulfil the budgeted targets in some years. Borrowers should be assured that the stream of new approvals will be maintained as scheduled, if orderly development as envisaged is to be achieved. It is not also clear why the 'promotional approach' should be decried as the Bank is primarily a development institution. If its expertise can be used to facilitate the preparation of worthwhile projects, need one object?

A factor which weighed with the task-force was the quality of the projects at the time of entry, however this attribute may be defined. Because of the highly diverse nature of projects assisted by the Bank, ranging from the capital intensive and localised projects, to widely scattered rural ones requiring extensive deployment of manpower, there may be conceptual difficulties in this regard. Intrinsically, it would mean the formulation of a project, which achieves the design objectives efficiently at minimum cost, and is implementable with the available manpower and institutional resources. Further, the project authorities should have designed it to take account of all relevant elements, which have a bearing on the beneficiaries and the environment.

The Staff Appraisal Report (SAR) is the instrument relied upon to achieve these goals. Unfortunately, the task-force report is somewhat critical of SARs as currently carried out, and laments that these are not what they were. Discussions with borrowers confirmed this view, and to their credit, borrowers demanded that there should be no relaxation of standards. The report approvingly quotes the finding of another task-force that the weakest part of economic work was risk and sensitivity analysis. Sensitivity to macroeconomic, financial and institutional risk can be considered during project identification, thereby influencing project selection. A major finding of the task-force was that Bank appraisals were not making clear the macroeconomic, financial and institutional assumptions and risks underlying the analysis. Sensitivity risk analysis and Switching values are used to a limited extent only. The task-force further buttresses the need for policy dialogue by arguing that even very well designed projects cannot succeed in a poor policy or regulatory environment. Hence, the need to link strategy even at the project level to the overall framework of policies at the country level. The implication, therefore, seems to be that the Bank is not very sanguine that the overall policies of the borrower will be sufficiently influenced by the Bank's advice, and by way of abundant caution it would rather reject projects where macroeconomic factors may prove unfavorable.

For decades, the Bank has been setting store on indices such as the Economic Rate of Return (E.R.R.), with shadow pricing of inputs, etc. for assessing the utility of a project. The report points out that these features were never fully operationalised. Also, reservations have been expressed about the dependability of such analyses, as inadequate attention is paid to macroeconomic issues, to institutional factors, as well as to the policy framework adopted by the borrower, though these have been found to be often responsible for slippages. The assumption is that everything goes according to plan, though the probability is that some factors may turn unfavorable. The result is said to be an upward bias in these figures. Another criticism is that portfolio performance is on a project-by-project basis, and countrywide implementation reviews are not standard practice. The task-force specifically recommends that a country portfolio performance review should be conducted annually for each country. This provides the occasion for assessing a country's overall portfolio performance, and for addressing any generic or systemic issues in the portfolio, as an input to *all* managerial decisions. Allocation of funds, whether from the IBRD or IDA, would thus be influenced by the review. The report candidly admits that a major failing is the absence of a systematic attempt to re-evaluate actual or expected benefits or the probability of attainment of the principal objectives. Consequently, the opportunity of restructuring or fine-tuning the project in the absence of this information is missed. From the borrowers' view point, the actual flow of benefits in relation to those envisaged at the inception of a project, and the physical attainment of its objectives, would be a more realistic index of the project's success rather than a high E.R.R. A further shortcoming mentioned is that Project Completion Reports tend to be prepared before full benefits from the project have materialised, as there is normally a considerable time-lag between physical completion and the flow of full benefits, vide irrigation and power projects. Little is done to ascertain the actual benefits on full development, and the sustainability of the project, with the result that knowledge of what really works, and what does not, is often deficient.

Loan agreements include a series of covenants which are legally binding. The report states that the evidence of gross non-compliance with these covenants is overwhelming and cites studies which found that only 22% of financial covenants in loan/credit agreements generally, and 25% of such covenants for water-supply projects were being complied with. The related finding is that Bank authorities, who are empowered to suspend payments or to cancel the agreements, infrequently do so and prefer to ignore the lapse, often because of macroeconomic developments or of unrealistic multiplicity of covenants. The question naturally arises whether such covenants should have been insisted upon in the first place, and also whether the stand of the Bank authorities during negotiations was realistic, resulting in the borrower being bamboozled into executing these covenants.

These discussions lead to what should be deemed to be the proper role of the Bank in project implementation. There will perhaps be little dispute that approved projects have to be supervised and monitored during implementation by the Bank as it has a responsibility to ensure proper end-use of the loaned funds, and the observance of procurement guidelines. It also has a role in ensuring compliance with the terms of the loan agreements and the legal covenants. What is not so clear is the Bank's role in facilitating implementation and in assisting borrowers in this regard.

The report finds that the Bank's role over the years has changed, and it is currently taking a more active interest in properly designing a project, having it implemented efficiently, and if necessary, modifying it in the light of changing circumstances. There will, perhaps, be agreement with the view that SARs should be improved, and only good projects should be taken up for implementation. Successful implementation is only possible if this basic requisite is met, and the design is sound. The report goes on to cite a document (OD 13.05) which enjoins that project execution and resolution of implementation problems "are the *joint* concern of the Bank and the borrower" (emphasis added). Staff are further directed to inform the borrower in writing what corrective action is to be taken "by whom, by what date, and what results are expected." The instructions appear to be tantamount to the Bank arrogating to itself managerial co-accountability for the implementation of projects.

A legitimate, well recognised and accepted role for the Bank is to provide finance, and to advise and counsel the borrower not only on project design and implementation, but also on the relevant policies. However, direct involvement in implementation could dilute the borrowers' own commitment towards the successful completion of the project, and may even be resented. The emphasis placed on ascertaining the actual flow of benefits during implementation, and up to full development, and on mid-course fine-tuning where required is to be welcomed. It follows that the requisite machinery for collecting the information in a meaningful way and analysing it, should be put in place, and the project vigorously monitored during implementation. The approach of viewing a country's overall portfolio, and identifying the generic and systemic shortcomings that emerge during implementation, also seems to be sensible, and should help in improving efficiency in the use of funds. As discussed later in this chapter, this aspect has been formalised and adopted as regular Bank practice. The incentive of regulating allocation of loans/credits on the basis of performance by the borrowers seems to be fair, and should ensure better use of funds, particularly, those of a concessional nature (e.g. IDA credits). However, the Bank should eschew the present tendency to take on operational responsibilities or assume joint accountability for a large number of disparate projects dispersed world-wide. The Bank does not have a comparative advantage in this regard, and unwarranted intervention may be resented, even if well-meaning. The Bank is already a very large organisation, verging on the unwieldy. It would be over-stretching it beyond acceptable limits if it were to be asked to run projects, even jointly, in Third World countries, with widely differing political institutions and beliefs, from Washington. The task-force's finding that the use of the Bank's resources, including staff time, in preparing, appraising and implementing projects in *not* correlated with the success rate, is not without significance in this context.

The current insistence on the execution of a large number of legal and financial covenants, etc. the majority of which are *not* complied with, is an indication, that the Bank gets distracted by multifarious issues, some of which are of subsidiary importance. It should concentrate on a limited number of crucial issues, insist on full compliance with the related covenants and ensure successful implementation within time and cost estimates, instead of frittering away its energies on minutiae. The view that overall policies at the country level are also material for success at the project level is fraught with risk. The Governments of the borrowing countries should be made squarely responsible for the successful implementation of the assisted projects, and where necessary, policy changes may be suggested by the Bank, if implementation is demonstrably found to be obstructed by those faulty policies. However, the Bank should not try to externally impose a straitjacket of policies on a borrower merely because of the current thinking. Circumstances differ widely from country to country, and there may well be powerful compulsions, which for political or other considerations, necessitate the adoption of particular policies. Governments of Third World countries have the right to chart and follow their own course of development based upon their endowments.

Of course, the Bank is in a unique position to make cross-country comparisons, and to ascertain what works and what does not. Advice based on such comparisons, and the wealth of data accumulated by the Bank, would be invaluable both for the design of new projects and the implementation of ongoing ones. This advice should be freely given, and would surely be welcomed by borrowers in their own interest, as they stand to gain most from the success of their projects, which though assisted by the Bank, are mostly financed with their own resources. Even the loan assistance received will eventually have to be repaid with interest. However, if the advice is rejected, or there are shortcomings in implementation, the Bank should still refrain from assuming direct, or even joint, responsibility. There are other remedies open to the Bank if the situation were to deteriorate beyond redemption. On the other hand, a different approach could be adopted if the borrowers were to solicit the Bank's assistance and direct involvement in the operational phase.

The World Bank has invested in a number of Resident Missions located in important borrowing countries. The report suggests that greater use should be made of these missions for supervising implementation, and advising on modifications to projects, etc. This is a reform which should be heartily welcomed. Since Resident Missions are in contact with officials of the borrowing Government, and are also aware of the difficulties faced by the project authorities, they can and should be entrusted with greater responsibilities. Sending missions from Washington repeatedly can be expensive in terms of transportation costs and manpower. It may be better to have additional senior level staff from headquarters visiting projects and holding discussions with officials of the borrowing Government, perhaps less frequently, and to rely more on the Resident Missions to deal with project modifications, monitoring, implementation bottlenecks, procurement issues, etc. Undoubtedly, borrowers have expressed a feeling that headquarters staff may be more impartial, but surely a proper balance could be struck, which would give the Resident Missions their rightful place resulting in some savings, and yet facilitating implementation. There also seems to be a case for decentralising loan payments to borrowers, which are currently made from Washington. These Resident Missions are supervised by headquarters, and can be given general guidance so that they operate within accepted Bank policies. The marvels of modern telecommunications would surely ensure that all Resident Missions were keeping in line.

During the closing stages of preparing this study, a Task Force reported on the role of Multilateral Development Banks (MDBs). As this report raised important issues, it was thought that the study would be incomplete if it did not refer to the report's salient features. The Task Force was set up at the instance of the Development Committee in October 1994, and its recommendations were broadly approved by the Committee at its April 1996 meeting, when it also urged the MDBs to act on the recommendations as a matter of priority. This endorsement enhanced the importance of the Task Force's findings. It had been asked *inter alia* to assess the implications of economic change for the development priorities, operations and management of the five principal MDBs (i.e. the World Bank and the four regional banks).

It is remarkable that the Task Force should have broadly endorsed the existing structure despite the vast political and economic changes in recent years, and in the context of a consensus on globalisation, and reliance on market forces. It suggested second order rather than fundamental changes, coupled with modifications in emphasis, and this approach was endorsed by the participating Governments.

The Task Force found merit in the complementary arrangement whereby the World Bank has a global reach, and the regional banks can attend to the more specific problems of their constituents. It recommended that the MDBs should focus on those countries which did not attract adequate and stable private capital flows. It recognised that there would always be critical development activities where governments would remain in the lead, citing roads, education and health activities as illustrations. The Task Force endorsed continuance of the intermediatory role played by the MDBs in mobilising financial resources for development, and their part in providing concessional assistance. While recommending a larger role for the private sector in creating infrastructure, the Task Force, nevertheless observed that well into the future, the requirements of publicly-financed infrastructure would remain large, and MDBs would need to support such ventures as are developmentally important and not yet attractive to private funding.

A reassuring aspect of the Task Force's report is the emphasis that it has given to helping the poorer countries and providing concessional assistance. It has accorded a central role to the MDBs for reducing poverty, and inducing borrowers to adopt policies for achieving this end by fostering agriculture and labour-intensive small industry. These observations constitute a resounding affirmation of the role played by the MDBs and a call for their continuance well into the future.

The Task Force found a strong relationship between good public policy and economic efficiency. Hence, strengthening government was identified as a legitimate role for the MDBs. This brought within their ambit, the clarity and integrity of public administration, the reform of the legal and financial systems, including tax administration, and development of the capital markets. Allocation of responsibility between the Central Government and the local administrations was also included. Clearly, these issues could prove to be sensitive, and undue attention by MDBs to taxes, military expenditure, subsidies, political oversight of the civil service, and allocation of functions between the different tiers of government could give rise to controversy. Predictably, the Task Force considered private sector development to be an important objective. The government was expected to provide an enabling environment in which the private sector could flourish, and this involved adoption of sound policies, and the provision of physical and social infrastructure at an acceptable level. Finally, the MDBs were to try and ensure that development proceeded along environmentally sustainable lines.

The Task Force made some relevant observations about coordination amongst the MDBs, which was envisioned at different levels. Primary responsibility for coordination at the country levels was thrust upon the recipient government. Admittedly, this suggestion has much to commend it, as the recipient alone has a comprehensive view of the full development process, the role played by each of the actors, and the precise frictional and administrative difficulties faced. However, the usual relationship prevailing between the borrower on the one hand and the donors or lenders on the other, may not be conducive for securing effective coordination amongst the latter. The former is primarily interested in making sure of getting the assistance, and is in a weaker position. The donor or MDB being in a stronger position may attach little weight to the recipient country's views, which may run counter to the views or pre-conceived notions of influential parties having a say in the functioning of the MDB or the donor government. A remedy that comes to mind is that an amplifying mechanism should be installed, which will persuade the donor or MDB to pay due heed to sensible suggestions. The World Bank would be the natural choice for performing this task and useful suggestions from recipient countries could be forcefully presented before the appropriate forums, with the requisite intellectual embellishments. Coordination was also suggested at the level of the MDBs, involving the heads of these bodies. It would but seem appropriate that there should be a convenor or chairman, who would be responsible for preparing agenda papers, and expediting collective decisions by the MDBs and donors. The natural choice again would be the World Bank because of its size, pre-eminence and past record. Besides, it is the only MDB with a global reach. It is noteworthy that the Bretton Woods Commission earlier envisaged such a role for the World Bank. Finally, coordination at the ownership level was also contemplated by the Task Force. The participating governments are usually the shareholders of the MDBs, and consequently, their owners. The Development Committee comprises the Finance Minister (or comparable dignitaries) of the various member-governments. It has its own secretariat. It is, therefore, natural that this Committee, with a long history, should play the role of coordinator, though its secretariat may have to be strengthened, and *ad hoc* task forces or groups specially constituted to deal with particular issues.

The Task Force observes that there are also opportunities for increased cooperation between MDBs and the IMF. It refers to the constructive initiative to undertake joint public expenditure reviews. Such coordination would reduce the work load on the recipient, and would ensure that contrary advice on policy issues was not tendered by the Bretton Woods twins. There is also considerable overlap between Structural Adjustment Lending by the World Bank, and the use of the Enhanced Structural Adjustment Facility by the IMF.

The Task Force has some pertinent comments on the functioning of the Executive Boards of these institutions. It recommends that the Boards should concern themselves with broad issues of strategy, and ensure that the institutions are functioning in accordance with the policies laid down. They should not be concerned with operational details. It will be recalled that this study too, quite independently, came to similar conclusions.

The Task Force reaffirms some of the findings of the Wapenhans report, e.g. quality of projects taken up for financing, emphasis on results achieved, and greater use of resident missions. Here, too, this study has made similar suggestions quite independently, based on whatever material was available, and the 'hands-on' experience of the author. Perhaps this affirmation of the Wapenhans report by the Task Force was predictable because Mr. Wapenhans was also included in the secretariat of the Task Force.

A final comment on a curious recommendation by the Task

Force may conclude this topic. As outlined later on, the World Bank, in particular, has set up an Inspection Panel which is required to investigate complaints of instances where the Bank is alleged to have disregarded or contravened its own guidelines, and as a result the interests of the people directly affected by the project have harmed. The Task Force recommends that the responsibility for compensation should rest with the borrower. The guidelines are those of the Bank, and it exercises tight supervision over the project at all stages, including missions from headquarters which carry out on-site inspections. It would be manifestly inequitable for the Bank to disclaim all responsibility and foist compensation on to the borrower, who probably had nothing to do with the formulation of the guideline, claimed to have been infringed!

In the early and mid 1980s there was an emphasis on co-financing. Perhaps the Reagan administration's reluctance to increase Bank resources, and its resolve to promote private investment for development projects acted as a catalyst. The reasoning appeared to be that the Bank's limited resources could be stretched, or 'leveraged' by associating other parties, and persuading them to also partly finance developmental projects. The Wapenhans task-force has been critical of co-financing, pointing out that 93% of the projects which were partly financed by external sources, involved *official* sources, i.e. bilateral and multilateral agencies. Their report rightly points out that the *additional* resources mobilised for the country as a whole have probably been minimal. Being official funds, and fungible, these resources would have been allocated to the concerned countries in any case, for use in projects or activities currently not financed by the Bank. The 1993 and 1995 figures relating to co-financing of 118 and 114 projects respectively may be of some interest, and are reproduced in the table on the next page.

It appears that of the total project costs about 1/3rd each is contributed by the World Bank, the other co-financiers, and by the borrowers themselves. However, of the total co-financing in 1993, 69% came from official sources, and private financiers contributed about 20%. Export credit accounts for about 11%. These proportions vary, and in 1992 private co-financing was $ 1,057 million or less than one-half the 1993 figure. Private co-financiers in 1995

Table

	$ millions		% of total project cost	
	1993	1995	1993	1995
Total co-financed amount	11,229	8,249	31.62	31.63
Official co-financing	7,758	6,626	21.84	25.40
Export credit	1,203	398	3.39	1.53
Private	2,268	1,225	6.39	4.70
World Bank contribution (IBRD & IDA)	11,066	9,983	31.16	38.28
Total projects costs	35,513	26,082		

Source: W.B. Annual Report, 1993 and 1995.

contributed about 14.85% of the total co-financed amount, and about 4.70% of project costs, a smaller share than in 1993. The export credit will generally be available to the borrower even without the Bank's intervention, as it is usually a part of the deal involving the supply of plant, equipment, etc. The task-force report has stated that each agency has its own rules, some of which are inconsistent with those of the Bank; they often tie their aid to donor country supplies, and have political and other restrictions. As a result, co-financing leads to many avoidable complexities, and significantly reduces the likelihood of successful implementation of the project itself. As has been stated, official co-financing may not result in a genuine additionality, and could be diverted to other projects in the same country. The trade off effectively means foregoing private co-financing of about 5% of the project costs, for considerable simplification. The choice preferably should be in favour of simplification. However, papers, issued during the Bank's 50th Anniversary take a contrary view.

The Bank is rather particular about procurement issues, and has evolved a well-considered policy on the subject. Its goals are stated to be (i) efficiency and economy in the implementation of the project and its subsequent operation, (ii) as a co-operative institution, giving eligible bidders (from both developed and developing countries) a fair opportunity of competing in providing goods and services funded by the Bank, and (iii) encouraging local contractors and manufacturers, within limits. The Bank generally insists on competitive international bidding, though for achieving the third goal, a modicum of preference is given to local contractors and suppliers. On the whole, the policy adopted by the World Bank is commendable. It does ensure fairness, and the borrowers are more or less assured of getting good value for their money. While the efforts to ensure a level playing field are welcome, there are some rigidities, and undue attention to detail which could be moderated with advantage. The task-force finds work done at headquarters, including procurement, accounted for 70% of the time spent on portfolio management, and field work accounted for only 30%. It also states that more than a third of total portfolio management time was spent on procurement. The heavy emphasis on procurement may, in fact, be counter-productive, as the borrowing agency should be made squarely responsible for the preparation of the tender documents, the drawing up of the specifications, advertising, and evaluation of the bids received. The Bank's role should be limited to supervising the work done by the borrower, and ensuring strict impartiality. It should be recalled that the borrower is vitally concerned in purchasing the right equipment, and executing the civil works, etc. efficiently and at the least cost. A broad examination rather than a duplication of the borrowers' work by the Bank should normally suffice. Such an approach would also cut down the time taken, and speed up execution. The staff time allocations indicated above suggest that this is not the approach adopted, and could perhaps, be reviewed, so as to avoid pettifogging detail.

Since procurement issues were raised by the task-force headed by Mr. Wapenhans, it may be appropriate to advert to some features, even though it means a digression. Over the years, projects assisted by the World Bank have procured goods and services as follows till June 30th, 1994:

Funded by IBRD	...	$ 96.310 billion
Funded by IDA	...	$ 34.984 billion
Total	...	$ 131.294 billion

For FY 1993 alone, payments to countries for foreign procurement amounted to $ 9.946 billion, while the FY 1994 figure was $ 9.010 billion. These amounts are by no means inconsequential even on a global scale. Analysing the cumulative figures till June 30th, 1994, the shares of the seven large industrial countries (USA, Japan, Germany, U.K., France, Italy and Switzerland) was aggregated. These countries supplied goods and services accounting for 69.87% of payments by IBRD. The corresponding figure for IDA was 61.4% approx. Considering both IBRD and IDA cumulative payments, the share of these 7 countries was 67.62%. If the recent figures for FY 1993 are considered, their share has fallen to 54.6%, but still is in excess of one-half. If payments are disaggregated by category, it is found that payment for equipment supplied by these 7 industrial countries during FY 1993 was as high as 65.5% of total payments for equipment. The shares of the USA and Japan in equipment payments were 14.3% and 15.2% respectively. For consultant services, the shares of the USA, France and U.K. were 16.1%, 13.7% and 13.5% respectively. These figures stand comparison with their respective shareholdings in the IBRD, viz. USA—17.4%, France—4.79%, U.K.—4.79% and Japan—6.47%.

The World Bank Annual Reports also contain figures showing IBRD and IDA disbursements for supplies and services, as between OECD countries and non-OECD countries, which would broadly correspond to the industrial and developing country groupings. These figures are reproduced from the 1995 Annual Report (p. 38) in the adjoining table.

Of IBRD procurement till June 30th, 1995 amounting to over $ 102 billion, the bulk went to the OECD countries (83%), and the remainder (17%) to the non-OECD countries. During fiscal year 1995, the IBRD spent about $ 5.9 billion, of which 78% went to the OECD countries. Over the years, there has been a tendency for the OECD share to fall, as the procurement sources get more dispersed, thus, the OECD share for the IBRD cumulative disbursements till June 30th, 1990 was higher at 86%. A similar pattern is discernible for IDA procurement, though the OECD share is somewhat lower, presumably owing to the more localised and less sophisticated projects financed by IDA, as compared to those financed by the IBRD. Nevertheless, out of the cumulative disbursements of $ 38 billion approx., 74% have gone to OECD countries. This figure,

Table

Disbursements for supplies and services

Million U.S. dollars

	IBRD					IDA				
	OECD		Non-OECD		Total	OECD		Non-OECD		Total
	Amount	%	Amount	%		Amount	%	Amount	%	
Fiscal 1995	4,584	78	1,312	22	5,896	1,987	62	1,210	38	3,197
Cumulative to June 30th, 1995	84,870	83	17,336	17	102,206	28,306	74	9,875	26	38,181

however, is lower than the OECD share of cumulative disbursements till June 30th, 1990, viz. 81%. For viewing these figures in perspective, it has to be mentioned that as of June 30th, 1995, the total voting strength of the OECD countries was 59.44% of the total, based upon their aggregate subscribed capital to the IBRD, i.e. they were benefitting more from World Bank procurement than their aggregate shares in the capital of the IBRD.

These figures show that the industrial countries stand to gain substantially from the lending activities of the World Bank, both in terms of trade and employment. The development process should result in rising living standards, and with the opening up of markets as a result of the Final Act implementing the GATT negotiations, the volume of international trade should increase substantially. Because of the widening technological gap between the developed and the developing countries, in an interdependent world, the industrial countries will continue to supply a dominant proportion of sophisticated and high-value goods to the developing countries well into the foreseeable future. This line of argument would suggest that industrial countries in their own enlightened self-interest should promote development, and assist the multilateral institutions by contributing to their capital and generally adding to their resources.

Returning to the findings of the task-force headed by Mr. Wapenhans, the extensive coverage given to the topic in both the 1993 and 1994 Annual Reports of the Bank, indicates that serious note was taken of these findings by both the Management and the Executive Board. Not only was the general thrust of their report endorsed, but also a detailed action-plan, designed to make the Bank more effective in achieving its objectives, was adopted so as to actually secure the planned results in the field upon completion. For this purpose, the necessary measures were adopted, including recruitment of staff with the requisite skills, special training, and changes in personnel policies to provide the desired incentives. Supervision over projects was strengthened, and the necessary budgetary resources were provided. As recommended by the Wapenhans' task-force, more rigorous analysis of project risk and sensitivity both during the preparation of a project and its implementation was insisted upon.

Two new instruments were called upon to play a major role.

One was the Country Portfolio Performance Review (CPPR), which would review progress for the country as a whole, and formulate solutions to problems that were encountered. The other was the Country Assistance Strategy Statement (CAS). This Statement is one of the primary vehicles for reviewing the World Bank's lending strategy in a given country. In determining the components of a country's lending programme, the CAS should provide a frank evaluation of factors constraining the effectiveness of aid. It is in this context that issues of good governance arise, and are discussed separately. There is a link between the CPPR and the CAS, and progress achieved with implementing current projects gets reflected in the strategy to be adopted for the country in future. The country findings were to be processed both at the regional and the apex levels, so that the Board was apprised of any generic or systemic issues calling for action. These reviews resulted in the restructuring of 104 projects by the end of fiscal year 1993, while the restructuring of 36 others was planned. Seventy-seven problem-projects were closed in fiscal year 1993, and 38 others in fiscal year 1992. Since peaking at over 20% in fiscal year 1991, the percentage of problem-projects fell to 18% in fiscal years 1992 and 1993. However, it is noteworthy that the Bank does not hold out any assurance of further improvement, cautioning that development is itself a high risk activity, and with the new generation of projects relating to structural and economic reforms, and covering the transitional economies of Eastern Europe and the former Soviet Union, these risks were heightened. It is, therefore, encouraging to read in the Annual Report, 1995, that the percentage of problem-projects has shown a fall since then. Out of 1,762 operations under implementation throughout the Bank, problem-projects in fiscal year 1994 constituted 15.2%, though this figure was slightly higher than the figure of 13.9% registered in the previous year. The report refers to the Annual Report on Portfolio Performance (ARPP) 1994, and mentions that of the 134 countries studied, there was a low likelihood of the development objectives being achieved in only 21 countries (including 13 countries in non-accrual status, or unsettled by civil conflicts), but that 72 countries had a high likelihood of achieving these objectives. The improvement can perhaps be ascribed to the steps taken to enhance quality at entry of new projects, e.g. by avoiding excessive complexity, requiring 'up-front' actions critical to the success of the project being taken *before* Board presentations, increasing borrower involvement, using pilot projects to test new approaches, etc.

Though not discouraging co-financing, the action plan seems to have paid partial heed to the Wapenhans report, and simplified the Bank's co-financing practices so as to minimise project complexity, often found to be associated with co-financing.

The importance attached by the Board to the follow up of the Wapenhans report will appear from a subsequent report which stated that almost all actions proposed to be taken pursuant to the former report had either been completed or were at an advanced stage of completion as on June 30th, 1994. A note of caution has been sounded, however, to the effect that the steps taken were only the beginning of what will be a continual, evolutionary process, and that specific goals of the programme of action will only be realised over time.

An innovation which may have far-reaching consequences was the establishment of an Independent Inspection Panel of eminent persons. This panel would look into complaints that the Bank was not adhering to the policies and practices that it had itself prescribed, when approving projects to be assisted, or when supervising their implementation. This Panel would report to the Board, and steps were taken to ensure that the President's accountability to the Board in this regard was not undermined. It is noteworthy that the Panel could only be activated on receipt of a request for an investigation from a group of people adversely affected by a particular Bank-financed project. The receipt of the request would be followed by a preliminary consideration by the Board, and by the Panel. If it was decided to proceed, the report of the Panel after completion of the investigation would be made public together with other papers. However, inspection in the territory of a country could proceed only with the consent of its Government. The Annual Report, 1995 states that the Panel has become operational from September 1994. Indeed, on the first request presented to it concerning the Arun III Hydroelectric Project in Nepal, the Panel found that apparent violations of IDA policy existed and recommended further investigations in three areas, viz. environmental assessment, involuntary resettlement, and treatment of indigenous peoples. The Board authorised the Panel to investigate these areas. It appears that the Panel has taken into account the remedial measures proposed by the Bank, and sent its report to the Executive Directors. It would be interesting to know the final outcome, but these developments highlight the added complexities in formulating and executing hydroelectric projects with Bank funding. The Panel is also seized of at least two more projects, viz. Power VI project in Tanzania and the Rondonia Natural Resource Management Project in Brazil.

The foregoing outline of the action taken serves to highlight the complexity of the development process, and the problems of dealing with projects under widely disparate conditions, and executed by borrowers having different capabilities for their execution. The cautions mentioned elsewhere about the Bank concentrating on essentials, and not being distracted by minutiae remain valid. While it should assuredly supervise implementation, it should avoid being drawn into a direct or even joint execution role. There is much to be said for the Bank as a financial lending institution, operating at one remove from the authorities directly responsible for the implementation of a project, and not intervening too actively with the borrower's administration and policies. Such an approach would generate closer understanding and be conducive to even more cordial relations between the Bank and its clientele.

The dramatic developments that have taken place in the erstwhile Soviet Union and in Eastern Europe will have far-reaching and massive implications for the functioning of the World Bank. There has already been a sharp increase in lending to the countries of Eastern Europe. The Report[17] states that there has been a sharp increase in the number of start-up operations for new clients in Eastern Europe, where supervision has only just begun. The region expects that the supervision effort will climb rapidly as these operations are implemented. The countries of the former Soviet Union have not been taken into account in this assessment, and it would be logical to conclude that Russia and the countries of the C.I.S. will be demanding assistance on a massive scale to cope with their formidable problems. The additional burden that will be thrust upon the World Bank will be enormous, both for appraisal of projects and for subsequent supervision, and reinforces the arguments put forward earlier in this chapter for decentralisation, and for concentration on broad, overall issues, leaving the minutiae to be handled by the concerned Government.

Some significant aspects need to be highlighted in anticipating the likely demands that will be made on the World Bank by these countries. The legacy left by the previous Socialist regimes is one of severe price and policy distortions, and a near absence of institutions that are taken for granted in market economics. To this extent, the threshold level for these countries may be more unfavorable than those obtaining in many developing countries of the Third World. Some countries are exposed to political turmoil, thereby compounding the problems, and the old production and distribution system appears to have been disrupted. On the other hand, most of these countries are very well endowed with human capital and with physical resources. With the collapse of the old order, there is little scope for gradualism, or for proper logical sequencing, as measures have to be taken within a much shorter time-horizon than what is normally available. A dominant feature is the proximity of several of these countries to Western Europe. The peoples of Eastern Europe and of the former Soviet Union are accepted as Europeans, and have considerable cultural affinity with the peoples of W. Europe. Consequently, the fear of a flood of refugees from Eastern Europe into Western Europe is real and potent, with the result that every measure feasible will be adopted to prevent undue hardship. For these reasons, the difficulties of the East Europeans are likely to strike a responsive chord in the people of advanced countries. Besides sympathy, another aspect which will exercise an influence in controlling disorder and avoiding hardship in these countries is the well-developed nuclear capacity of the Russian Federation and some members of the C.I.S. The World Bank estimates[18] that the upper middle-income countries of the former Soviet Union and Eastern Europe would require ODA of the order of $ 4.5 billion annually. This estimate has been arrived at on the basis of recent actual receipts, indicating balance of payment needs. Doubts arise about the validity of these estimates having regard to the large population involved and the need for major structural adjustments, coupled with the requirement of building up a proper institutional framework. It is not unlikely that actual requirements will be higher, once the programmes are implemented. The figures given in the Annual Report 1995 (pp. 69, 60 and 75) show that overall commitment figures by the World Bank to Europe and Central Asia during FY 1995 ($ 4.5 billion) are well in excess of the corresponding figures for Africa ($ 2.3 billion) and South Asia ($ 3 billion). The five year figures for 1990-95 for Europe and Central Asia at $ 20.3 billion are already in excess of the corresponding figures for Africa and South Asia.

If press reports are to be believed, the recent cessation of armed conflict in Bosnia Herzegovina will result in additional demands upon the World Bank for financing a major reconstruction programme in that war-ravaged region. The World Bank President, Mr. Wolfensohn, is reported to have unveiled a $ 4.9 billion three year plan at a recent conference in London (Nov. 1995). How this programme will be eventually financed, and what the World Bank's share will be has not been clarified, but senior Bank officials are reported to have confirmed that estimates of initial financing for the first three months of 1996 were of the order of $ 550 to $ 600 million. Mr. Wolfensohn is reported to have said that he expects other donors such as the E.U., the Islamic Conference Organisation and individual member-States of both bodies to come up with specific proposals. The overall final demand is likely to be very substantial, as the war damage was colossal, with over 250,000 killed, 200,000 wounded, and two-thirds of the buildings destroyed or damaged.

The East European countries and the C.I.S., including the five Central Asian Republics are not the only claimants for aid knocking at the door. Another category includes re-activated aid recipients who were excluded because of war or other exceptional reasons e.g. Afghanistan, Cambodia, Iran, Jordan, Vietnam and Sudan. Recently, because of the agreement between Israel and the P.L.O., the latter has become a strong contender for ODA. A newspaper article[19] mentions that a study carried out by the World Bank has found the economy of the Gaza strip and the West Bank to be in shambles, and the infrastructure, etc. there requires immediate improvement. The study estimates that this area will require at least $ 3 billion during the next decade by way of aid to improve schools and other services. Having regard to the publicity accorded to the

Israeli-Palestinian accord, and the importance attached by the USA and other major powers to peace in the Middle-East, it seems likely that substantial funds for Gaza and the West Bank will have to be provided on a priority basis.

Some other countries are also entitled to multilateral concessional aid (e.g. IDA funds) as they have suffered a regression in per capita income. These countries include Cote d'Ivoire, Egypt, and Honduras. Countries such as Angola and Mongolia are said to be able to service only concessional aid, and their claims will also have to be considered.

The World Bank has attempted to estimate the requirements for ODA from these countries. It assumes that a rough order of magnitude for the potential additional requirements for ODA from all new low and lower-middle-income claimants can be found by assigning ODA on the basis of population and per capita income, and comparing each claimant to countries of similar per capita income level. On this basis, the potential call on ODA by new claimants would be roughly $ 5.5 billion per year, equivalent to 13% of 1991 net ODA to all developing countries. Hence, adding this figure to the requirements of the East European countries and the countries of the erstwhile Soviet Union, extra requirements would be of the order of $ 10 billion per year, or about 23% of 1991 net ODA This figure excludes requirements for the P.L.O. and Bosnia-Herzegovina.

Environmental issues are attracting much attention, as mentioned earlier, and an aroused consciousness demands the tackling of these issues for the benefit of all mankind, both for the present and the future generations. On the other hand, poverty alleviation is an avowed objective of the World Bank, and is essential for environmental purposes, as poverty is acknowledged to be an important cause of environmental degradation. Development, almost axiomatically, causes some damage to the environment, and the objective should be to minimise such damage to the extent possible by good design, and installation of devices to reduce pollution. However, as has been mentioned in Part A of Chapter 5, these measures call for extra expenditure and add to the burden of the developing countries, and benefit not only their people, but also humanity as a whole. Enlightened self-interest on the part of the industrialised countries should persuade them to provide additional resources for the purpose through multilateral financial institutions, the G.E.F. or similar body. In addition, the expertise they have developed for pollution control should be widely disseminated at minimum cost so that developing countries can also use this knowledge for reducing pollution in their plants and equipment.

Against the demands for ODA from new claimants, and for pollution control measures, aid prospects are dim. Germany and Japan are still hit by recession, though there are signs of improvement. Even a normally generous country like Sweden has cut back aid because of budgetary constraints. What is disconcerting is the lack of public support for development, and this indicates the need for the proper projection of development activities, as being of mutual benefit to both donors and recipients. Against the U.N. goal of 0.7% of GNP, which was reaffirmed at the Rio conference, net ODA flows fell to 0.29% of GNP of the OECD's Development Assistance Committee countries in 1994-95, the lowest level since 1973.[20] The Nordic countries were the most generous, contributing 1% or a little more of their GNP, with the Netherlands close behind. The large contributors in absolute terms were Japan ($ 13.2 billion), USA ($9.9 billion) and France ($8.5 billion) but as a percentage of their GNP, their contributions were low. Japan's contribution was slightly below the 0.29% average figure, while the USA contributed about 0.15% of its GNP, ranking last amongst 21 donor countries. Arab aid is also declining because of lower real oil prices, and in the aftermath of the Gulf War, which has entailed a major reconstruction effort. The 'peace dividend' about which much was heard, has not been translated into aid for the developing countries, though military expenditure has been cut back by some advanced countries. Domestic concerns have received priority.

There is thus a serious mismatch between the additional requirements of ODA arising because of new claimants and environmental considerations, and the stagnancy of the available aid. Clearly, the issue is important enough to demand serious rethinking on the part of the donor community, and the international financial institutions, spearheaded by the World Bank. Unless timely remedial measures are adopted, there is a strong likelihood that ODA will be diverted to the East European countries, and to members of the C.I.S. for the reasons already outlined. The first step is to evolve a consensus that ODA to the East European countries and to the C.I.S. will be *additional* to existing levels, thereby safeguarding the interests of the current recipients in other regions. The consequences of ODA being diverted to the new claimants from the present recipients in other regions can be little short of disastrous. Many programmes are of a continuing nature, and require to be pursued over a relatively long period. It has already been stated that adjustment measures frequently require about a decade to yield results, and it would be tragic and most inequitable if these adjustment programmes were aborted midway. To take India's case by way of illustration may be of interest. India took a courageous step in July 1991 and opened up its economy. Later, it has made its currency convertible on current account, and further liberalised trade. Industry has been largely de-regulated. These changes are irreversible, and having induced India to make the changeover, the world community has a continuing responsibility to create conditions which permit the reforms to succeed. At this juncture, when the reforms have yet to be consolidated, and private investment has yet to surge ahead, India should not be left dangling, by reducing the aid package, and diverting funds to new claimants. Such a step would be all the more unjustified because of India's exemplary record in servicing her debt, despite major setbacks, both internal and external, e.g. the Gulf war which had severe repercussions on the Indian economy. This unblemished record maintained at great sacrifice is in marked contrast to the record of Latin American and African countries. These countries have benefitted in the former case from the Baker and Brady initiatives, and in the latter case from the Toronto terms and the enhanced Toronto terms.

Debtors received further relief under the 'Naples terms', which were agreed upon by the Paris Club in December 1994. These terms provide deeper stock reductions on non-concessional bilateral debt than what was available under the earlier Toronto and London terms. The objective is to find an exit strategy for eligible poor countries from repeated reschedulings by establishing a debt service profile that, with sound policies, can be sustained over the long term. An option allowed for a 67% reduction in debt stock or in future debt service payments. Five agreements provided debt relief to middle-income countries including some countries which are inherently more advanced than the traditional Third World countries, viz. Algeria, Croatia and the Russian Federation (which accounted for $ 4.1 billion of the interest capitalised in 1995).

These initiatives are laudable, and have helped to ease the debt crisis. The fact, however, remains, that these were expensive, and diverted funds from other countries which have followed prudent policies. It is up to the international community not to allow profligacy and wrong policies to be rewarded at the cost of other countries, which followed the path of financial rectitude, and maintained an unblemished record. How much these initiatives have cost has been estimated by the World Bank. Debt forgiveness to the heavily indebted poor countries alone during 1990-94 is put at $ 10.8 billion. The total for all developing countries is put at $ 28.5 billion. Besides, the IDA debt reduction facility was drawn upon. The principal extinguished is put at $ 2.5 billion approximately, and the total resources used for the purpose is shown as $ 336 million.[21]

Further debt concessions appear to be in the offing. Pursuant to the request of the Development Committee in October 1995, the Boards of the IMF and the World Bank came up with a 'framework of action' to help the heavily indebted poor countries (HIPCs), which was considered at its April 1996 meeting. While the Committee agreed with much that was outlined in the 'framework', it called for further study, and requested that a 'programme of action' be prepared speedily, preferably in time for the next Annual Meeting of the Fund and the Bank.

The problems of the debtor countries, especially those of HIPCs, have been allowed to grow over the years by the international community. Currently the HIPCs are seriously affected and urgent measures for the amelioration of their problems are needed quickly. The 'framework' is a realistic document, which addresses these problems squarely, but whether the measures proposed will be adequate, and will be formulated and implemented within the time available, remains to be seen.

The 'framework' builds upon existing mechanisms for providing debt relief, and recommends a case-by-case approach for the eligible countries. The approach is sensible because of the diversity amongst the countries. A preliminary analysis of some 38 countries, shows that about 18 of these are in a 'sustainable' position, i.e. within a period of 5 years or so these could be expected to reduce their debt problem to manageable proportions relying on existing relief mechanisms. Some 12 others have been categorised as 'possibly stressed'—i.e. within a period of 5-10 years, these too would have manageable debt problems after utilising the existing relief measures and perhaps some additional help from the international community. Some 8 other countries are expected to be in an 'unsustainable' position even after 10 years, and would require exceptional assistance from the international community. The broad guideline adopted for assessing whether the debt problem is manageable or not, is whether at the end of the adjustment period, the debt stock exceeds 200 to 250% of the annual export earnings, and whether the debt-service charges exceed 20-25% of those earnings. The exceptional assistance suggested is reduction by commercial creditors etc. of the net present value of the debt of the particular country by up to 90%, a substantial improvement over the 67% relief admissible under the Naples terms, and a generous measure indeed.

A guiding principle recommended is that *all creditors* should participate in the relief measures in an equitable manner. However, special provisions have been introduced for the multilateral development banks (MDBs). Their preferred creditor status is to be safeguarded, and there is to be NO write-off or write-down of the loans made by them. The reason given is powerful, viz., to preserve the high standing of these banks in the world's financial markets, so that their intermediation role is not prejudiced in any way. The stipulation is eminently sound as it ensures that the MDBs capacity to help other countries is not impaired. Apparently, reschedulings will be in order as the requirement is that these loans are eventually repaid in whatever way feasible. Concessional assistance, grants etc. from IDA, Bank profits, and single-country or multi-country trust funds are the devices suggested for providing relief. The 'framework'suggests a key role for the Boards of the IMF and the World Bank. Emphasis is placed on the track record of the borrower, and the adoption of sound policies. Claimants would be required to undertake IMF adjustment programmes, and *inter alia* the quality of their public expenditure would come under close scrutiny. At the end of the first stage, a 'decision point' will be reached, and the Boards will decide whether

i) the relief under the 'Naples' terms and other existing benefits are adequate for the claimant, or
ii) exceptional relief will be required under the present initiative.

Only countries in the second category will be eligible. A further round of adjustment programmes will be required. The initiative will be presently available for a period of two years only after which a review is proposed.

It will be seen that the initiative is elaborate, and subject to continuous monitoring, with safeguards built in at various stages to ensure compliance with conditionalities imposed by the Fund and the Bank. The timeframe is long, and only the most deserving will be eligible. On the basis of certain assumptions, the costs have been tentatively estimated by these bodies at $ 7-8 billions, of which about 1/3rd will fall to the share of the MDBs. Inherently, these estimates should be treated as order of magnitude figures only because of the many imponderables.

The London *Economist* in its issue of June 23rd, 1996 has commented on the initiative for debt relief to the HIPCs and mentions the cost figure of $ 5.6 billion, of which $ 3.6 billion would be borne by the commercial creditors etc., and the balance by the MDBs. The share of the World Bank, and the IMF is put at about $ 1 billion. This journal raises questions whether a 90% reduction would be acceptable to creditors, and how the IMF could help, especially since its head has selected the Enhanced Structural Adjustment Facility as the instrument of choice, and its resources would be exhausted soon. Its replenishment by selling gold stocks is said to be unacceptable to Germany. At the instance of the French President, Jacques Chirac, the G-7 was to sort out the issues at the Lyons summit, but the Saudi Arabia bomb outrage appears to have intervened. Many intractable issues are, therefore, still to be resolved.

Certain comments on the admittedly inchoate initiative for helping the HIPCs may be in order. The African countries predominate amongst those studied. Out of the 12 'possibly stressed' countries, 8 are African. Of the 8 'unsustainable' countries, which will require the most help, 7 are African. The South American countries are a small minority, while the single Asian country, may not require massive help as it is in the 'possibly stressed' group. The distribution of concessional assistance amongst the regions is thus likely to be further distorted.

The further question to be considered is how the HIPCs came to the present sorry pass, requiring massive debt relief. The problem has acquired its present dimensions over a relatively protracted period, and has resulted from poor judgement or worse, on the part of both debtors and creditors. A serious indictment is that the problem should have been allowed to fester despite the elaborate paraphernalia of country assistance strategies, policy dialogue, IMF consultations, economic and sector work by the MDBs, and repeated missions from the Bretton Woods twins. Both the World Bank and the IMF ARE CONCERNED WITH THE MACROECONOMIC POLICIES ADOPTED BY THE DEBTOR COUNTRIES, and their development projects. It can be legitimately asked whether the guidance and advice given, and the supervision exercised by these bodies was the most appropriate. Prof. Jeffrey Sachs has in fact drawn attention to this aspect.

The solutions proposed, if eventually accepted without major changes, would draw heavily on the resources of the World Bank, including IDA, and the IMF. It can be argued that diverting profits of the Bank to this initiative adversely affects IDA and other borrowers, as these resources otherwise could have gone to supplement IDA resources for general use. It can be further argued that the HIPCs initiative pre-empts funds from other borrowers, who have managed their affairs more efficiently and prudently.

It is incumbent on the international community to bear this aspect in mind. Countries which have managed their affairs prudently at considerable sacrifice, and have maintained an unblemished record of servicing their loans should be rewarded, and assistance to them should not be curtailed. Since concessional assistance is limited, and its prospects remain bleak, some special measures should be devised for the 'blend countries' which are likely to bear the severest impact of the pre-emption of funds by the HIPCs debt initiative. The ability of these countries to take on further debt at market-related rates is severely limited, and F.D.I. is unlikely to be available for social and physical infrastructure in these countries in the foreseeable future for the reasons detailed in Chapter 7, although essential for creating an enabling environment in which the private sector can flourish.

India's strict adherence to the original debt servicing norms, for example, has allowed the lending agencies to make the financial gains as planned. Good behaviour should get its due reward, and not be penalised by curtailing aid at this critical stage.

For these reasons, in the short and medium term, the only feasible arrangement to meet the additional demands for ODA as outlined above, and to transfer funds for development purposes, is to augment lending by the multilateral institutions. The World Bank being the premier developmental institution should take the lead in increasing the quantum of loans. The World Bank President could emulate the example of Mr. Robert McNamara and increase the volume of Bank lending manifold, by displaying the same dynamism, and foresight, and using his political acumen and contacts with world leaders. While other donor countries should also be encouraged to increase their contributions to bilateral aid, it is perhaps not too early to think in terms of another capital increase for the World Bank, now that the demands of the East European countries and of the countries of the former Soviet Union also have to be met by the World Bank, at least for the time being. As elaborated in the beginning of Chapter 3, though the requisite 'headroom' may be available now for lending at current levels, the additional demands made by the East European countries, and the members of the former Soviet Union could erode this 'headroom' quite quickly, in which case the constraint imposed by the Articles of Agreement could become operative. Experience shows that it takes a long time to negotiate a capital increase, and for the additional subscriptions from the shareholders to flow in. A further aspect needs stressing. The influence that the World Bank can exercise when proffering its policy advice is directly related to the financial resources that it can provide to the borrower, as pointed out by Prof. Cassen. For the Bank to be effective, therefore, it must be in a position to command large enough resources for influencing *all* its clientele. Most borrowers accept Bank advice not so much on the intrinsic merits of that advice, but more because of what they perceive as their gain in financial terms. During parleys with Government officials, it is basically the Bank's money that counts. There is, besides, a certain dynamics to World Bank lending. A reason why borrowers make every possible effort to service Bank loans is that any default will stop further releases by the World Bank, and this has proved to be a very effective deterrent to default. To preserve the position, the World Bank would have to be sanctioning more loans, particularly to those countries which are facing problems, and are likely to require assistance for some more time, and as distinct from countries which have already crossed the development 'hump', e.g. East Asia and Pacific countries. The previous table (p. 283) showing gross disbursements and net transfers has some relevance to the present discussion. Illustratively, for the L.A.C., and the Caribbean in 1992, gross disbursements were $ 3,927 million, though net transfers were *minus* $ 3,317 million, i.e. the difference was because of debt servicing obligations. If a particular country is placed in similar circumstances of having to meet massive debt servicing obligations, and is simultaneously facing other financial problems, then the urge to default would be powerful. A possible neutralising factor, which would induce the country to abide by its obligations to the World Bank, is the probability that fresh money would be provided by the Bank. For the safety of monies already loaned, the Bank should, therefore, be prepared to continue lending during periods of crisis, and should build up adequate financial resources for developing that capacity.

The question then arises where these additional resources for increased Bank lending are to come from. As we have seen, the IBRD plays a vital role of intermediation by tapping the global financial markets, and re-lending these sums to its borrowing members. As such, these activities do *not* impose a direct burden on the budgets of the concerned Governments and, in all fairness, should not be opposed by these Governments. The issue is, therefore, whether the Bank is in a position to raise additional resources from the financial markets. The views expressed by Mr. Eugene Rotberg, former Vice-President and Treasurer, are relevant.[22] He mentions that during the 1970s and early 1980s, there were many hurdles to clear before being allowed to access the important financial markets and these have been referred to in Chapter 1. He goes on to state, however, that at some magic point (and it is hard to identify even in retrospect exactly when it occurred) the Bank had more flexibility than it needed—after so many years of having to overcome an adverse political and financial environment. Further, it was claimed that the Bank could raise in one bond issue amounts which previously took 10-20 issues narrowly focussed on specific markets. By the 1990s the Bank had reached the stage where there was no political or financial constraint on its ability to fund virtually any size lending programme.

Mr. Rotberg has ascribed this sea-change in perceptions to a variety of reasons, a few of which can be briefly stated. *First*, the markets were impressed by the quality of the policy advice given by the Bank, and underpinning the loan operations. *Secondly*, the quality of the lending operations, and the dedication with which the loan economists, engineers, and specialists appraised and supervised the lending operations were recognised. *Thirdly*, the safety of the investment, based upon the Bank's callable capital, and its inherent financial strength, and the policies adopted in managing its affairs were considered to be positive factors. The Bank also came to be identified as a preferred creditor, and this factor further enhanced the safety factor. The Bank's paper became a 'prestige' symbol for institutional holdings.

Finally, with the globalisation of the various economies, Governments as a practical matter, began to lose control over their capacity to constrain the flow of savings and currencies across borders. The Bank was a major beneficiary of this change. The Bank capitalised on this opportunity by the institution of global bonds in a variety of currencies. These bonds were the primary cause of an even further narrowing of the spread between World Bank bonds and Government obligations to about 15 basis points, on average, in virtually every market. The achievement of these fine rates undoubtedly benefitted the borrowers.

The foregoing would indicate that availability of financial resources on reasonable terms is unlikely to prove a major obstacle to enhanced World Bank lending, and this too, without imposing any additional direct burden on the budgets of the member-Governments. On the other hand, Mr. Rotberg draws attention to the stagnancy, if not the decline, in lending by the World Bank in recent years. He deplores that this should happen when the Bank has the expertise, motivation, idealism and the delivery system to increase its lending and disbursements, and with it the capability to deliver sound economic advice. His advice is that the Bank must create a more flexible product. While acknowledging that the Bank has permitted borrowers to choose a floating rate loan in designated currencies, he thinks that this initiative is not enough, because quite narrow conditions have been stipulated, and the amounts are modest. He suggests that borrowers should be allowed to choose:

(a) the currency among at least half a dozen that are permissible,
(b) its rate fixity, and
(c) a maturity range and amortisation schedule more closely aligned to what they need.

He warns that unless the Bank changes its financial product, it will soon find, given the access of borrowers to alternative ways of financing, that it will become a side-show for many borrowers. This warning should be heeded in the light of another factor cited by him, viz. the rate of cancellations of loans by borrowers. Bank borrowers have now cancelled over $ 21 billion loans committed but not yet disbursed, of which $ 3 billion were cancelled in FY 1993 alone, and more are being cancelled at an even higher rate in FY 1994. It will be recalled that recently the IBRD has made a genuine effort to widen the choices available to prospective borrowers, and there is now substantial compliance with Mr. Rotberg's suggestions (vide Chapter 3). One may recall also what we have argued elsewhere, that the Bank should place less stress on policy dialogue, and conditionality, and pay more attention to the needs of the borrower, its capacity and the constraints that it is facing. The approach should be broader, with concentration on essentials, and with less attention to pettifogging detail.

Even after the existing sources of financial transfer, and the intermediation role of the World Bank, etc. are buttressed further, serious thought should be given to tapping new sources as finances will always be a constraint. World trade appears to be growing faster than the GNP of the trading countries. Volume growth estimates of world trade now range around 4%, some 2.5% faster than growth of world output.[23] Perhaps a small levy on world trade to be collected by an international financial institution may be acceptable at this juncture, especially now that the Uruguay round has been completed successfully. Again, perhaps, the time has come for a small levy on the produce garnered from the international 'commons', e.g. fish catches outside the exclusive economic zone of any country, and minerals raised from the ocean depths.

To conclude this Chapter, it might be helpful for the reader to *summarize* the salient points made, so as to provide some focus to the discussions. The plea is that urgent need exists for increased lending by the World Bank even in the context of liberalisation, globalisation, and the consensus on developing the private sector. Various studies have indicated that the projects financed by the World Bank have been generally successful, and even the structural reforms undertaken with World Bank or IMF assistance have mostly yielded favourable results. The strengths developed by the World Bank and the excellent organisation built up by it over the years, should be fully utilised for development, thereby helping both the developing and the developed countries.

A striking finding of the Third Report on Adjustment Lending is that the outcome of such lending has been different as between the low-income and the middle-income countries, the former benefitting less than the latter, because of their lower level of development. The State has an important role to play in advancing the long term development of these countries, and in attaining an acceptable threshold level, which would be conducive to the growth of private enterprise. Even in the present altered circumstances, the State's role remains crucial as it is required to pay attention to the development of the social sector, besides creating an efficient regulatory environment. Development calls for the provision of infrastructure at acceptable levels, e.g. power, transport, railways and telecommunications. These tasks are in addition to the normal functions of maintenance of law and order, administration of justice, and safeguarding security, both internal and external. In the absence of these essential pre-requisites, private enterprise cannot thrive and neither domestic nor external capital will be forthcoming. Vast resources will be required for these purposes, and in the foreseeable future, the multilateral institutions such as the World Bank, will be called upon to further the development process by assisting appropriate projects. These institutions should thus be prepared for a long haul. Foreign Direct Investment, though growing, is highly concentrated in a few countries where conditions are already favourable, making it essential for ODA to come to the assistance of others, currently left aside.

A Task Force comprising eminent persons was constituted to examine the role, management and operations of the MDBs, including the World Bank, in the changed economic conditions, and has reported recently. Its findings have been endorsed by the Development Committee (April 1996). Despite globalisation and the consensus regarding greater reliance on the private sector:

(a) It re-affirmed that the MDBs have an important role to play well into the future. While no fundamental changes are proposed, some changes in emphasis are suggested.
(b) It found that governments will continue to have a major role to play in countries and sectors which are not attractive to private capital flows. These include sectors such as infrastructure, roads, education and health. It recognised that MDBs would have to finance these activities.
(c) It emphasised reduction of poverty, and advocated assistance for agriculture, and labour-intensive small scale industry.
(d) It advocated that the Boards should concern themselves with strategic issues rather than operational details.
(e) It advocated closer coordination between the different MDBs and also the IMF.

Basically, these findings are a resounding endorsement of the functioning of the MDBs and their continuance well into the future. Where necessary, these finding have been commented upon, and their strengths or weaknesses identified. The congruence between the Task Force report's findings, and the suggestions made in this study have been noted.

The dissolution of the USSR and the reforms both in the C.I.S. and in Eastern Europe, have cast an additional load on the World

Bank and other multilateral agencies. Large resources, and technical assistance will be required for the transition of these States to efficiently functioning market economies. It is essential that these resources are *additional* to resources currently being deployed to Third World countries, as any diversion from the latter may abort the adjustment process launched by several countries. The apprehension is that Eastern Europe and the C.I.S. countries would be in a position to exert irresistible pressure owing to their affinity and propinquity to Western Europe.

Many countries have launched structural adjustment programmes with advice and assistance from the IMF and the World Bank. The measures adopted have frequently conformed to a pattern involving macroeconomic stabilisation, trade and industrial liberalisation, and public sector reform. There has been heavy emphasis on policy dialogue with the borrowing countries. Military expenditure has been sought to be curtailed, even though beyond the mandate of the IBRD. Priority has been sought to be given to primary education as against higher education, to primary health care and preventive medicine as against curative medicine, attempts have been made to reduce subsidies on food and fertilisers and to target these to the deserving, reduction in the size of Government has been advised. Many of these suggestions have been acquiesced in by borrowers because of their dire need, and their weak bargaining power vis-a-vis the Bretton Woods twins. In many cases the results of the reforms have been spectacular—but there can be no gainsaying that these have been achieved at a cost. Stabilisation often leads to cuts in investment, and inevitably to slower growth in future. Expenditure on higher education and on hospitals cannot be pared without jeopardising future progress and well-being. Moreover, resistance generated by these reforms has to be faced by the people's representatives (in democracies), while the Fund and Bank personnel responsible for the advice remain faceless and anonymous. The Bank has a formidable supervisory machinery, which is likely to be strengthened further. Also, legally binding covenants are entered into when the loan or credit is approved, covering all aspects of the project or adjustment programme. Policy dialogue is now insisted upon even for investment projects, and treated as part of the same continuum with adjustment lending.

The Wapenhans Task-Force Report has provided some illuminating insights into the Bank's functioning. It is reported that the bulk of the legal covenants are not complied with, and there is reluctance on the part of the concerned authorities to enforce the available sanctions, presumably because the covenants may not have been required in the first instance, or because the transgressions were in themselves inconsequential. The task-force also finds that there is no correlation between the staff strength deployed in appraisal and supervision, and the eventual success of the project. The primary determinant appears to be the sense of 'ownership' induced in the borrower by the project, and the resultant involvement. Comparisons have been drawn between the performance of Ghana and Bolivia in one instance, and Ghana and Kenya in another, which show acute differences (favouring Ghana), despite the panoply of Bank supervision and monitoring instruments. The inference is that the development process is still imperfectly understood, with many imponderables, not captured by the available data, and systems of analysis. The capacity of the Bank to influence implementation is limited, and the borrower's capacity and will are the predominant factors governing success. If the object of such supervision is to enhance the safety of the Bank's funding, then it could be argued that this safety depends solely on the solvency of the concerned Government, and emphasis on project supervision may be misplaced. The task-force refers to avoidable complexities, and to preoccupation with new loans at the cost of supervision of on-going projects.

Despite the successes achieved by the Bank, there is thus scope for improvement, and for a change in attitudes. Divorce between power and accountability of the Bank, as now exists, is undesirable. The Bank should be more attuned to the political costs incurred by borrowing Governments, and contrive to moderate their economic advice so that the borrower is prepared to go along willingly, and is able to marshal the relevant material and arguments to convince and educate the public and the electorate about the soundness of the reforms. Measures which generate fierce opposition can be counter-productive, and endanger the entire reform process. There is also a case for simplification, and for concentration on basics, without being distracted by trivia. Further, there is much to be said for reposing more confidence in the judgement and perspicacity of those in power in the borrowing country, rather than depending on theoretical considerations based on statistics and data, which may be less than perfect, and incapable of capturing all the nuances of a complex development process. Mr. Rotberg's suggestion that the Bank's instruments be made more flexible, so as to be better able to cope with the genuine needs of the borrower, has much merit. Finally, there is scope for easing off somewhat on policy dialogue and the resultant conditionalities. The pace and modalities of reforms should be designed to accommodate the ground realities in the borrowing country.

The attempts by the Bank to improve the quality of the projects selected for lending, and the focus on the country as a whole through the mechanism of the Country Portfolio Performance Review and the Country Assistance Strategy Statement, deserve a warm welcome. Cross-country comparisons and the lessons drawn deserve to be fully utilised for on-going and future projects in order to improve efficiency. While supervision and monitoring of projects should be strengthened to the extent required, the Bank should desist from undertaking direct responsibility for execution, even jointly with the borrower. As mentioned elsewhere, there is much to recommend adequacy, regularity and continuity of lending by the World Bank.

Finally, there is expert opinion on record to vouch for the availability of adequate resources from the global financial markets to finance enhanced World Bank lending, which is deemed to be essential in the altered circumstances. Since there is no direct impact on the budgets of member-Governments, enhanced Bank lending should be encouraged, and not discouraged, as appears to be the case from present indications.

Notes and References

1. Speech to Board of Governors, Nairobi, 1973.
2. Third Report on Adjustment Lending, p. 69.
3. Third Report on Adjustment Lending, p. 7/8.
4. Ibid., p. 14, para 1.7 et seq.
5. Ibid., para 2.57 and Annex.

6. Box 4, p. 12, ibid.
7. Global Economic Prospects and the Developing Countries, 1993 p. 59.
8. Global Economic Prospects and the Developing Countries, 1994, p. 47.
9. Third Report on Adjustment Lending, p. 38.
10. Ibid., p. 58, para 3.37.
11. Ibid., Annex 2, p. 77.
12. *New York Times*, Sept. 13th, 1993.
13. Third Report on Adjustment Lending, 1992, p. 99.
14. Ibid., para 3, 54.
15. P. 8, Box 1.
16. P. 68, Annual Report 1994.
17. Third Report on Adjustment Lending, p. 85, 3.19.
18. Global Economic Prospects.
19. *New York Times*, dated Sept. 12, 1993.
20. World Debt Tables, 1996, p. 25.
21. World Debt Tables, 1996, pp. 31-35.
22. The financial operations of the World Bank, BWC Report, p.c. 185 et seq, particularly p.c. 202.
23. Global Economic Prospects, 1993, p. 55.

CHAPTER 7

CONCLUDING OBSERVATIONS

It may be appropriate to close by commenting broadly on the achievements of the World Bank over the last five decades or so, the role that it has adopted for itself, and peering into the future, to try and discern, however dimly, the role it should be expected to discharge, and its relevance to the international community in the then prevailing circumstances. Taken overall, it would appear that during the past few decades, the Bank has made a valuable contribution to the international community, and has profitably used the monies provided by the participating Governments, who are its shareholders. To its credit, it has earned handsome profits, and though no dividends have been paid to the shareholders, these profits have been ploughed back and used to further the development effort. By and large, the overall success rate of the many projects it has partially financed is high, being 87% in financial years 1979-81, though it has declined to 65.7% in financial years 1989-91. It is undeniable that multitudes of persons, including the poor and the disadvantaged, have benefitted from the Bank-assisted projects, and in taking this view, one is favourably impressed by the wide gamut of projects taken up, to name a few sectors: irrigation, power, agricultural extension, social forestry, health, nutrition, education, roads, railways, ports, and fertiliser units. In the densely populated countries, most rural projects such as irrigation, social forestry and agricultural extension directly benefit the poor, because of the small size of the agricultural holdings, and the pervasive poverty. Undoubtedly, the Bank's activities have attracted the ire of environmentalists and some earlier projects involving the resettlement of persons by clearing virgin forests, and driving highways through such forests, e.g. in Brazil and Indonesia, would today raise their hackles, but at that stage, environmental consciousness had not been aroused and both the project authorities and the Bank acted in good faith oblivious of these aspects. To its credit, the Bank has been quick to adapt, and has built the necessary machinery to ensure that environmental considerations are given due weight. It has also responded to pressures, resulting in its withdrawal from some controversial projects, e.g. Narmada project in India. As already mentioned in Part A of Chapter 5, press reports suggest that the Bank has over-reacted, and is contemplating withdrawal from all multi-purpose development projects, because of its bruising confrontation with environmentalists. It is to be fervently hoped that wiser counsels will prevail and the Bank will not turn its back on the poor and the underprivileged who would gain immensely from well designed multi-purpose projects.

The Bank can claim credit for having made possible some momentous developments with far-reaching consequences. It can be argued that but for the active interest taken by the Bank, the Indus Waters Treaty would not have been negotiated. This agreement led to the utilisation of the waters of the northern rivers of the Indian sub-continent, to the benefit of both India and Pakistan and resolved the impasse following partition. A series of Bank missions visited China during the late 1970s and early 1980s, and carried out detailed studies of the Chinese economy. It can be argued that these studies, reinforced by the intellectual under-pinning provided by the Bank, happened to synchronise with political developments both in China, and abroad, particularly in the USA and were well-received by the Chinese authorities. These studies, together with the lure of Bank funds, particularly the highly concessional IDA funds, may have contributed in a significant measure, to the Chinese authorities liberalising their economy, and allowing greater play to market forces. The globalisation of the vast Chinese economy cannot but have profound implications for the international community as a whole. The Bank for long has been a persistent advocate of liberalising the Indian economy, removing trade barriers and reducing import tariffs. It has consistently favoured competition, transparency and an outward orientation. The Gulf War, and other factors precipitated a foreign exchange crisis, which concentrated the minds of the policy-makers, and led to the economic reforms of

July 1991. Much of the advice given by the Bank previously, now fell on more receptive ears, and it was backed up by assistance in the form of quick-disbursing loans/credits from both the Bank and the IMF. It can be argued that the intellectual inputs, and detailed studies by the Bank staff, coupled with the assurance of funds, did tilt the balance in favour of globalising the Indian economy.

The World Bank is essentially a developmental institution. As the World Development Report 1991 points out,[1] "development is the most important challenge facing the human race." It mentions that more than 1 billion people, one-fifth of the world's population, live on less than one dollar a day per head. Essentially, the challenge of development is to improve the quality of life, and the task is daunting but not hopeless. Though the process of development even now is not fully understood, there is a consensus that an increase in productivity is required to improve the well-being of the people. Reforms may be called for over a wide front. As the W.D.R. 1991 points out "Development has emerged as a fragile and multi-dimensional process. It depends on complex interactions among institutions, policies and the global economic climate." Perhaps an indication of the Bank's success in propagating its view is that it can claim that a consensus is gradually forming in favour of a market-friendly approach to development. The Bank has done much work to examine the interaction between Governments and markets and to suggest complementary ways by which markets and Governments can pull together. Far from minimising the role of the State, the Bank calls for the development of institutions essential for a modern economy. Specific mention is made of legal and financial institutions. It advocates that supporting institutional development requires a State with well-developed administrative structures, and agencies responsive to market needs. Also, for reforming the public sector enterprises, and making these perform better, it calls for an improvement in the administrative capacity of the State.

Clearly, successful development will call for political courage and statesmanship, and economic vision of the highest order, on the part of the borrowing Government, and a sympathetic understanding by the Bank of the difficulties faced by the borrower, coupled with a genuine desire to help. It may be of interest to mention that the Bank foresees that *decades* of rapid growth will be required to make inroads into poverty. This gives some indication of the time-frame within which the development process has to operate.

There is a touch of irony in that the World Bank is a creation of the member-Governments, which are its sole shareholders. It is a cooperative institution, having development as its primary objective. It is not motivated by the need to make large profits for the benefit of its shareholders. It is, therefore, an archetypical public sector endeavour. Nevertheless, it is a strong and effective champion of the private sector. Further, the Bank has been an unqualified success, though of course, scope for improvement remains. Its performance over the years demonstrates that the profit motive is not essential for success, and public sector organisations *can* be run efficiently. It would thus appear that the functioning of the World Bank holds lessons for public sector enterprises worldwide, because such a large proportion of these enterprises have performed poorly, and eroded public resources which otherwise could have been put to better use. The Bank has been fortunate in some of its Presidents, who have functioned superbly. Tribute is also due to the generations of Executive Directors drawn from different countries, who have built up and maintained high traditions, and successfully accommodated different viewpoints, resulting in the creation of a magnificent institution. It also has to be acknowledged that the member-Governments have been actuated by a high sense of public purpose, and have eventually taken the correct decisions, resulting in the Bank holding the pre-eminent position that it does today in the field of development. Finally, the Bank owes a deep debt to different generations of its staff, especially at the senior levels, who have contrived to devise solutions, despite conflicting views, and ensured that the Bank was always able to press forward and to fulfil its objectives.

Over the years, the World Bank has been doing a lot of work in defining what, in its view, should be the proper role of the State in a developing economy. It is a measure of its confidence, and the favourable climate that it has been able to create that it can unequivocally assert "Competitive markets are the best way yet found for efficiently organising the production and distribution of goods and services. Domestic and external competition provides the incentives that unleash entrepreneurship and technical progress."[2]

Of course, the Bank readily concedes that markets cannot function in a vacuum and a legal and regulatory framework is required, which the Government alone can provide. It agrees that for basic infrastructure too, the market may prove inadequate. The W.D.R. 1991 goes on to say "Put simply, Governments need to do less in those areas where markets work, or can be made to work, reasonably well. In many countries, it would help to privatise many of the State-owned enterprises. Governments need to let domestic and international competition flourish." The Bank has been severe on policies fostering infant industries, and on import substitution. Also, it is critical of industrial licencing, and of restrictions imposed on entrepreneurs regarding entry and exit. Conversely, the Bank advises that Governments need to do more in those areas where markets alone cannot be relied upon. Priority is given to investment in education, health, nutrition, family planning and poverty alleviation. It also sees a legitimate role for the State in providing both the physical and the social infrastructure. Further, the State would, of course, be expected to provide the regulatory and legal machinery, and to run the administration. The Bank also expects an improvement in the quality of these services. Finally, the State would be expected to raise the requisite resources, and to ensure macroeconomic stability, by operating within its means, and not incurring large deficits. The Bank further underscores the need for the State to protect the environment. The list is thus formidable, and casts an onerous burden on the State, particularly because of the earlier caveat that the State machinery should be responsive to market needs. For the normal law and order Government machinery to take on these sophisticated tasks, which call for a basic understanding of the development process, and the interaction of the economic and political forces, would require an intensive period of re-orientation and training.

In recent years the World Bank has been probing deeper into sensitive areas, which constitute the essence of governmental authority and sovereignty. It is now concerned with 'governance', which it defines as the manner in which power is exercised in the management of a country's economic and social resources for development. The reason is claimed to be that good governance is necessary for the sustainability of the programmes and projects it finances. It is stated that in its absence, much of what the Bank expects to achieve through its lending will be put at risk.[3]

The practices of having Country Portfolio Performance Reviews (CPPRs) and Country Assistance Strategy Statements (CASs) referred to earlier, focussed attention on 'governance'. Unsatisfactory implementation of Bank-assisted projects and the results turning out in practice to be less than planned, uncovered by these exercises, were attributed to governance factors. The Bank states that experience in all regions confirms that *public sector management* is a key issue of development effectiveness.[4] This conclusion is in response to a change in the paradigm of the State, as Governments seek to adjust from a pattern of control and intervention to one in which the role of Government is to provide an enabling environment for the private sector. The requirement is for sensible macroeconomic management, selective intervention, and a proper regulatory environment, besides use of indirect means rather than administrative fiats. This model requires a smaller State equipped with a highly professional bureaucracy that is accountable for results (p. 56, ibid). The subject has been considered under various sub-heads, some of which will be discussed below. One item is *civil service reform*, which is generally recognised as necessary for restoring a professional bureaucracy, and dealing with problems caused by historical over-commitment of functions, and excess staffing. It is admitted that the transition is proving difficult, a major constraint being the Government itself. The unreconstructed State is acting as a resource drain, and an obstacle to market-oriented adjustment and to effective social action. The challenge for the Bank is said to be to assist in restructuring the public sector in ways that go beyond employment reduction and rationalisation to effect a new synergy between smaller, more focussed Governments and a renewed private sector. There is a caveat that in countries where the mismatch between the ability to pay, and numbers on the pay-roll, is severe, the problem may prove intractable. A second item meriting attention is *financial management*. The suggestion is for having an integrated system and modernising both the management functions and the auditing system. However, the Bank finds that progress with budget reform has been uneven, and some governments (e.g. in S. Asia) have been ambivalent, and the commitment for reform has been weak. A third item which has been repeatedly addressed by the Bank whenever the occasion arose, has been *reform of the public sector enterprises* (PSEs). It has been an important element of structural adjustment lending, and the need to eliminate the crushing burden on the Government's budget, owing to loss-making units, has been stressed. The Bank has also recommended divestiture or privatisation of PSEs.

In keeping with the Bank's philosophy of stimulating the private sector, the model envisaged of a smaller State manned by a professional and competent bureaucracy is understandable. However, such a paradigm may not be universally applicable. Primary reliance is placed upon the private sector to provide the goods and services, while the role of the State is relegated to providing an *enabling environment.* Where a robust private sector is already flourishing, such a paradigm may be feasible, subject of course, to the qualifications outlined below. However, the Third World comprises countries in various stages of development, and a vibrant and dynamic private sector having command over adequate resources may not exist in many countries. For the private sector to flourish, it must also be provided with the requisite basic infrastructure, and the appropriate legal, administrative and financial supports. To minimise the role of the State in countries lacking these essential pre-requisites may not be advisable. In certain cases, the role of the State may well be to first create an adequate and dynamic private sector, and thereafter to provide all the wherewithals by way of infrastructure, and the legal, financial and regulatory paraphernalia. These comments are based upon the Indian experience at the time of independence (1947), when private entrepreneurs with the requisite financial and human resources were few, the country was woefully deficient in power, irrigation systems, ports and telecommunications, the railway system was badly run down after World War II, and technically trained personnel were in chronic short supply. The country had yet to recover from the trauma of partition and bloody riots, and the aftermath of the war and the Bengal famine. The only stark choice was either that the Government took upon itself the task of development, and of industrial reconstruction, or the country had to go without many essentials, and endure an even lower standard of living and forego economic growth. Market failures occur even in industrialised countries, and undue reliance on the private sector, where markets themselves are rudimentary, as is the case in many Third World countries, may be unsound. After the catastrophic Bengal famine, the Government of India has been careful to keep in place a public distribution system for foodgrains and other essentials. Such intervention is eminently desirable not only to cater to the poor and underprivileged, but also to ensure basic supplies to the mountainous and far-flung regions of the country. Left to the private sector, the people of these regions would have to incur prohibitive costs even for their basic needs.

Apart from these lacunae, however, the message of the Bank, that the bureaucratic machine has to be reoriented to adequately face the challenges posed by the consensus on allowing greater play to the market, and more scope to the private sector, has merit. The peoples of many countries are not served as well as they should be by their administrative machinery. It appears to be only appropriate that borrowers should utilise the expert knowledge of the World Bank, and its ample resources to modernise and reorient the governmental machinery to ensure that the development process yields the desired results, and the allocated funds are properly utilised. A well-conceived public sector reform programme, with the necessary local inputs from an expert body fully aware of the deficiencies, and competent to devise remedies, would yield considerable benefits, and allow the development process to proceed efficiently. Such a programme could be confined to the technical and administrative aspect of putting in place a responsive, speedy and impartial machinery for implementing accepted policy decisions efficiently. It could also redress the gross imbalance that is widely prevalent between the numbers of professionals at the upper levels, who assume responsibility and take important decisions, and those at the lower levels engaged in routine duties, and who often serve as appendages from a feudal past. This programme need not prejudge the role of the State. It should, of course, be free of ideological bias. However, such reforms can be successful only if there is the necessary political will, and the concerned Government is earnest in its efforts. The Bank will have done a signal service if it can persuade many Governments to undertake such reforms.

Apart from these somewhat familiar concepts on which the

Bank has been focussing earlier also, it has now launched some other concepts under various rubrics, which suggest new approaches. One such is *accountability*. It is claimed that this is at the heart of good governance. At the political level, it means making rulers accountable to the ruled. Elaborating, it adds that accountability can be reinforced by measures such as decentralisation, participation and competition. These measures are said to enable the public to influence the quality and quantity of the service provided. The publication refers to the experience with the participatory approach in the water sector, and states that on the basis of extensive documentation, it can be claimed that the approach works. The evidence is not so clear cut for sectors such as education, health and poverty reduction. The OED's finding with regard to 24 projects evaluated in 1992 as being outstanding, was that borrower ownership and beneficiary participation played an important role in these projects.

It is argued that modernising accounting and auditing to improve overall accountability means putting better financial management systems at the disposal of both Government leaders and legislatures. These are the tools of greater accountability. In a remarkable admission, the Bank adds that the demand for accountability has to come from Government managers, the legislature and the press; the Bank can only facilitate the process, and not substitute for it. Perceptively, the publication states that its experience confirms the importance of rooting accountability in *local* processes and institutions, and the need to *avoid* substituting international governance for local governance. It would appear that the approach advocated by the World Bank in this regard is eminently sensible, and we can all profit from it.

Another concept is *transparency* and dissemination of information. Without transparency, it is pointed out that there would be resistance to change. It is argued that information is power. It is claimed that transparency is a deterrent to corruption, and specifically refers to competitive public procurement. The Bank states that it is assisting many countries in reforming procurement systems. Budgetary systems should also be more open. These comments by the Bank are generally acceptable, and are closely linked with the previous concept of accountability. There can be no doubt that more openness in Government would be welcomed by the public, as it would permit scrutiny of the role played by bureaucrats and political functionaries. Tearing aside the veil of secrecy would assuredly put decision-makers on their guard, and would be a disincentive to taking improper decisions. However, it would be as well to recognise the limits to which transparency and openness can be pushed in a harsh and unforgiving world. No Government can be expected to divulge defence secrets, or details affecting security, whether internal or external. Even commercial intelligence can be of value to competitors and others. Trade deals between countries, and involvement of Governments in such deals is not infrequent, and it would be naive to expect all such details to be disclosed.

A further concept is the rule of law, and the establishment of a properly functioning *legal framework.* It is contended by the Bank that such a framework is essential for economic activity to thrive, as property rights have to be legally safeguarded, and civil and commercial behaviour has to be regulated. Notions of fairness and social justice should permeate statutes. Further, for businessmen to invest, they would first like to be assured of an adequate return in due course. Stability and predictability would be essential for investors to be able to take their decisions. While laws may be incorporated in the statute books, their administration and enforcement depends upon the governmental machinery and the courts. It is often found that courts are clogged, and unconscionable delay occurs. Since justice delayed is justice denied, reform would be welcome. The Bank correctly points out that legal reform cannot be successful without full conviction and political commitment of the concerned Government. There is also the sensible caveat that wholesale transfer of particular Western-based legislation, without due regard for the legal traditions of a country, should be avoided. Currently, the emphasis happens to be on Eastern Europe and the countries of the former Soviet Union. However, the problems raised by the World Bank under this heading are real. Many countries even with well developed judicial systems, and established traditions could profit from World Bank funds and expert advice. In many countries, judicial processes are too slow, and courts are grossly over-burdened, with too many tiers providing opportunities for appeal, so that finality is delayed to an unacceptable extent, and the judicial process itself has become ineffective. The losers are the indigent and the under-privileged, whose resources do not permit them to take full recourse to the judicial process. The field is one that appears to be eminently ripe for wholesale reform.

Another aspect referred to by the Bank, is respect for *human rights*. By way of introduction, the Bank first points out that within the donor community the *political dimensions* of governance are becoming increasingly important in determining the allocations of bilateral aid flows. It reports that the Development Assistance Committee of OECD sees an overall agenda emerging in aid policies with several links, respect for human rights and rule of law being one such. The publication then goes on to refer to Art. IV, section 10 (discussed in Chapter 1), and reaffirms that because of this prohibition, the Bank does *not* take into account the political dimensions of human rights in its lending decisions. However, it does concern itself with human rights that are economic and social in nature. The first element involves poverty reduction, and the utilisation of the one resource the poor have in plenty, viz. labour, and its productive use in rural development, etc. The Bank's strategy for safeguarding economic and social rights also means specific policies to improve participation of the poor in activities promoting growth by increasing their access to land, credit, public infrastructure and services, and reducing environmental degradation. The second element is to provide basic services to the poor, such as health care, nutrition and education. This trend has been reinforced by increased lending for human resource development (which has been commented upon elsewhere) and for the provision of safety nets especially meant to insulate the poor from any adverse effects of structural adjustment.

The disclaimer by the Bank in respect of the political dimensions of human rights may require some clarification to be judged in the right perspective. The Bank points out that bilateral aid donors have made performance in the political dimensions of governance a criterion of aid allocations, and this applies also to respect for human rights and the rule of law (pp. 57 & 52, ibid). The Bank chairs consultative group meetings where aid allocations to particular countries are settled, and there issues of human rights and rule of law are raised by the bilateral donors. As the Chairman, the Bank has a coordinating role including all aspects of governance, political or otherwise. The political issue thus *does* arise, and the Bank appears to function as the mouthpiece of the bilateral donors, and negotiates to arrive at a mutually acceptable solution for the aid package. To this extent, therefore, the prohibition on political considerations influencing Bank decisions gets significantly weakened. Similar considerations also apply to *military expenditure*, another sensitive item, which figures in discussions about good governance, but are not dealt with here, as this aspect has been covered in Chapter 6.

The publication suggests that the Bank has been somewhat selective in addressing good governance issues in different regions. There has been concentration on the Latin American countries and on the African continent. Special emphasis has been placed on governance aspects in the countries of Eastern Europe, and the former Soviet Union, partly because of the totally different régimes that prevailed there earlier, and the lack of entities taken for granted in market economies. The Bank finds that East Asia is already well served by a highly competent and motivated bureaucracy, which is also reasonably well paid. In South Asia, there is some ambivalence, and weak commitment towards public sector reform.

The issue calling for comment is: How should borrowers react to the new-found zeal displayed by the Bank for good governance? Clearly, reactions will depend upon the circumstances in each country, and the political commitment to reform. However, there are some general issues which call for discussion as they can cause misgivings. These include items such as the role of the State in the altered situation, public sector reform, and improvement in the functioning of PSEs, with a possible curtailment of their functions. We have already dealt with the role of the State, and the need to offset market failures and imperfections. Public sector reform has been linked with aid effectiveness, and the general sense of aid-fatigue. In Part D of Chapter 4 we have considered aid effectiveness broadly, and referred to various important factors *beyond* the control of the recipient, which reduces aid-effectiveness, e.g. aid has to be adequate and regular, and suited to the prevailing circumstances in the recipient country. The Development Committee, in particular, has repeatedly brought up this issue—and these other factors, besides public sector reform, need to be addressed simultaneously and solutions evolved. On issues such as respect for human rights and the rule of law, as well as military expenditure, it would appear that the Bank is at risk of transgressing the limits imposed by its own articles. To make aid packages dependent on the recipient country's attitude to these issues is unjustified, and the Bank should scrupulously avoid giving the impression that it is a party to any such link. Countries may be faced with vicious insurgency and militancy, often fomented by foreign countries, and in some cases amounting to an undeclared war. The concerned country may be forced to take counter-measures in self defence. Issues of alleged human rights violations by the victimised country in such circumstances are meaningless, especially when the human rights of the hapless victims, often murdered in cold blood, are ignored.

The next issue deserving consideration is: Does the World Bank have the comparative advantage to deliberate on issues of good governance and give impartial and sound advice? Heretofore, the Bank has concerned itself with economic and social issues, and has primarily raised resources, and re-lent these to developing countries. It has developed great strengths in financial management, and in appraisal and implementation of a multitude of projects. It is also concerned with macroeconomic policies. Against this background, the Bank can hardly claim to have proficiency in administrative matters and to advise on good governance with its political dimensions. Of course, it can hire consultants, but they are likely to be ignorant of local conditions, admittedly a grave deficiency. Third World borrowers may find it expedient to encourage the Bank to only consider those aspects of good governance shorn of political overtones. It might be possible to segregate elements of good governance which are mostly administrative and technical, and to utilise the financial resources and expert knowledge of the World Bank to streamline the administration, so that it is responsive to the needs of the people, and efficiently pushes through the development agenda. Such a non-controversial approach may prove to be a real boon to the peoples of many Third World countries. The World Bank in its approach to governance has been admirably impartial and objective, and has also pointed out the pitfalls, as well as drawn attention to the sensitivity of some issues. Probably, it will respond favourably to these and similar urgings, especially when, as we shall see later, it sets such great store on partnership and client orientation.

The World Bank has recently celebrated its 50th Anniversary, and this provided the occasion for much debate, and the release of a series of publications outlining its achievements, and also indicating the lines along which it was expected to change in order to cope with the vastly altered global conditions arising, in particular, from the dissolution of the USSR, and the consensus on greater reliance on the private sector, and a market economy. An important document to emerge was the report of the Bretton Woods Commission (BWC), chaired by Mr. Paul Volcker, the former head of the U.S. Federal Reserve Bank. It comprised a number of eminent persons with vast experience of international finance as the Co-Chairs, and Members of the Commission. The report, with a series of background papers prepared by the staff, and some of the Members, is a mine of valuable information, and provides an indication of how the IMF and the World Bank Group can be expected to function in the altered global scenario. The Commission's report will doubtless influence the views of the participating Governments, because of the weight carried by Mr. Volcker and his associates. Though a lot has been said about the IMF, it is proposed to confine ourselves here to the Commission's recommendations about Development Assistance. The Commission conceded the need for continued assistance to support provision of social and physical infrastructure in the poorest countries. It pointed out that investment in human resources was neglected during the debt crisis of the 1980s in some countries, and lost ground has to be made up. The World Bank is exhorted to maintain general support for development, and the BWC draws attention to the acute problem faced by the poorest developing countries that receive IDA and other concessional assistance.

However, the central challenge seen by the BWC is the creation by the participating Governments of the institutional and policy environment in which the private sector can flourish. The premise is that in today's world, economic resources and growth potential have come to reside largely in the private sector. The World Bank is advised that ODA should be directed *only* at what the private sector cannot or will not do. Its activities should be confined to areas where markets fail, where poverty must be directly confronted or where public goods must be provided. The BWC believes that the World Bank should do *more* to speed up the transformation from 'State' to 'Market' and criticised it for still supporting too many State-owned enterprises. The Bank is told to deal directly with the private sector, and to catalyse investments. Greater use should be made of the IFC, but instead of changing the articles of the Bank which prohibits lending to the private sector without Government involvement, the Bank is advised to route its funds through the IFC to the private sector. The heavy emphasis on the private sector and the discouragement of lending by the World Bank to the extent feasible, and that too confining it for investment in the social and physical infrastructure of the poorest developing countries, is clearly apparent.

It may be appropriate to pause here, examine the factual position, and relate it to the recommendations of the eminent Commissioners. Undoubtedly, World Bank figures indicate a surge in private capital flows to developing countries in recent years. In 1986, the figure was $ 19.9 billion. Net private capital flows to developing countries continued to rise sharply from $ 44 billion in 1990 to $ 154.2 billion in 1993, or by a factor of 3.5 in just four years. Thereafter, there has been a perceptible slowing down, as the 1994 and 1995 figures were $ 158.8 billion and $ 167.1 billion respectively, resulting in increases of about 3% and 5.2% over the previous year. These trends suggest that though private capital flows may continue in future also, it would be risky to assume that they will continue to grow briskly and some saturation may occur as the emerging markets mature.[5]

A striking feature of these private flows is their highly concentrated pattern of distribution amongst various recipients. The top twelve recipient countries, mostly located in East Asia, Latin America or Europe, received 80 to 85% of net private capital flows during each of the years 1990 to 1995. The smallness of the share received by the low-income countries is noteworthy. During the same years, their share has ranged between 19.2% and 36.6%. The low-income countries group includes China, which is somewhat atypical because of its size, military might and economic potential, and it has succeeded in attracting much FDI through its skilful diplomacy. If these private flows destined for China were to be excluded, the other low-income countries' share of these flows has been minuscule, ranging from a high of 9.5% in 1990, to a low of 3.29% in 1992. In the latest year, 1995, these other low-income countries were able to attract a mere $ 7.7 billion or 4.6% of the total private capital flows, i.e. lower than their share in both 1990 and 1991.

Private capital flows are not homogeneous, and different components display dissimilar characteristics. One component, viz. portfolio investments, again comprises distinct elements in the form of equity and bonds. Both these elements are sensitive to many factors, such as the level of interest rates in the industrial countries, particularly the USA, the price movements in the U.S. Stock Exchanges, and the contagion effect of financial crises, such as the recent Mexican crisis. These capital flows can be volatile, and can desert the host country in anticipation of adverse price trends or other factors. It would be risky for a host country to rely on these resources to finance long term development. In assessing the potential of portfolio investments, it should be recalled that globalisation trends made it worthwhile for foreign financial investors to diversify their portfolios with the dual objectives of reducing risks, and enhancing returns. Most operators have in mind a pre-determined proportion to be invested in the emerging markets. Once these limits are approached, the reasonable anticipation is that fresh investments in these markets will be curtailed. Portfolio investments grew rapidly from $ 6.6 billion in 1990 to $ 83.9 billion in 1993, but have subsequently declined to $ 67.1 billion in 1994, and further to $ 55.7 billion in 1995.

The second component, viz. Foreign Direct Investment (FDI), is less volatile than portfolio investments, and sometimes is linked with transfer of technology, export promotion, and integration with global markets through MNCs' out-sourcing components, etc. From the host country's viewpoint, it thus has decided advantages, especially since the investment need only be serviced when it is profitable and dividends become payable. FDI, too, has grown fast, from $ 25 billion in 1990 to $ 68.3 billion in 1993, an almost three-fold increase in four years. Thereafter, growth has decelerated, FDI in developing countries increasing by 17.2% and 12.7% in 1994 and 1995, to reach the figure of $ 90.3 billion. Currently, developing countries are estimated to have attracted 38% of global FDI. FDI, like aggregate private capital flows, displays much skewness in distribution amongst the recipient countries. The top twelve recipients during each of the three years, 1993, 1994 and 1995 have attracted around 80% of the total, and they are located mostly in East Asia, Latin America or Europe. Low-income countries, including China, have succeeded in attracting almost 50% of the total. For the reasons mentioned earlier, if China's share is excluded, then the share of the other low-income countries falls precipitately to 6.3% in 1993, 7% in 1994, and 5.09% in 1995. Significantly, their share is smaller in 1995 than it was in 1990 (viz. 8%). In absolute amounts, the FDI to these countries is of the order of a mere $ 5 billion. The regional distribution of the FDI is also significant. East Asia was the most favoured region, absorbing over 59% of the FDI in 1995. Latin America did quite well, attracting about 19.7% though its share in 1995 was well below what it achieved in 1990-92 (viz. 32.7%). The decrease may be an aftermath of the Mexican crisis. In contrast, sub-Saharan African received 2.4%, but even so, its share was slightly higher than South Asia's paltry 2.2%. A significant feature, which may be a harbinger of future trends, is that according to the World Bank, Eastern Europe and Central Asia saw a big increase of 49% to about $ 13 billion, with Hungary emerging as the leading FDI recipient in the region.

The pattern of distribution outlined above will appear rational, when it is recalled that private investors are out to seek the best return for their clientele. They have certain desiderata in mind, e.g. stability, good growth prospects, an acceptable level of basic infrastructure, an abundant supply of skilled labour, which should also be cheap. It is difficult for many low-income countries to live up to these expectations, and hence they lose out to middle-income countries. The poor performance of sub-Saharan countries and of South Asia, can be similarly explained. Infrastructure is abysmally inadequate, and large investments are required for the purpose, as also for the social sectors, including health and education, which may not be forthcoming owing to budgetary constraints. It is most unlikely that private funds will be available for meeting these deficiencies, and in the absence of a suitable environment, FDI will not be forthcoming to the extent required to alleviate poverty and promote desirable economic growth. It will be recalled that after the Mexican crisis, investors have become more discerning, and differentiate between markets on the basis of fundamentals. Till such time as these low-income countries have not reached a minimum threshold level of development, and created a congenial and enabling environment for private business and industry to flourish, it will be necessary for ODA, including a reasonable proportion on concessional terms, to be injected into their economies. This was also the conclusion arrived at by various reviews of structural adjustment lending, which emphasised the differences between the low and the middle-income countries, and the relatively long time horizon within which development issues have to be tackled. It would be futile to expect private capital to flow into the most deserving countries in adequate amounts before they have attained the minimum threshold level of development. Withdrawal or decrease of ODA and other bilateral assistance prematurely would only lead to frustration, and impart an inward-looking orientation. This approach is fraught with the danger that it may result in many more Cubas emerging in the Third World.

The W.D.R. for 1994 shows disbursements in 1992 of long term public external capital, and of private non-guaranteed external capital for various countries. A few countries have been tabulated below for comparison. Some countries do show higher private flows than public flows:

Disbursement ($ million) in 1992

	Public	Private (Non-guaranteed)
Indonesia	6,270	6,527
Thailand	1,547	3,223
Chile	670	1,066
Brazil	2,129	6,947
Malaysia	1,323	1,358

It is noteworthy that these countries are in E. Asia or in Latin America, and the *public* flows are by no means insignificant as well.

For other countries, including some from Latin America, the public external flows are significantly higher than the private flows.

	Public	Private
Mexico	6,750	5,113
Argentina	1,209	679
India	6,134	254
China	15,232	0
Philippines	5,431	274

Judging from these flows, ODA will be required for some decades at quite high levels, especially by those countries located in regions which prima facie do not appear attractive to private entrepreneurs. Some of these countries are necessarily not the poorest or the least developed. It may, therefore, be somewhat premature to accept the BWC's finding that as privatisation proceeds world-wide, it may well be that demand for official development financing diminishes in the decades ahead.

A noteworthy recommendation of the BWC is that the Bank group should concentrate its assistance in those countries where the need is greatest. It is elaborated that this means a more aggressive policy of graduation, from both IDA and the Bank as a whole. IDA resources should be reserved solely for the poorest and least developed countries, whose institutional and technical capacity is weakest. Bank resources, according to the BWC, should be concentrated more intensively on lower-income countries, and economies in transition, which lack ready access to international capital markets.

It is interesting to juxtapose this recommendation of the BWC with the views expressed by another Commissioner, Dr. I.G. Patel, on page C-70 of the report. Referring to the experience of the 1980s, he writes "The Bank was clearly encouraged, by recalcitrant donors, to graduate borrowing countries too soon—from IDA to the Bank and from the Bank to private capital markets. There can be little doubt that this haste had something to do with the debt crisis in Latin America and even to the present difficulties in India. The right balance between finance and adjustment is always a difficult question. But doling out inadequate finance on inappropriate terms to a large number of reforming countries is like playing a game of musical chairs with too few chairs, so that a substantial number of players must remain stranded in turn." Perhaps, the BWC may be somewhat hasty in again pressing for graduation prematurely.

Other recommendations of the BWC have far-reaching implications for prospective borrowers. The Commission emphasises good governance, proper allocation of public expenditure, and reduction in military expenditure. Borrowers, if they want funds, must be prepared to shed their sensitivity regarding possible inroads into their sovereignty, and answer questions on these issues to the satisfaction of the Bank. The BWC calls for cooperation with regional Development Banks, and for rationalisation and harmonisation of their procedures and requirements. There is also the sensible recommendation that the World Bank and the regional banks should eliminate overlaps and rely more on one another. Further, the World Bank should be given an enlarged role in aid co-ordination globally. These recommendations, if implemented, would ease the burden on borrowers—and may call for further comments subsequently. The BWC calls for protecting the environment and improving the quality and effectiveness of ODA. There are also remarks on the quality of projects, which can be considered as an endorsement of the thrust of the Wapenhans report considered earlier.

Finally, the BWC has given the same medicine to the Bank, as that which the latter doles out often to borrowers. The World Bank group's governance should be strengthened, and the Development Committee (of the Governors) needs to become an effective forum in which to provide direction to World Bank group policies. A similar conclusion has been independently arrived at in Part D of Chapter 4. The Commission believes that the World Bank group must give high priority to increasing its own internal efficiency and effectiveness. It thinks that there is scope for the Bank to shed staff significantly as it became more efficient.

Amongst the spate of publications released by the Bank group on the occasion of its 50th Anniversary, outlining its achievements, goals and functioning, is a small brochure titled "Learning from the Past, Embracing the Future." This brochure is noteworthy for its contents, and its balanced approach which appears more attuned to existing global conditions than that of the BWC. It also gives an inkling of the Bank's future functioning in the altered circumstances by identifying the 'challenges' and the 'guiding principles' which would influence its activities.

The brochure identifies the Bank Group's dual roles of mobilising financial resources, and investing in development (its financial role) and its advisory role of distilling and disseminating its own cross-country experiences, and helping clients to contact the best available sources of knowledge and expertise. It claims that the combination of the financial and advisory roles gives it its comparative advantage. The Bank differentiates between the middle-income and the low-income countries, and anticipates that its financial role will diminish in the former group, as they gain improved access to global financial markets, though its advisory role in those countries may remain important. By contrast, in low-income countries, large levels of external financing, as well as technical advice would remain essential.

The key development challenges foreseen by the Bank are as follows:

(a) *Continuance of economic reforms*, which are necessary to improve living standards, enhance growth, and reduce poverty. There is no mistaking the emphasis on deepening policy and institutional reforms, and the removal of constraints imposed by institutional features. There is the assurance that countries which have completed the first stage by achieving economic stabilisation, will be assisted in undertaking the second generation reforms, involving items such as good governance, civil service and judicial reforms, development of capital markets and reform of public sector enterprises.

(b) *Investing in people:* The objective is laudable, viz. human capital should no longer be a constraint on development. The emphasis is on good quality primary education, and on effective health care. Special mention is made of early childhood development, immunisation from certain crippling diseases, and provision of nutritional supplements. The focus is commendable, and benefits from such programmes in the long term will be enormous, while the costs may be relatively modest.

(c) *Protecting the environment:* The brochure points out that during the next 35 years, GNP of developing countries is anticipated to grow 5-fold, with its consequent toll on the environment, unless sound policies and strong institutions are put in place to minimise damage. The urban problem is highlighted, as 90% of the projected population increase will occur in towns. Agricultural research finds mention. The Global Environment Facility is jointly managed by the UNDP, UNEP and the World Bank. There is a welcome reference to the needs of developing countries, particularly low-income ones, and to the defraying of incremental costs of global environmental protection by this body. This assurance is re-assuring as industrial countries have benefitted from earlier programmes for the Danube and the Mediterranean, and a reasonable balance between the two groups would be universally welcomed. The one lacuna that comes to mind is the absence of any mention of transfer of technology to developing countries for treating effluents from chemical and other polluting plants, so as to protect the environment for the common good of *all* countries, and the concessional resources to be made available for the purpose.

(d) *Stimulating the private sector:* The general consensus now prevailing of enhancing the role of the private sector for higher economic growth, employment generation, and even for infrastructure projects, is likely to inform the Bank group's future activities. In an era of budgetary constraints, developing countries find it expedient to tap the potential of the private sector. The instrument for stimulating the private sector would be the IFC and its strong endorsement by the BWC is likely to influence the participating Governments, so a sharp boost in the resources of the IFC and in its activities is likely to be seen in the foreseeable future. Other organisations such as MIGA, will also be enlisted for the purpose. Capital markets of developing countries, re-structuring of banks, and mobilisation of long term finance for development are all within the World Bank group's agenda. There would, of course, be World Bank support for privatisation of public sector enterprises.

(e) *Re-orienting the Government:* The strategy is to enable the Government to perform its core functions of maintaining public safety, and providing access to key services such as health and education, and protecting the environment. Without these services, markets cannot function efficiently. As the brochure puts it, the challenge is to assist in restructuring the public sector in such a way as to effect a new synergy between a leaner and more efficient Government and a revitalised private sector. Even more emphasis is likely in the future on policy dialogue, to achieve the goal of good governance. No let up on military expenditure issues can be hoped for, though these are to be introduced indirectly, by calling for allocation of more resources to the social sector. Judicial, civil service and public enterprise reform will also receive attention. Borrowers should, therefore, be prepared to debate these issues in a professionally competent way if they desire Bank funds, and are not to be overwhelmed by the Bank group's expert studies, and vast cross country experience.

For the future, the Bank group has adopted six guiding principles, viz:

(a) *Selectivity:* Sensibly, it has decided to identify the strategic activities in consultation with its borrowers, where its involvement in support of *market-oriented* structures is likely to have the most impact. It will try to maximise the contributions from others.

(b) *Partnership:* The Bank group will seek to build strategic alliances with its partners. These include, besides the borrowing Governments, international organisations such as the IMF, and the World Trade Organisation. Bilateral aid agencies, and regional Development Banks also fall within the scope of the partnership arrangements. The objective is to maximise the leverage obtainable from the Bank's own funds. It will be recalled that the Wapenhans' report had criticised co-financing on the grounds that additionality of funds was somewhat dubious, and because of different procedures followed by various aid agencies and suppliers, there were avoidable complications. It appears that this criticism has been only partially heeded, and the World Bank will try to involve other agencies, wherever feasible. Nevertheless, the criticism was not unfounded, and it is hoped that the BWCs suggestion to give the World Bank a bigger role in co-ordinating international assistance, would help to redress the deficiencies. It should be feasible for the World Bank to streamline and harmonise the practices and procedures of different agencies, so that the minimum dislocation and inconvenience is caused to the borrowers. Efforts directed towards this end should serve to mobilise resources from different sources, and allocate these to achieve the optimum results.

(c) *Client orientation:* The Bank group assures borrowing countries that it will be more responsive to their needs. A reduced role for the Bank over time in project preparation, and greater flexibility in the project cycle are anticipated.

(d) *Results orientation:* There is to be greater emphasis on the development impact of projects, and to focus more on the performance of the project portfolio, shifting management of projects centre stage. Quality of projects entering the pipeline will be ensured. It will be recalled that these points were earlier made by the Wapenhans's report, and what is now stated is an emphatic endorsement of that report's suggestions.

(e) *Cost effectiveness:* Efforts will be directed to contain costs, enhance efficiency, improve coordination and simplify processes.

(f) *Financial integrity:* The Bank has always jealously safeguarded its high financial standing in the world's capital markets. There is an assurance to maintain its high standing, which enables the Bank to deliver the best terms to its

> clients. Borrowers would obviously endorse and welcome this principle. It is noteworthy that the World Bank proudly claims that its high standing in capital markets comes *in part* from shareholders' guarantees but for the *most part* it has been *earned* by prudent financial management. Its record to date would validate this claim.

The Bank group has, of its own volition, assessed the likely impact of the application of these principles on its work, and institutional culture. An early mention of the Bank's improved ability to respond to new challenges in the countries in transition from centrally-planned to market-oriented economies, shows the importance attached by the top echelons to this group of countries. As we have pointed out earlier, additional resources should be especially mobilised for this large group of countries, and the traditional borrowers of the Bank in the Third World should not go by default. The concern for quality in project portfolio performance, and for simplification of business practices, should command general support.

A suggestion that some tasks currently undertaken at headquarters might be performed in the field made in the brochure, indicates that the Bank group management may be receptive to similar suggestions made in this study, e.g. greater use of Resident Missions.

The application of these principles, and the new emphasis on efficiency is claimed to mark the beginning of *fundamental changes* in the Bank group's way of conducting business. The objective appears to be to transform it into an institution that is leaner, more agile, more focussed on priorities, and more responsive to changing client needs. There follows a statement which could arouse misgivings amongst Third World borrowers. The Bank group, it is claimed will continue to grow but it will not measure its growth by the amount it lends. Rather, the criteria will be the quality and efficiency of its services, and the depth and quality of the partnerships it develops. This general thrust towards reduced lending may not be in the interest of Third World development, where resources continue to be a constraint. The tangible and measurable flow of financial resources can hardly be substituted by intangibles such as the quality and efficiency of the services provided. Some general comments on the direction of change introduced by the World Bank may be called for. Social infrastructure, and human development, with the provision of key services in education and health, are likely to be allocated more funds. The allocation was about $ 287 million p.a. during 1970-79, but has risen to $ 1,290 million p.a. during 1990-93. These funds benefit the borrowers, and the poorer sections of the community, and must be given priority. Even so, these funds do not result in tangible physical assets such as a power station or a fertiliser plant in the case of traditional project lending. Nor do these resources result in direct, tangible, financial flows. The Bank's high financial standing depends on the perception of financiers and decision-makers in the financial markets of the world. Some education and clarification may be called for so that the absence of physical assets, which are hypothecated to the loan does not alter current perceptions. Similar questions of direct financial returns also need to be answered. The World Bank will have to ensure to an even greater extent, that its profitability and its low default rate continue to engender confidence and its prudent financial management continues to strengthen the high financial standing already earned.

With increasing reliance on market forces and the private sector, and the dilution of the previous system of administered prices, and of centralised command and control, in the developing countries, a different style of functioning will be demanded from borrowing Governments. Vigilance will still be essential, and the Government will have to retain the power to pull the levers, and to make corrections in order to make the economy move in the desired direction. The new system calls for a deeper understanding of the development process, and higher degree of sophistication than the previous one. The design of the appropriate incentives and disincentives calls for skill and competence. The World Bank group with its wide cross-country experiences, should be in a position to offer sound advice on what works and what does not. There should also be a degree of empathy between the Bank and the borrower, so that a measure of trust and confidence develops.

It is said that 80% of the world's peoples reside in the developing countries. More significant is the statistic that 94% of *all* the babies born, are born in the developing countries. In the course of time, therefore, the present population imbalance between the developed and developing countries is likely to get accentuated. Efforts are being made to improve living standards in developing countries, and consequently their needs will be growing rapidly.

Industrial economies are bedevilled by the problems arising out of cut-backs in military expenditure, and the difficult employment situation resulting from automation and rapid technological change. Contrary to the near stagnation witnessed from time to time in the developed countries, because of these and allied trends, the economies of the developing world have enormous potential for steady growth, as living standards improve. These economies could provide a welcome supplementary outlet for the products of the industrial world, including plant and machinery. Enlightened self-interest of the developed countries would suggest that measures should be taken to speed up the development process in the developing world, and external flows, whether through multilateral agencies and bilateral aid donors or from the private sector, should be enhanced. Procurement figures from World Bank assistance have been referred to earlier in order to indicate the benefits likely to flow to the industrial countries from speedier development.

It is, therefore, not clear why the BWC and the World Bank itself envisage a reduction in lending by the World Bank. While private flows would be welcome in most countries, the fact remains (as pointed out earlier), that these flows are highly skewed. The low-income countries, in particular, do not attract private flows, which are concentrated in the more advanced middle-income countries. The need for ODA and multilateral assistance to the former group is, therefore, acute. Why World Bank lending should be de-emphasised is also unclear, as such lending has no direct impact on the Governments' budgets, additional funds being raised from the financial markets. Again, while there is a general consensus on enlisting the services of the private sector, and relying more on market forces, some caution may be indicated. Markets may be rudimentary, and their functioning may be perfunctory in many developing countries, as the basic requirements for efficient functioning may not be in place. Experience shows that interventionist States have achieved rapid development, e.g. Japan and Korea—but, of course, the intervention has to be sensible. Dr. I.G.

Patel, one of the Bretton Woods Commissioners, thinks that making banks invest a certain proportion of their funds in a few neglected sectors makes abundant sense. It may not be prudent, therefore, to be dogmatic about reliance upon the private sector. Such a course may be the most appropriate where the private sector is already robust, but a different mix may be required when the private sector has first to be nurtured, and conditions for the efficient functioning of markets have yet to take shape.

For many developing countries, and the transition countries of Eastern Europe and the former Soviet Union, ODA may be required in large amounts for many more years. In a world of harsh realities, the World Bank group's voice will be heard and respected in the counsels of nations only if its advice and views are backed by adequate resources that it is prepared to commit. Advice is seldom persuasive because of its technical excellence, and requires financial commitment. There is the further point that many countries have borrowed heavily from the World Bank over the years, and questions of creditworthiness and undue concentration on a few countries can arise. It would be essential to ease such problems by providing adequate concessional assistance.

The engine for economic growth in recent years has been the truly remarkable advance of technology, which shows no signs of slowing down. Because of the commanding lead established by the industrial countries, and the evidence that the technology gap is widening, the developing countries are perhaps destined to play a game of "catch-up" well into the foreseeable future. Even the essential tasks of poverty reduction and provision of key services such as quality primary education, and basic health, can prove intractable owing to the magnitudes of the numbers involved, and the burgeoning population in the Third World. Further, even with much greater reliance upon the private sector than before, the proper environment for it to flourish has to be created by the State. This also calls for a well developed physical infrastructure, e.g. power, telecommunications, ports, railways and transportation. Not only are these activities highly capital-intensive, but also most developing countries would find that the private sector is uninterested except on terms which borrowing Governments would find difficult to accept. ODA and World Bank loans/credits may therefore have to be provided to such countries for quite some decades yet. To argue that with liberalisation and greater involvement of the private sector, the World Bank's role and the quantum of its assistance will diminish, may be somewhat premature at this stage.

Notes and References

1. Page 1, World Development Report, 1991.
2. World Development Report, 1991, p. 1.
3. Annual Report 1994, p. 76 (Box 4.3).
4. Governance—The World Bank's Experience, 1994 (p. 3 + p. xvi). This publication has been drawn upon to indicate the World Bank's approach to and views on relevant issues of governance.
5. Table 1.1 of World Debt Tables, 1996 (p. 7). Many other figures have also been taken from these tables and other tables in that publication.

References

1. Aid Effectiveness, Independent Consultants' Study (Prof. R.H. Cassen).
2. Adjustment Lending, Third Report on.
3. Agenda 21.
4. Brandt Commission, Report of.
5. Bretton Woods Commission, Report of.
6. Development Committee, Origin & Achievements of the.
7. Development Committee, Communique of Sept. 1993.
8. Development Committee, Communique of October 1994.
9. Economist, The (issue dated Nov. 12th, 1994).
10. Environment & Development, Report of World Commission on (Our Common Future—Brundtland Report).
11. Global Economic Prospects & Developing Countries, 1993.
12. Global Economic Prospects & Developing Countries, 1994.
13. Governance (World Bank 1994).
14. I.D.A. in Retrospect.
15. I.F.C. Annual Report, 1994.
16. Implementing World Bank's Strategy to Reduce Poverty.
17. Investing in Development (Baum and Tolbert).
18. Maintenance of Value. Report of ad hoc Committee on. (July 1986).
19. M.I.G.A. Annual Report, 1992.
20. M.I.G.A. Annual Report, 1994.

21. Portfolio Management & Performance, Report of Task Force on. (Wapenhans Report).
22. Project Cycle, The (Warren Baum).
23. Project Performance Audit Results, Seventh Annual Review.
24. Rio Declaration.
25. U.S. Treasury Paper on Role of Multilateral Financial Institutions.
26. World Bank Annual Report, 1985.
27. World Bank Annual Report, 1988.
28. World Bank Annual Report, 1989.
29. World Bank Annual Report, 1990.
30. World Bank Annual Report, 1991.
31. World Bank Annual Report, 1992.
32. World Bank Annual Report, 1993.
33. World Bank Annual Report, 1994.
34. World Bank Annual Report, 1995.
35. World Bank Budget, 1990.
36. World Bank Budget, 1994.
37. World Development Report, 1991.
38. World Development Report, 1992.
39. World Debt Tables, 1996.
40. World Bank since Bretton Woods. (Mason & Asher).

INDEX